A Year With Michael Green

365 reflections to challenge
and inspire your faith

Stephen Poxon

First published 2023 by Authentic Media Limited,
PO Box 6326, Bletchley, Milton Keynes, MK1 9GG.
authenticmedia.co.uk

British Library Cataloguing in Publication Data
A catalogue record for this book is available from the British Library.
ISBN: 978-1-78893-310-0
978-1-78893-311-7 (e-book)

Stephen Poxon, Authentic Media and the Tony Collins Literary Agency
wish to thank the Wakebankes Trust for granting permission
for the use of the works of Michael Green in this book

Cover design by Claire Marshall
Printed and bound by Bell & Bain Ltd, Glasgow, G46 7UQ

Foreword

Michael Green had a rare combination of gifts (and I ought to know – I was married to him for 61 years!). He was an academic, with First Class degrees in Classics from Oxford University and in Theology from Cambridge. But, unlike many academics, he was also a good communicator – whether speaking or writing – connecting with people regardless of their levels of education or ability. Third, he had a passion for evangelism; he loved to see others turning to the Christ whom he himself had begun to follow in his teenage years. That combination of depth of scholarship, clarity of communication and gift in evangelism is very unusual. He particularly loved working with students of all ages because of their potential for influence in the world, especially with university students and their vitality!

He discovered his gift for writing almost by mistake. In the days when there was a dearth of 'popular' Christian books it was suggested that he might write one. 'I don't know what I could write about,' was his reply. 'Haven't you got some talks you could turn into a book?' 'Well, I have just been to South Africa and gave a series of evangelistic talks in Cape Town University.' So his first non-academic book, *Choose Freedom*, was born. He wrote about 70 books over more than half a century, most of which fall into three main categories. One group was written for the not-yet-Christian, who needed to be convinced of the truth of Christianity and shown how to embark on a journey of faith; the second group is for those who want to understand the New Testament better, the third for those who want to be equipped to help other people to come to faith. He wrote as he spoke; many have said that they could hear his voice as they read.

Stephen Poxon has had quite a challenge to choose 365 extracts from a small selection of those 70 books. Read, enjoy, and learn more about living in relationship with Jesus.

Rosemary Green

Introduction

Michael Green was a man of many parts: a vicar in the Church of England, a scholar and lecturer of international renown, an ardent and passionate evangelist, a teacher whose colossal intellect burned with a lifelong desire to communicate Christian truths (to university students in particular), a devoted and deeply loved family man and, last but certainly not least, a dedicated fisherman!

Given Michael Green's love of souls and his willingness to engage in careful, reasoned, intelligent Christian apologetics, it is perhaps no surprise that his (rare) moments of relaxation saw him at the riverbank or in a stream. Match that with the call of Christ to his disciples to become fishers of people (Matt. 4:19) and it is not difficult to catch a glimpse of Reverend Green's heart. We can but speculate as to how many prayers were included in his fishing excursions, as he no doubt communed with the Man of Galilee whenever the lines of his hobby and his vocation blurred and merged.

If God's people are called to love the Lord with all their mind (Mark 12:30), then it is stating the obvious to tell you that Michael Green took that injunction very seriously indeed – but not without glimpses of a sparkling wit and a ready acknowledgement of life's absurdities and our patent need of a Saviour. The perilous state of the human soul without Christ appalled him, and motivated his mission. He felt the weight of his personal responsibilities as an evangelist and as a witness to the saving grace of Jesus Christ, but that is not to say he was unable to see the comical side of life too; not least when gently poking fun at many of the reasons people gave for avoiding God.

Michael Green's academic achievements are a matter of record and can easily be viewed online, so I shan't repeat them here. Suffice to say, though, his was no boringly dry attachment to academia, for his was a living faith full of energy, dynamism and relevance. There was nothing dusty about Michael Green's intellectual approach to doctrine and biblical exegesis. Far from it! Possessed of a God-given brainpower that fizzed and sparkled in multiple directions all at once, his ministry as a pastor, an educator, a writer (and some – with over seventy books to his credit) and a missionary took him all over the world and brought him into contact with thousands of people, all of whom he longed to reach with a message grounded in studious contemplation and married to a radiant personal experience of the love of God. His were no dull philosophical theories, but, always, vibrant testimonies.

It is no exaggeration whatever to state that Dr Green's scholarly reputation places him at least on a par with St Paul as a learned theologian. History will place him amongst the greats of English theologians, and rightly so. Not for nothing was he Professor of Evangelism at Regent College, Vancouver and advisor to the Archbishops of Canterbury and York.

This book, then, represents a mere dip of the toe into the deep waters that were Reverend Canon Michael Green's life of service and dedication. As Editor, I am acutely aware of the fact that I have barely even begun to paddle in those waters. I freely acknowledge that, but then this book is not meant as a study guide. Rather, it is, first and foremost – and this needs to be stressed and understood – a *devotional* composition; an aid to prayerful reflection and quiet thought.

I have attempted to excavate some of Michael Green's works (albeit, a tiny fraction of them) in order to unearth *devotional* gems. You will be the judge of whether I have succeeded in locating any such jewels, but honesty compels me to advise you not to treat this excavation as any sort of exercise in education. For one thing, that is beyond me, and for another, I have a sneaky feeling that Michael Green, nowadays spending his time as one of that 'great cloud of witnesses' referred to in Hebrews 12 and therefore watching over me as I have handled his material, would enjoy the thought that anyone reading these pages would sense the presence of God the Holy Spirit brooding over them as they do so, so that matters of prayer, contemplation, discipleship and devotion are enhanced.

Do not, though, for all that, leave your Bible at the door when you pick this book up. You will need a Bible alongside you so that you can refer to the copious number of texts mentioned. And a pen. And a notebook. This is not for the faint-hearted or the lazy!

Putting this book together has been a terrific privilege, a learning curve and a labour of love. I am truly indebted to everyone who has helped, advised, corrected and encouraged me along the way: my family, of course, who put up with me typing away in the corner, and without whose love, unwavering support and interest I would be sunk. That is never taken for granted. My erstwhile literary agent, Tony Collins, who sparked this project into being and generously entrusted me with its welfare. I owe Tony a great deal for placing this one on my desk, even though the responsibility has sometimes appeared overwhelming. Likewise, I am so very grateful to everyone at Authentic Media, perhaps especially Donna Harris and Claire Gough, with whom I have worked most closely, for the kindness they have shown in patiently sharing their expertise. These guys, like Tony Collins, know their trade, and I am humbled to work alongside them. Their friendship in this collaboration is appreciated. I freely acknowledge my dependence upon the goodwill and advice of the aforementioned.

Special thanks, though, are reserved for Rosemary and Tim Green, Michael's widow and one of his four children, respectively. I can but hope I have rewarded their confidence in me. Rosemary and Tim have been nothing less than co-operative and supportive throughout, and their enthusiasm for this project has been inspiring. I am most thankful to have met them, and to have undertaken this endeavour on their behalf, in memory of Michael.

I was privileged to meet with Rosemary and Tim in what was Michael's beloved Oxfordshire. Having spent some hours with them discussing this work, Rosemary, a veteran pilgrim, caught me with her parting words: 'Tell them about the cross.' That sentence says it all. The cross of Christ was Michael Green's driving force. I have tried hard to capture Rosemary's advice within these pages. You have my word that I am praying for you as I type, that in some way, as you turn each page, your heart will be led afresh to Calvary. If that becomes your experience, then I will have done what I was invited to do.

One important point to note is that my reference material has all been 'of its time'. That is to say, the works of Michael Green's into which I delved do not include references to gender as we would expect to discover them in modern times. Michael Green, throughout, referred predominantly to 'he' and 'him', and 'man' and 'men', and so on. Rest assured, no offence whatever is intended by this, and certainly not any intention of gender exclusion. It is simply the case that, in keeping faith with the reproduction of Michael's works as they were originally written, they reflect the commonplace terminology of his day. This caveat is included with more than a nod to the sensitivities of readers who might pick up on this detail. There is no slight or insult within any such phraseology, merely an authentic replication of original works.

1 January

**I will establish my covenant with you, and you will enter the ark –
you and your sons and your wife and your sons' wives with you.
(Genesis 6:18)**

'The creed of Israel is, in brief, "Yahweh saves".'[1] So wrote T.B. Kilpatrick[2] half a century ago,[3] and he was not far wrong. Salvation is the great central theme not only of the Old Testament but of the whole Bible. From the story of God's rescue of Noah and his family from the flood (Gen. 6 – 9) to that graphic picture of the final destiny of God's saved people as the Bride of Christ in the heavenly Jerusalem (Rev. 21), God is seen to be at work in the rescue of men . . .[4]

Much of the Old Testament could be seen as a veiled prediction of the salvation later achieved through the life, death and resurrection of Jesus [emphasizing] the continuity between the Old and the New Testaments. But it had two great weaknesses. It enabled the commentator to read what he liked into the Old Testament text; and it hardly allowed the Old Testament message to mean anything to its original hearers. With the rise of modern critical scholarship has come a strong reaction against this sort of approach, and a refreshing recognition that the makers of the Old Testaments were *men* speaking from God to the situation of their own day – and not mere machines recording a timeless echo of his voice. Much greater attention is paid today to the writer himself, and the political and historical situation to which he addressed his message and the philosophical and cultural heritage in which he was nourished. The Old Testament is seen nowadays as less as the *Book of the Oracles of God* than the *Book of the Acts of God*;[5] God's self-disclosure is seen less in biblical statement than in biblical history . . .

It cannot be denied that God's acts in rescuing his people are even more important than the interpretation given to those acts in the pages of the Bible. The theme of . . . 'salvation history' is what the Bible is all about.[6]

Thank you, Heavenly Father, for this helpful insight: the pages of the Bible, not as evidence of formal and austere divine dictation but, altogether more gloriously, details of a deity permanently at work. You are the God of covenant, and God of Calvary. How wonderful!

2 January

**Philosophy, which depends on human tradition . . . rather than on Christ.
(Colossians 2:8)**

So far as the study of salvation is concerned, it makes very little difference whether one adopts the old static conception of the Old Testament as first and foremost a *praeparatio evangelica*,[7] or the newer, more dynamic approach, which sees it as the record of God visiting and redeeming his people. On any showing, salvation is basic. On this the theologians are agreed; not so the man in the pew. To him, 'salvation' carries one of two connotations. It may conjure up in his mind the open-air preacher, the high-pressure evangelist, or that earnest but rather daunting acquaintance who is always enquiring whether he is yet saved. His immediate reaction is to resent this unwarranted intrusion into his private life, and indeed to defer all such ungentlemanly considerations of ultimate issues.

On the other hand, mention of salvation may induce in the modern churchgoer a soporific, numinous feeling of well-being; it is a word which he associates with church and clergy, with archaic prayer-books and black-bound Bibles. It belongs, in short, to the world of religion, not of life. This is of course a caricature of the ordinary Christian's attitude to salvation, but it is not a misleading distortion. It serves to emphasise how far we have strayed in our religious thinking from the teaching of the Bible. The Hebrew would not understand the distinction we so often make (at all events by implication) between religion and life. What would be the good of a religion that made no difference to life? The Hebrew would find it hard to understand our familiar distinction between the sacred and the secular.[8]

A fine line, Lord, and an important distinction; the subtle difference between religious teaching which leads to something perfectly true, but quite dusty and relatively lifeless, and the teaching of the Bible, leading to life abundant. Guide me, I pray, as I attend to my own personal church commitments while simultaneously exploring fullness of faith in Christ, the divine Visitor and Redeemer, the architect of salvation. Lead me, I pray, towards a belief system that is holistic, wholesome – and alive.

3 January

Is it nothing to you, all you who pass by?
(Lamentations 1:12)

I was standing at the church door after a service when one of our church workers introduced a friend, who said, 'I believe in God – but why bother about Jesus? Could you recommend something to read on the subject?' On the spur of the moment, I could think of nothing. And when I racked my brains subsequently, I still could not come up with a single title designed to disturb modern apathy about Jesus. Why bother with Jesus?

It seemed to me – and it still seems – utterly astounding that so many people today can glance at the greatest life which has ever been lived and say, 'So what? Why bother?' I want to disturb that apathy.[9]

A disturber of the apathetic! That is quite a calling, Lord, yet, as a follower of Jesus, it is one that must sit close to my heart. Let me begin by praying for a mind-set sensitive to apathy; that is, any indifference I encounter regarding the claims of Christ. Help me to take it from there, in terms of formulating my own approach to evangelism. I may never write a book or give lectures, but allow me at least the privilege of forming the best responses I can, within my personal sphere of influence. I pray too for my church fellowship and any efforts we, collectively, might make at witnessing. Guide us and use us, so that those who pass by might somehow feel your gracious touch upon their lives.

4 January

I baptise you with water for repentance. But after me comes one who is more powerful than I, whose sandals I am not worthy to carry. He will baptise you with the Holy Spirit and fire.
(Matthew 3:11)

The Christian Church has always had a good many professing members who are rather like those disciples at Ephesus who, when asked by Paul, 'Did you receive the Holy Spirit when you believed?' replied, 'No, we have never even heard that there is a Holy Spirit' (Acts 19:2). Of course, this group at Ephesus must have heard something about the Holy Spirit if they listened at all attentively to John the Baptist, but they did not realise that the promised Spirit was available for them; that he could make a difference to their lives. Many adherents of all denominations have been in the same state. They have, of course, heard about the Holy Spirit, but have either put it all down to typical ecclesiastical in-talk, or assumed that it was not intended for ordinary folk like themselves. For all practical purposes, the Holy Spirit could be discounted. Christianity was a matter of churchgoing, of soldiering on and trying to do one's best, and of believing in the existence of God and the historical life and death of Jesus (even if his deity and resurrection were not to be taken too seriously). On the other hand, there have always been people in the Christian Church who were very sure about the Holy Spirit. It was simple. He was the divine backer of their particular emphasis in theology and practice.[10]

'Available for them' – what a beautiful description of God the Holy Spirit; not a distant God, remote or unfeeling, but 'available' as companion and counsellor. Such grace. Holy Spirit, abide with me. That is my first plea, my priority prayer. Grant me that grace whereby the Holy Spirit inhabits my churchgoing, to keep it fresh and dynamic and full of love. By the same token, grant me the wisdom to remember that my own 'particular emphasis in theology and practice' is always subject to the Holy Spirit's Lordship (and not the other way around).

5 January

By his wounds you have been healed.
(1 Peter 2:24)

I have found during many years as a university and theological college teacher that the subject of the cross of Christ is often a matter of debate and argument. It is interpreted in different and often contradictory categories. It is treated as an item in dogmatic theology.

But what has the cross to say to the man in despair, to the heartbroken and the guilty? How does it relate to human situations such as loneliness and bereavement, to struggles between races or power blocks? What has it to say in the face of terrible natural disasters or ghastly expressions of human wickedness like Auschwitz?[11]

God is love, the cross is saying. I thank you, Lord, for the cross of Christ. I thank you that in my moments of desperation and heartbreak, I may yet gaze upon the cross and consider hope, even then. I thank you that all my sin is there; the great emblem of pardon resonates across the ages. I thank you that the divine response to wickedness is seen at Calvary. My prayers today are for those mentioned in this excerpt. In your mercy, enable them to lift their heads and see the cross. Impart healing according to their need and situation.

6 January

**He was delivered over to death for our sins
and was raised to life for our justification.
(Romans 4:25)**

All too often the cross of Jesus is boxed away in a theological compartment, and books are written by professional theologians for and against one another on the subject. But Jesus died for human beings, not only for theologians. Accordingly, the cross is too important a matter to be left to the theologians. If it is true that God Almighty was in Christ redeeming the world on Calvary, which is certainly part of the New Testament claim about the death of Jesus, then we need to understand what that cross can mean for ordinary individuals and communities . . .

The first Christians did not lay a great deal of emphasis on the cross *tout simple*. They did not isolate it . . . and regard it as *the* saving event, with the resurrection being a mythical way of stressing its saving nature. On the contrary, the overall emphasis of the New Testament proclamation is preserved very typically in the account of Peter's sermon on the Day of Pentecost.

This Jesus, delivered up according to the definite plan and foreknowledge of God, you crucified and killed . . . This Jesus God raised up, and of that we are all witnesses. Being therefore exalted at the right hand of God, and having received from the Father the promise of the Holy Spirit, he has poured out this which you see and hear (Acts 2:23,32f).

The cross was not generally proclaimed by itself, but in union with the resurrection and in the power given by the Holy Spirit. The cross and the resurrection of Jesus belong together. They should never have been divorced into separate and all but hermetically-sealed compartments of dogmatic theology. It is not the cross which saves. It is Jesus, crucified and risen.[12]

'It is not the cross which saves. It is Jesus, crucified and risen.' Lord, you have completely arranged my salvation, with not one detail overlooked. Likewise, you have granted eternal life in resurrection power. I praise you for that blood-stained old cross, and for my blood-stained, risen, living Redeemer.

7 January

Even if there are so-called gods, whether in heaven or on earth (as indeed there are many 'gods' and many 'lords'), yet for us there is but one God.
(1 Corinthians 8:5–6)

Years ago people were saying that science had proved that God did not exist and that there was very little to know beyond the physical world of the here and now.

Today people are far less sure. There seems to be mounting evidence that a spiritual world exists beyond what we can merely see, touch, taste, hear and smell. Many are trying to make sense of this and are looking in all sorts of places to find some answers. Surprisingly, in our supposedly sophisticated world, witches and black magic have never had it so good. Islam is becoming more popular in Britain and elsewhere. Hinduism has never had such an influence as it has today, along with transcendental meditation, Eastern mysticism, New Age thinking . . .

New religions and spiritual causes are mushrooming all over the place. It's not just the Jehovah's Witnesses and the Mormons that come round to your door nowadays: the Hari Krishna crowd may be dancing in your street. General bookshops now stock a wide range of New Age titles and the interest in spiritualism supports many specialist bookshops as well. If you take the UFO addicts and the horoscope readers into account, it is plain that we are not merely religious: we are positively hooked on the supernatural. The supermarket of gods is here with a vengeance.[13]

How gracious and faithful you must be, Almighty God, to keep patience with a confused world that seems to explore every spiritual avenue except the truth of Christ, and prefers supermarket searching to safety and salvation. Thank you for such forbearance. My prayers today reach out towards those who are sincerely seeking authentic spirituality, but barking up several wrong trees. By your Spirit, lead them home. I think especially of any known to me personally. Lead, kindly light.

8 January

**There is no other name under heaven given to mankind
by which we must be saved.
(Acts 4:12)**

The sovereign rescue of men and nations by God is the main burden of the most common and important Old Testament root concerning salvation. The [Hebrew] word *yasha'* and its cognates has the basic meaning of 'bringing into a spacious environment', 'being at one's ease, free to develop without hindrance'. It is the opposite of the [Hebrew] verb *tsarar*, 'to be in discomfort, in cramped or distressing circumstances'. It deserves close attention, not only because it is normative for the whole concept of salvation in the Old Testament, but because it forms part of several of the best-known names in the Bible, such as Isaiah, Hosea, Joshua, and supremely Jesus. If we are to understand what is implied by Matt. 1:21, 'Thou shalt call his name Jesus, for he shall save his people from their sins', it will be imperative to grasp something of what this word *yasha'* had come to mean to the Hebrews.[14]

> **Lord, this is an exciting insight. I thank you for it, and I pray that it will slowly but surely settle into my heart. In my prayer-time today, assist me to reflect upon this gracious act of 'sovereign rescue' and, in doing so, to find that I come to love you more dearly. Help me to appreciate these facts, then grant my soul their application.**

9 January

**God's love has been poured out into our hearts through the Holy Spirit,
who has been given to us.
(Romans 5:5)**

A good deal has been written in recent years about Primitive Catholicism, the tendency apparent even within the New Testament period itself to domesticate the Holy Spirit, to make him the perquisite of the Church. The man who is validly baptised or rightly instituted into office in the Church is assured that he has the Holy Spirit.[15]

Lord, preserve my thinking from simplistic, unexplored, assumed theology. As I sit here with you, I invite you to challenge my certainties and assumptions, and to introduce corrections as you see fit. And never allow me to think of you, gracious Spirit, as someone I might domesticate, for you are the untameable God Almighty. Meet with me as I pray. Help me to bear that in mind. I worship you.

10 January

**I have been the Lord your God ever since you came out of Egypt.
You shall acknowledge no God but me, no Saviour except me.
(Hosea 13:4)**

Salvation is the work of God. One cannot help being struck from the very out-set of any study of this word by the remarkable fact that in the vast majority of references to salvation, however it was conceived, God was seen as its author. It is God who saves his flock (Ezek. 34:22), who rescues his people (Hos. 1:7). He alone can do it (Hos. 13:10–14) for, in the last analysis, there is none else (Isa. 43:11). Wherever we look in the books of the Old Testament this fact stares us in the face. It is the Lord who saved his people from Egypt (Ps. 100:7–10). He it is who saves them from Babylon (Jer. 30:10). He will always be true to his saving character (Deut. 20:4). For he is the high tower, the refuge, the Saviour of his people (2 Sam. 22:3). He is their God and their Saviour (Isa. 43:3), the Hope of Israel and his Saviour in time of trouble (Jer. 14:8).

In short, the whole Old Testament revelation portrays a God who intervenes in the field of history on behalf of his people. To know God at all is to know him as Saviour. 'I am the Lord thy God from the land of Egypt, and thou shalt know no god but me; for there is no saviour beside me' (Hos. 13:4). 'God' and 'Saviour' are synonymous throughout the whole of the Old Testament.[16]

Heavenly Father, this is a terrific analysis of your saving grace, and I thank you for it. Draw alongside me, I pray, as I contemplate these verses of Scripture. Draw that picture of salvation upon my heart. Thank you for the love these texts beautifully represent. My God. My Saviour.

11 January

The Lord is the Spirit.
(2 Corinthians 3:17)

It is not only Catholic Christendom which has been guilty of domesticating the Holy Spirit . . . Protestants have been no less anxious to do so, for the Holy Spirit is a disturbing influence. Let him therefore be paid lip service, but for all practical purposes be shut up in the Bible where he can do no harm. Let his presence attend the confessional statement of our particular brand of Protestantism. Let the bizarre and miraculous elements which the New Testament documents narrate about his activity be relegated to those far-off apostolic days: it would be very embarrassing and doctrinally untidy if the Holy Spirit were to speak to men today, or to enable miracles to be performed and men to speak in tongues not their own. The Bible, accordingly, is the safest place for the Spirit. That is where he belongs; not in the hurly-burly of real life.[17]

Thank you so much, Holy Spirit, that you are a humble deity, who deigns to be right there with us, in the thick of it, in 'the hurly-burly of real life'. Thank you for staying alongside us, your people, day in and day out. Forgive us, I pray, for ever once trying to minimize you, to trap you, to organize you, or to even imagine that we can keep you in our collective pocket. You are God, and we stand in need, not only of your abiding presence, but of your gifts and miracles too.

12 January

We believe that Jesus died and rose again.
(1 Thessalonians 4:14)

Exemplarism . . . is a way of looking at the cross as if it were simply and solely an example of self-sacrifice. Jesus had taught that 'greater love has no man than this, that a man should lay down his life for his friends'. And on the cross we find him practising what he preached. But is that all there is to it? . . .

To be sure, his death was the supreme example of total self-sacrifice, not just for his friends, but for his enemies. But that is one of the lesser heights of the Everest of Calvary. Exemplarism springs from failing to grasp that the cross and the resurrection belong together. Nobody could have seriously put forward an exemplarist doctrine of the cross if they had held it together with the resurrection of Jesus. For his rising from the tomb – if it be true – is just what did *not* happen to others and martyrs for a thousand causes.[18]

Dying God; ever-living God. God of the cross, God of the tomb, God of the resurrection. My God. I may not ever really grasp that paradox, but by faith I believe, and I thank you for the death that put an end to my guilt, and the rising from the dead that promises me everlasting life. Help me to proclaim redemption's plan to the best of my ability, and also to live within its range of benefits.

13 January

Jesus said . . . 'I am the resurrection and the life.'
(John 11:25)

At the opposite extreme from exemplarism lies another doctrine of the atonement which also fails to grasp the significance of the resurrection. I mean, of course, that doctrine of satisfaction which has been found in some parts of Christendom since Anselm. Christ's death on the cross was the means whereby satisfaction was made for sin, and harmony restored in a world which had clearly run amok. A variation on this view can be found in many evangelical circles which see a crude substitution as lying at the heart of the cross. God's affronted justice required payment in redress by somebody: on the cross Jesus paid it instead of sinners.

I would not deny for a moment that there is a substitutionary element in the cross, but it cannot be expressed fittingly by claiming that God arbitrarily substituted Jesus for the sins of all the world. That would be a bookkeeping transaction, and would give us a very strange doctrine of the justice of God who was happy for the wrong person to suffer; it would also give us a very subpersonal understanding of Jesus, almost as if he were some commodity to be exchanged. But once the cross and the resurrection are held together, a very different picture emerges. It is the picture the New Testament itself gives us, of a living Christ who died for us and rose again. The one who entered our alienation and estrangement at the most profound level is alive to welcome us back, 'ransomed, healed, restored, forgiven' into the Father's home of love.[19]

Jesus Christ, in whom is found everlasting life, I worship you as my resurrected Saviour; the one whom death and the tomb could not hope to hold. Your resurrection signalled the vanquishment of death, the last great enemy, so that we might be welcomed home one day. Hallelujah! Receive my homage, humble though it be.

14 January

My Father's house has many rooms; if that were not so, would I have told you that I am going there to prepare a place for you?
(John 14:2)

A faith to live by has got to offer hope for society at large. If a faith is merely individual, it is petty. If it is merely social, it is impersonal.

Part of the wonder of the Christian faith is that it has nerved reform, education, medical care, idealism in whole nations, as well as transforming individuals. Unlike Communism, it offers the hope of fulfilment in which all subjects of Jesus will have their share, not merely those who happen to be alive at the end. Unlike Buddhism, which offers us a future with individuality rubbed out (as we will all be absorbed into the One), Jesus promises people that they will for ever be in his Father's house. Every individual will be there. Everyone will matter. And love, not oblivion, will be the order of the day.[20]

> **What a thrilling mystery, Heavenly Father – a saving love that is something deeply personal, yet which also gladly embraces the whole world. What a depth of mercy. Lord, touch the hearts of those for whom I pray this day, that they too may 'be there'. May those I pray for – family, friends, neighbours, colleagues – come to know your love in a way that leads them home. God of the universe, God of individuals, hear my prayers.**

15 January

The Spirit searches all things, even the deep things of God.
(1 Corinthians 2:10)

What . . . is the Christian to make of the Holy Spirit? Where shall we begin? It is important to remember that we are mere men, talking about God. And it is not possible for us to know anything at all about him unless he is generous enough to disclose himself. Another book [I have written] has tackled the question of revelation; suffice it to say at this point that without revelation we cannot say anything about the Lord who is Spirit. St Paul makes this very clear. 'What person can know a man's thoughts,' he asks, 'except the spirit of the man which is in him? So no one comprehends the thoughts of God except the Spirit of God' (1 Cor. 2:11). In other words, it takes God to reveal God. And Paul claims that God has done so, through the Spirit interpreting spiritual truths to men who possess the Spirit . . .

Theologians often distinguish between God as he is in himself, and God as he has revealed himself to us. It seems to me to be both useless and presumptuous to attempt to pierce the incognito of the essential Godhead. It is quite enough for me to try to grasp the way in which God has disclosed himself to us.[21]

'It takes God to reveal God.' Heavenly Father, I thank you for love revealed. Help me as I ponder that concept today. It would take me several lifetimes, Lord, to even attempt to comprehend the wonders of such revelation, and that would scarcely be time enough. Thank you for making yourself known; Creator to created, King to subject. What a stunning hallmark of grace this action really is. Thank you for the gracious agency of your Spirit in this respect.

16 January

This is what the LORD says –
Israel's King and Redeemer, the LORD Almighty:
I am the first and I am the last;
apart from me there is no God.
(Isaiah 44:6)

The Law, the Prophets and the Writings (the three divisions of the Old Testament Scriptures) combine to teach one basic lesson. It was this. There is one God, and no runners up. That is the lesson Abraham learnt in polytheistic Ur of the Chaldees. It had to be learnt time and again by his descendants throughout the succeeding twenty centuries. Yahweh, the God of Israel, was the only deity. The other gods of the heathen were idols (literally 'nothings' in Hebrew).

The downtrodden captives in Egypt at the time of the Exodus came to realise that Yahweh, the only self-existent one (Exod. 3:14), was a mighty deliverer who could be trusted. The Mosaic Law underlines the fact that their whole social, religious and daily life must be governed by loyalty to that one God who brought them out of the land of Egypt, out of the house of bondage. They forgot the message times without number. The Old Testament records them running after false gods, the gods of the nations around them, whenever opportunity offered. Elijah has to drag them back from the worship of the heathen fertility gods introduced by Jezebel. Hosea has to recall them to Yahweh, their first love, when they have gone and committed adultery, like Hosea's first wife, with some other 'Lord' on whom they have lavished their worship and devotion. Jeremiah and Isaiah never tire of reminding the people that there is one God who can save his people, and that all other refuges are in vain.[22]

'One God, and no runners up'! Remind me too, Lord, time and again, to hang my helpless soul on you, and you alone, for I seem to need reminders. Forgive me for those times in my life when I have chased idols and have listened to their voices; of popularity, wealth, cheap success, material gain, and so on. Thank you, Lord, that when the 'other gods' of doubt, faithlessness and temptation have held sway, you have never once failed, or hesitated, to draw me back. Faithful God. True God.

17 January

I am the Living One; I was dead, and now look,
I am alive for ever and ever!
(Revelation 1:18)

A . . . weakness which springs from separating the cross and resurrection can be seen in the popular Roman Catholicism of Latin America. Everywhere there are images of the Virgin Mary, at times no more than a mild Christianisation of the feminine fertility principle endemic in animism. Where Jesus is recognised at all, he appears in one of three guises. Either he is the helpless baby held in the arms of his Mother; or he is the dying hero, his pains depicted with a very gruesome realism in the Stations of the Cross; or else he is the awesome future Judge. At no time while visiting a number of Latin American countries did I get any sense that Jesus was risen and alive, except in circles that have been revived by the Catholic charismatic movement. Everywhere else it seemed to be a powerless Jesus, a dead Jesus, or a threatening Jesus that was presented. The balance was only put right when the cross and resurrection were held together.[23]

Risen Lord Jesus, live in my heart this day; in my thinking, my motives, my words and my actions. By your living presence, guide and guard me. (And, Lord, I offer a prayer for friends of mine across different denominations. We all stand in need of mercy, though we worship in different ways. Bless them richly.)

18 January

If we are faithless, he remains faithful, for he cannot disown himself.
(2 Timothy 2:13)

'The Lord saved Israel that day out of the hand of the Egyptians.' It is no exaggeration to say that this rescue from Egypt, the land of bitter bondage under the threat of imminent death at the hand of harsh taskmasters, determined the whole future understanding of salvation by the people of Israel. The Exodus was a great drama in which God was the central actor. It was played out against a backdrop of divine judgement on Egypt, carried out in the plagues. Its plot was God's faithful mercy and love to Israel displayed in their rescue from judgement through the death of a lamb, sealed in the great deliverance of the Red Sea, and issuing in the covenant of Sinai in which God undertook to be their God, and they undertook to be his people (Ex. 19:1–6) . . . God comes to the rescue of his people who cannot help themselves.

Once again his salvation is accompanied by judgement on the impenitent and unbelieving. Once more, throughout the long story of the wilderness wanderings, marred as it was by rebellion and even apostasy on the part of the Israelites, we see the *hesed*[24] of God lavished upon a people who both forgot him and disobeyed him.[25]

'God comes to the rescue of his people who cannot help themselves.'
You are a God of exceeding faithfulness. Let that faithfulness be the
theme of my song this day. Saviour. Rescuer. Judge. Merciful Lover.
Deliverer. Helper of the helpless. A God of lavish mercy. Meet me here
as I meditate upon these aspects of your nature.

19 January

Everyone who calls on the name of the Lord will be saved.
(Romans 10:13)

A faith to live by has to appeal to everyone. If it is true at all, it must be true for all. Islam is primarily for Arabs and the areas they have conquered. Buddhism and Hinduism appeal, for the most part, to the Eastern temperament. Communism appeals to the oppressed. Zen appeals to the overworked. But Jesus is the man for all races, and for all seasons . . . the sheer universality of the gospel is just what you would expect if it is the truth of God.

These are some of the things I would look for in a faith that will bear my weight through life and in the face of death. It must be true, relevant, able to change the lives of individuals and whole societies; it must meet the deepest needs of man, and it must be applicable with equal appeal to all men everywhere. Try that for size with other faiths and you'll see why I am an enthusiast for Jesus of Nazareth. None but he can meet all those conditions of a faith to live by. That is why it is worth bothering with Jesus.[26]

God of the whosoever, your plan of redemption is inclusive; a reflection of your entire being. With that in mind, I pray for those known to me personally who might be labouring under the impression that Christianity is okay for Christians, but is not for them. Reach out to them and impart faith. I pray too for anyone who feels that they fall outside the remit of grace, perhaps on account of some kind of sin or misdemeanour. Whisper to them that this is not so. Whisper and woo, I pray. Let them know you are the God who stands the test.

20 January

Remember the wonders he has done.
(Psalm 105:5)

When the individual worshipper is recording God's deliverance and giving him thanks (e.g. Ps. 66:13–20), he cannot refrain from beginning with a recital of God's salvation of his people in the Exodus (66:5–7); he sees the national rescue and his own as belonging together. When Habakkuk is speaking of God's deliverance from foreign enemies and from drought and pestilence, he still cannot escape from the normative influence of the Exodus (Hab. 3:8ff.). Because of the salvation of God experienced then, he has confidence in continuing preservation by the God of his salvation (3:18).

It is just the same when the king celebrates the deliverance which God has wrought for him and his people (e.g. Ps. 18). He describes the victory (or salvation) in terms coloured by the ancient conflict-myth and by the historic Exodus. His God is the God who saves. When the prophet looks forward to the ultimate deliverance, the final salvation in the new age, he returns to the symbol of the destruction of Leviathan by Yahweh which had found historical expression in the Exodus (Is. 27:1) . . .

Past, present and future are comprised in the intervention of the Saviour God.[27]

Thank you, Lord, for this encouragement to look back before I look forward – not in any rueful way, but in order to stock up on fresh confidence in a God who has never failed his people, and isn't planning to do so. As then, so now. Bring to mind those times of deliverance from my own past years, so that I too may all the more trust you for that which is still to come, Alpha and Omega.

21 January

**'Very truly I tell you,' Jesus answered, 'before Abraham was born, I am!'
(John 8:58)**

God comes in person to make himself known. After years of scrutinising Jesus of Nazareth, of listening to his teaching, of watching his character, of observing his miracles, after witnessing that shameful death and experiencing that glorious resurrection, the men who had known him best were sure of it. This man had brought God into focus. 'God, who spoke of old in many and varied ways to our fathers through the prophets, has in these last days spoken to us in a Son. Him he has appointed the heir of all things. Through him he created the worlds. He reflects the glory of God, and bears the very stamp of his nature, upholding the universe by the word of his power.' 'In him dwells all the fullness of the Godhead in bodily form.' 'He is the image of the invisible God, the firstborn of all creation; for in him all things were created, in heaven and on earth . . . all things were created in him and for him. His is the priority over everything, and in him all things hold together.' 'No man has ever seen God; the only Son, himself God, who is in the bosom of the Father, he had made him known.'

In words like these Paul, John and the writer of the Epistle to the Hebrews struggle to express the unheard-of claim, that they themselves would have deemed blasphemous but for the irrefragable evidence of the life, death and resurrection of Jesus, that God had indeed visited and redeemed his people. The one it was unlawful to name had taken the name of 'Emmanuel' ('God with us') and 'Jesus' ('God saves').[28]

So many Scriptures, Lord, and yet, even all of them combined merely, inadequately, scratch the surface of the glory that is the incarnation. Nevertheless, thank you for descriptions of wonderful love, coming to me from heaven above. You are a God who visits! Visit me this day, and do so as a welcome guest.

22 January

**On my account you will be brought before governors and kings
as witnesses to them and to the Gentiles.
(Matthew 10:18)**

Literary Romans were very aristocratic creatures. Why should they bother about
a peasant teacher who lived on the very edge of the map, in Judaea? Nevertheless,
some of them did bother. Pliny was the Governor of Northern Turkey, right up
by the Black Sea, in about AD 112. He wrote lots of letters to the Emperor, and
they have survived. He tells us about the Christians, their numbers, their influence
(sale of sacrificial victims for the pagan temples had dropped to nothing!), their
worship (early in the morning, with hymns to Christ as God), their loving and
harmless lives, and their regrettable unwillingness to stop being Christians when
he told them to! Many of them he executed, but the movement refused to lie down
and die. You can read all about it in his *Epistles* 10:96. Another aristocratic Roman
writer was Cornelius Tacitus, the Governor of the rich province of Asia Minor
(our central and coastal Turkey). He writes of the way in which the Emperor Nero
picked on the Christians as scapegoats for the Fire of Rome in AD 64. He tells of
the incredible cruelty practised on them: some were clothed in the skins of wild
beasts and torn apart by dogs, while others were covered with pitch and set alight
at night in Nero's gardens. Tacitus felt sorry for them, but he did not like them.[29]

**Lord Jesus, you came to us as 'a peasant teacher' whose destiny was to
be ordered to explain your actions in the praetorium, such was your
brave humility. Maybe I don't acknowledge your courage as often as I
should. How frightening it must have been for you, to be hauled before the Roman authorities and subsequently beaten to within an inch
of your life. And yet you bore it all. Hear my prayers today for those
around the world who continue to suffer for your sake, at the hands
of despots at least as sadistic as Nero ever was. Grant enabling grace
to the suffering church whose witness is badged and distinguished by
bruises and blood.**

23 January

Brothers and sisters, we do not want you to be uninformed about those who sleep in death, so that you do not grieve like the rest of mankind, who have no hope. For we believe that Jesus died and rose again, and so we believe that God will bring with Jesus those who have fallen asleep in him.
(1 Thessalonians 4:13–14)

The early Christians went to their funerals with a real measure of joy over their departed loved ones; they saw death through the lens of the resurrection hope. They dated the deaths of their martyrs by the appropriate year and added, *regnante Jesu Christo*, 'in the reign of Jesus Christ'. They were able to hold disaster in perspective because they saw the cross, the central mystery of faith, through the light of the resurrection.

Well, is that early Christian resilient faith apparent in Christian circles today? Do clergy normally enable their congregations to face agony with at least one eye on the empty tomb? Is there in the average Christian funeral anything distinctively different in attitude from atheist funerals? I fear there is often no difference at all. And part of the reason is that we have separated the cross and resurrection in our minds, have lightly said to a suffering friend 'It's your cross, dear' and have failed to set tragedy and pain in the light of the resurrection. Instead of a robust faith which can face suffering with quiet confidence in God who raises the dead, we have denigrated into a selfish eudaemonism which regards pleasure and good times as our right, and complains that the first touch of adversity destroys our faith. 'Why does God allow it?' would not be stilled, but it would be heard a lot less often in church if we had not separated cross and resurrection.[30]

Thank you, Lord, for this insight. Thank you, too, for the great Christian hope of life beyond the grave. Thank you for the way in which that was made available. Thank you. Lord Jesus, in your mercy, draw close to those who are dying without you, even as I pray now. Touch the hearts of those whose earthly existence is reaching its natural conclusion. May they find resurrection grace, even at the last minute, like the thief you spoke to moments before he took his final breath. Rescue the perishing.

24 January

**They bound him, led him away and handed him over to Pilate the governor.
(Matthew 27:2)**

There is plenty of other Roman evidence that Jesus was a real person of recent date. The cities of Pompeii and Herculaneum were overwhelmed by a volcano in AD 79, and Christian mosaics, wall paintings and inscriptions have all been found there – also, in all probability, an early Christian chapel. Archaeology has also come up with a decree from the Emperor Tiberius (AD 14–38) or Claudius (AD 41–54), discovered in Nazareth, which threatens with the death penalty anyone who disturbs tombs: it looks as if this is official reaction to Pilate's report of the empty tomb of Jesus. There can be no doubt in the mind of anyone who takes historical evidence seriously that Jesus actually lived and died in Palestine under the governorship of Pontius Pilate, which ended in AD 36.[31]

**Your incarnation is a matter of fact and historical record, Lord Jesus.
God with the skin on, for my sake. History and humanity are touched
by this unique intervention. Jesus came down, my ransom to be.**

25 January

**You will receive power when the Holy Spirit comes on you;
and you will be my witnesses.
(Acts 1:8)**

God the Creator, the God who had come alongside men in Jesus, now made him-self available to come within their very personalities. It is inconceivable that any-one sat down to think out any doctrine so intrinsically improbable as the Trinity. It was forced upon them by experience. Convinced as they were of the unity and uniqueness of God, the disciples became confident that he was present in Jesus. After Pentecost, they became assured that their experience of God's activity in their midst and in their mission was nothing less than the continued work and presence of Jesus among them. Accordingly, they did not shrink from speaking indifferently of 'the Spirit of God' and 'the Spirit of Jesus' or 'the Spirit of Christ'. Jesus of Nazareth was now the prism through which the various shafts of light in the Old Testament about the Spirit became luminous and in focus to them.[32]

And what a prism! I think, Lord, the key thought here is 'experience'. What good is it if I go to church simply because it's what my family has always done? What good, even, is sound doctrine if it has failed to pen-etrate my ears? I pray, Holy Spirit, for an ever-increasing experience of your activity within my life. Gentle as a dove, maybe, and probably incremental, but that's what I need. Grant me an experience that grows and matures.

26 January

He breathed on them and said, 'Receive the Holy Spirit.'
(John 20:22)

The Spirit of God is no natural quality of man. It is no hidden recess within our bodies. For one thing, the Hebrews did not divide man up into spirit, mind and body as we tend to do; they thought of him as a single entity, an animated body, a living person. For another, they had a perfectly good word to describe our human vitality, the quality that marks off a living person from a dead one: and that was *nephesh*. Only comparatively rarely is this word brought into contact with *ruach*,[33] though we cannot expect, and do not find, complete consistency. It is true that *ruach* is used of man's spirit in a number of ways. It is used in the story of the Flood, for instance, to denote 'the breath of life' (Gen. 6:17) which God gives – And takes back again. It is used to denote full vitality, real spirited living; contrast the deflation of the Queen of Sheba when she saw all Solomon's treasure – 'there was no more *ruach* left in her' (1 Kgs. 10:5). It comes to mean the seat of the emotions, intellect, and will – particularly often applied to the governing impulse in a man's life (e.g. Prov. 25:28; Ps. 32:2; Numb. 14:24). Occasionally, therefore, a man's *ruach* 'spirit' seems to be equated with his *nephesh*, his 'life', but this is by no means the normal usage. *Ruach* and *nephesh* can be thought of as each having their own circle of meaning. Occasionally, the circumferences of those circles intersect, but the main content of each is clear. *Nephesh* is natural; it belongs to man. *Ruach* is supernatural; it belongs to God. Though *ruach* may be found in man, it is always, so to speak, on loan, and not a possession; a resident alien, not a native.[34]

And what a loan! The divine guest of the soul – imparted by grace to be my teacher, counsellor, guide, enabler and friend. Lord, perhaps the moral of today's reading is that I should remember not to rely upon my own strength. The arms of flesh will fail me, and my resources will fail, that's for sure. Yours, though . . .

You will be a blessing.
(Genesis 12:2)

The voice of Zechariah after the Exile brings the . . . message from the Lord, 'As ye were a curse among the heathen, O house of Judah and house of Israel, so I will save you, and ye shall be a blessing' (Zech. 8:13). Saved, to be a blessing. And the way in which they are to be a blessing is emphasized. 'These are the things that ye shall do; Speak ye every man truth to his neighbour; execute the judgement of truth and peace in your gates' (8:16). Perhaps the most famous expression of the purpose of salvation in the whole of the Old Testament is in Isa. 49:6–7. The obedient Remnant of Israel will fulfil the function that properly belonged to the whole nation (49:3) and so *be* the Servant of the Lord their Redeemer that they can actually be called his 'salvation'; a people so dedicated to God that he can use them not only to summon the exiles of Israel from all the places into which they had been dispersed, but in some sense to be a light to lighten the Gentiles, and bring even kings to worship the Lord. Whatever the detailed explanation of this much-canvassed passage, it is a plain expression of the fact that salvation has a purpose. God who gives the saving power to men expects them to use it to his glory.[35]

Saved to save and saved to serve. The mandate is clear, Heavenly Father: with great pardon comes great responsibility. I wait upon you to lead me in your ways of service. Master, speak.

28 January

**He made himself nothing
by taking the very nature of a servant,
being made in human likeness.
(Philippians 2:7)**

He was a travelling teacher, a jobbing builder by trade, and he had fallen foul of the authorities. After a burlesque of a trial he was led out to die outside the city walls of Jerusalem, the main town of one of the most significant provinces on the edge of the Roman map. The year was about AD 30. The date, Easter. The time, nine o'clock in the morning. They crucified him. Not at all pleasant, but it happened to a great many people in those days. No worse than what takes place in the torture chambers of more than seventy countries in the modern world.[36] And yet it has become the most famous death in history.

It was a messy business. The Romans, who seem to have got hold of the idea of crucifixion from the Phoenicians in the Punic Wars, became expert at this most grisly method of execution. They reserved it, however, for the *humiliores*, the lower classes in the Empire. And in particular it was what Cicero called a *servile supplicum*. It was the penalty for slaves. Apart from them you might find a deserting soldier being crucified, or someone who had interfered with the Vestal Virgins. This 'most cruel and most terrible punishment' (Cicero, *In Verrem*, 2.5.165) was a death reserved for the lowest of the low.[37]

'Of no reputation'. 'A travelling teacher'. 'A jobbing builder'. 'Led out to die'. One of 'the *humiliores*'. 'The lowest of the low'. These are but some of your names, Lord Jesus; descriptions of your lowly humanity. Each of them, though, in the context of your incarnation, says so very much about you, and about your love for fallen humanity: my God and King, swathed in majesty.

29 January

Do not treat prophecies with contempt but test them all;
hold on to what is good.
(1 Thessalonians 5:20–21)

Christianity soon became a great threat to Judaism, and there is evidence to show that the very mention of Jesus was frowned on in Jewish documents. Nevertheless, scattered through the Mishnah[38] there are allusions like these. 'Rabbi Eliezer said, "Balaam looked forth and saw that there was a man, born of a woman, who would rise up and seek to make himself God, and cause the whole world to go astray."' We read of his miracles, with the disparaging comment, 'He learnt magic in Egypt.' We read, too, of his death: 'They hanged Jeshua of Nazareth on the eve of Passover.'[39]

A disparaged and lied-about God, suspected of being little more than a magician. Help me, Lord, I pray, to discern that which is truth and that which is error. It's a minefield out there sometimes, Lord, spiritually speaking, and I need your guiding hand upon my thinking. Protect me from lies and falsehood.

30 January

**It is by grace you have been saved, through faith –
and this is not from yourselves, it is the gift of God.
(Ephesians 2:8–9)**

It is time to consider the conditions of receiving God's salvation which emerge in the pages of the Old Testament. The prime condition is a simple trusting reliance on God alone, not in any fancied goodness or strength of one's own. This applies both in the national and in the personal sphere. Israel is not to look for alliances with Assyria or Egypt as a solution to their military problems, but to God alone (Hos. 5:13 – 6:3; Isa. 31:1; Ps. 33:16–20). This is the way they have always received God's salvation, and this is the way they will continue to experience it. 'They got not the land in possession by their own sword, neither did their own arm save them, but thy right hand and thine arm, and the light of thy countenance, because thou hadst a favour unto them' (Ps. 44:3). In the same way, the individual, too, is to rely exclusively on God for his salvation (Ps. 55:16; 86:2; 138:7, etc.). God will not share the glory of his salvation with another, and certainly not with man, who is so quick to forget what God has done for him, and to boast of his own puny abilities and strength (cf. Ps. 106:21). Consequently, it is when men are at the end of their tether, cast solely upon the mercy of God, that he can risk saving them without the danger of their becoming proud.[40]

What a message, Heavenly Father! This is heart-warming and reassuring. Just as I am, I come. Nothing do I bring, except faith in the blood of Christ. I have no other argument. 'A simple trusting reliance on God alone'. Help me, I pray, as I ponder these words, to accept them, and to lay aside 'any fancied goodness or strength' of my own. Let that be my strength and hope. I want no other plea.

31 January

Not that we are competent in ourselves to claim anything for ourselves, but our competence comes from God.
(2 Corinthians 3:5)

It is the poor, the humble, the weak that God saves (Job 5:15; 22:29; 26:2). It is, the psalms assure us, those who trust in God (Ps. 17:7; 37:40; 86:2), those whose hearts are right before him (Ps. 7:10), the heartbroken and contrite (Ps. 34:6),[41] the afflicted (Ps. 18:27), those who call upon him (Ps. 107:13) and fear him (Ps. 85:9), those who know themselves to be poor men in need of his succour (Ps. 34:6 – and this includes the king, Ps. 20:6). These are his people (Ps. 119:94). These are the men who are not too full of themselves to receive the salvation he proffers them. Nothing could make more plain than Ex. 14:13 the truth that man's place in salvation is one of trusting response to the loving initiative and intervention of God. 'Fear ye not,' says Moses in God's name to the people of Israel, when God is about to seal the deliverance from Egypt with the crossing of the Red Sea, 'Fear ye not, stand still, and see the salvation of the Lord which he will show to you today.' Such faith is the proper attitude in man towards a God who saves; and so it is represented from one end of the Bible to the other.[42]

A study of salvation in the Psalms! Help me, God of my salvation, always to remember that this is your altruistic gift to me (and to all who call upon your name). Help me always to remember to bring my nothing – no merit – and exchange it for your everything, and to find that sufficient. My rags for your robes.

1 February

He must reign until he has put all his enemies under his feet.
(1 Corinthians 15:25)

Josephus was an influential Jewish refugee-general, writing in Rome in the 90s, and very keen to keep his nose clean and get the best deal possible for his conquered countrymen, who were smarting under the sack of Jerusalem in AD 70. So you would not expect him to say much about a controversial figure like Jesus. What, then, do you make of this?

> And there arose about this time (i.e., Pilate's governorship) Jesus, a wise man, if indeed we should call him a man; for he was a doer of marvellous deeds, a teacher of men who receive the truth with pleasure. He won over many Jews and also many Greeks. This man was the Messiah. When Pilate had condemned him to the cross at the instigation of our leaders, those who had loved him from the first did not cease. For he appeared to them on the third day alive again, as the holy prophets had predicted, and said many other wonderful things about him. And even now the race of Christians, so named after him, has not yet died out.

When you get a piece as explicit as that in an anti-Christian writer it is pretty shattering. No wonder lots of people have attacked the text. Nevertheless, this passage is there in all the manuscripts of Josephus. Some of it may well be ironic. But there can be no doubt from this Jewish evidence that Jesus was a real historical person.[1]

Ironic or not, this extract speaks volumes in terms of your life and its unique impact, Lord Jesus. Even your enemies and opponents took note of your presence and recorded the mark you made, here on earth. What a God you must be, to command such acknowledgements; powerful and remarkable. There is none like you.

2 February

**Carrying his own cross, he went out to the place of the Skull
(which in Aramaic is called Golgotha).
(John 19:17)**

[When a crucifixion took place] the condemned man was invariably scourged, and men were known to die under that punishment alone, so severe were the wounds inflicted by this cruel cat-o'-nine-tails inset with pieces of metal. It is possible that Jesus suffered this punishment from both the Jewish and from the Roman authorities (Matthew 26:67f; John 19:1). Thereafter he had to carry the *patibulum* of his cross, and was led out under armed guard to die.[2]

'That punishment', Lord Jesus, which, rightly, belonged to me. You were punished like this for my sake, when you had done no wrong; the innocent scourged in place of the guilty. And because of this, I go free. Such love, written in crimson and rust.

3 February

You shall have no other gods before me. You shall not make for yourself an image in the form of anything in heaven above or on the earth beneath or in the waters below. You shall not bow down to them or worship them; for I, the LORD your God, am a jealous God.
(Exodus 20:3–5)

Faith can easily degenerate into superstition, just as prayer can degenerate into the attempt to force God's hand. In 1 Sam. 4 the Israelites realize that their defeat by the Philistines is to be seen as a chastening from the Lord, and so they send for the ark of the covenant (4:3), the visible pledge, the sacramental symbol of God's presence in their midst. They are sure that, provided they are armed with this talisman, the victory will be theirs. Instead, they suffer a signal defeat and the ark is captured (4:11). They have to learn that God cannot be manipulated, nor will he tolerate trust in any other than he, be it never so sacred a symbol. In contrast, as this same first book of Samuel makes plain, once men come in sincere penitence to God and are willing to obey him rather than attempt to use him for their convenience, then he does save. The following sequence of events is illuminating.

> Samuel spake unto all the house of Israel, saying, If ye do return unto the LORD with all your hearts, then put away the strange gods and Ashtaroth from among you, and prepare your hearts unto the Lord, and serve him only; and he will deliver you out of the hand of the Philistines . . . Then the children of Israel did put away the Baalim and Ashtaroth and served the LORD only . . . And the children of Israel said unto Samuel, Cease not to cry unto the LORD our God for us, that he will save us . . . And Samuel cried unto the LORD for Israel, and the LORD heard him . . . And the Philistines drew near against *Israel*; but the LORD thundered with a great thunder that day upon the Philistines and discomfited them, and they were smitten before Israel . . . Then Samuel took a stone . . . and called the name of it Ebenezer, saying Hitherto hath the LORD helped us. So the Philistines were subdued, and they came no more into the coast of Israel. (1 Sam. 7:3–13)[3]

Saving God, dissolve any idols that linger in my heart today; any traces of superstition, however righteous those traces might appear to be, that I too might serve you only.

4 February

He spoke and stirred up a tempest
that lifted high the waves.
(Psalm 107:25)

Perhaps the first thing that strikes us as we come to the Old Testament is the tremendous emphasis on the Spirit of God as a violent, invading force. It is like the wind that hurtled across the desert or whistled through the cedars or rushed down the wadis. 'The grass withers, the flower fades when the *ruach adonai* blows upon it. Surely the people is grass,' cried Isaiah (40:7), and that is typical. There is a whole host of places where we are told that God's action is like the wind, strong, boisterous, uncontrollable. He sends the wind. He controls it. He causes it to cease.[4]

Boisterous God! Come, blow through your beloved church afresh; gusts of glory, flurries of forgiveness, and rushes of renewal. Invade us in love.

5 February

The Spirit came into me and raised me to my feet.
(Ezekiel 2:2)

In speaking of the 'Spirit of the Lord' the Old Testament writers significantly retain this emphasis on God's violent invasion from outside our experience, disturbing and mysterious like the wind. It is their way of stressing that the Beyond has come into our midst, and we can neither organise nor domesticate him. This comes out very strongly in the Book of Judges. The oppressed people of Israel cry to the Lord to send them deliverance. His response is to 'raise up a deliverer for the people', Othniel. The Spirit of the Lord came upon him; he judged Israel; he went out to war; and his hand prevailed (Judg. 3:9–10). Again, Gideon was a very ordinary man until 'the Spirit of the LORD took possession of him' (Judg. 6:34). Then he became instrumental in a signal deliverance for his country. It was most noticeable in the case of that famous strong man, Samson. It was when 'the Spirit of the LORD came mightily upon him' that he 'tore a lion asunder as one tears a kid' (Judg. 14:6).[5]

Spirit of the living God,
Fall afresh on me.
Spirit of the living God,
Fall afresh on me.
Break me, melt me, mould me, fill me.
Spirit of the living God,
Fall afresh on me.[6]

6 February

I was a stranger and you invited me in.
(Matthew 25:35)

[Jesus] had a genius for friendship. However, it never turned to favouritism. Time after time in the gospels you find Jesus talking to a single Pharisee, a blind man, a beggar, a lame man, a mourning widow, a Roman soldier. A tremendous variety of needs, and he cared about them all so much that each one must have felt that he was the only person that mattered to Jesus for the time being. That's quite right: he was. His friendship with the women who accompanied him, his friendship with the dozen disciples who left house and home to stay with him – this is one of the most attractive traits of his character.[7]

O Lord – that person who wanders into a church service and sits, somewhat apprehensively, by themselves. Let me go and sit with them, or at least offer them a handshake and a smile. O Lord – that newcomer who makes their way into a coffee morning at my church and patently doesn't know anyone there. Let me take them a cup of coffee, on the house. And so on, Lord Jesus. O Lord, forbid that I should ever assume that visitors and guests will be welcomed by someone else.

7 February

They offered Jesus wine to drink, mixed with gall.
(Matthew 27:34)

[Jesus] was exposed naked on the cross. The cause of his being there was written above his head and fixed to the cross; and he was left there to die slowly in intense agony from exhaustion, thirst, and wounds. The criminal had, of course, no recourse but to curse, spit and urinate on his tormentors. Often the kindlier execution squads would offer a draught of drugged wine before nailing the man up. This went some way towards dulling the pain. And sometimes a rough *sedile* or saddle was fixed to the cross. This offered support to the crucified man, and often prolonged his life. By raising himself up on his lacerated feet and the saddle he could give some respite to heart and lungs which were put under immense strain by the position of crucifixion.[8]

What does Calvary mean to me? A distant place near Galilee?
Somewhere I've never been?
A far-off venue, foreign hill, where Roman soldiers used to kill
The enemies of state?
A patch of grass, not much to see; is that what Calvary means to me?
A garbage heap, the council tip; symbol of Rome's efficient grip?
Or is it more than that to me?
The man impaled upon a tree; my Saviour, drenched in blood.
In actual fact, what kept him there, naked (not even underwear),
Was my long list of sins.
For God hung there, the God-man, Christ,
For me (for me!) was sacrificed.
The purest Lamb of all was slain; innocent, yet wracked with pain;
Each blood-drop marking wrong.
I'll never really comprehend why God the Father chose to send
His loved, begotten Son;
But somehow, thanks to love, I'm free.
That's what Calvary means to me.[9]

8 February

The Lord is the Spirit.
(2 Corinthians 3:17)

We have grown used to expecting the Spirit of God to speak in a gentle whisper, not a roaring wind. We have sought him in the promptings of our hearts or the resolutions of our committees. We are in danger of forgetting that it is God we are talking about: the God who created us, the God who sustains us and has sovereign rights over us. This God can and does break into human life, and sometimes he does it through the violent, the unexpected, the alien. It was this same spirit that drove Jesus off into the desert to be tempted after his baptism, that pioneered the mission of the early Church often in the most bizarre, unexpected and 'unorthodox' ways; that gripped a man like Philip, removed him from a flourishing evangelistic campaign in Samaria and drove him into the desert – because there was one man who needed his help. When that help was given 'the Spirit of the Lord caught up Philip', just like Ezekiel long before him, and 'Philip was found at Azotus, and passing on he preached the gospel' (Acts 8:26,39–40).[10]

Ezekiel's God, Philip's God, my God. Holy Spirit, grant me a clear picture of just who you are: Almighty God, and nothing less; a status utterly unparalleled.

9 February

Walking and jumping, and praising God.
(Acts 3:8)

I once met a girl who awoke to find herself gripped by the Spirit of God at 2 a.m. She was a cripple, and at once her hip was cured – a hip, incidentally, that had defied the efforts of the country's best doctors – and she found herself praising God in tongues. Now she is doing a remarkably useful piece of Christian service.[11]

> Healing God, I pray today for anyone known to me who is in need of your touch; those in pain, whose bodies aren't working very well. Great Physician, draw near to them as I bring them to you. Grant them a glimpse of your wonder-working power, according to their need. Jehovah-Rapha.[12]

10 February

We have been justified through faith.
(Romans 5:1)

One of the important elements in the deliverance God affords to men is victory (e.g. 1 Sam. 14:45). As F.J. Taylor puts it, 'To save meant to be possessed of the necessary strength, and to act on it so that it became manifest. David gained salvation when he reduced the surrounding peoples to obedience' (2 Sam. 8:14). Any chieftain who had sufficient strength to gain victory over the foes of the people could be described as a saviour (Judg. 2:18; 6:14), but as it was God who had raised up the saviour (Ex. 14:30; 1 Sam. 10:19), he was pre-eminently their Saviour . . . To save another is to communicate to him one's own prevailing strength (Job 26:2), to give him and to maintain the necessary strength. Only God is so strong that his own arm obtains salvation (victory, security, freedom) for himself (Ps. 98:1; Job 40:14), and everybody else must rely on a stronger than himself (i.e. God) for salvation.[13][14]

Let me never think, Almighty God, that I can in any way save myself. It's tempting to make that assumption, but I have no strength or ability in that regard. Rather, teach me to lean very hard on grace, and to find it sufficient, both in this life and the next. That's a much safer option. You save to the uttermost, wherein is all my confidence.

11 February

May I never boast except in the cross of our Lord Jesus Christ.
(Galatians 6:14)

No subject has been such eloquent shorthand for the acme of heroism and self-sacrifice, as the cross of Jesus Christ. It was the cross and resurrection which set the new faith apart from Judaism. It was the cross and resurrection which seemed to the early Christians so to encapsulate the central truth of God that they would tolerate no other gods, even if it meant courting execution for their narrow-mindedness. It was the empty cross which founded a missionary religion which has spread into every country and tribe in the world, and which has attracted more followers than any other religion. Every revival of Christianity has had that empty cross very near its core. The cross has had a profound effect on education, medicine and the relief of social injustice wherever the Christian gospel has been given a chance to spread.[15]

A cross in a car in an everyday street
(A little one, hanging, quite cute, really; sweet),
An ornament, there with an old Disney doll,
Hung for good luck?
(With Jesus AWOL)
A bit like a Bible that's kept on a shelf,
A family heirloom stored next to the elf
That Gran bought in Blackpool, a holiday charm,
A trinket for bingo,
A cheap pseudo-balm.
Is this what I've shared with a world that is lost,
When I've stopped to consider what witness might cost?
Have I mentioned salvation?
That blood-stained red tree?
Does it matter too much what that world thinks of me?[16]

12 February

LORD, my Rock and my Redeemer.
(Psalm 19:14)

God's salvation is no light and easy thing. Though it costs man nothing, being offered him in sheer grace, it costs God dear. The emphasis on the costliness of salvation is important, and is brought out in a variety of ways, notably in the sixth-century prophets. Sometimes the title 'Redeemer' is linked with that of 'Saviour' (e.g. 'I am thy Saviour and Redeemer, the mighty one of Jacob', Isa. 49:26; 60:16). Sometimes the two ideas are linked in the context, e.g. 'Thus saith the LORD, the Redeemer of Israel . . . In an acceptable time have I heard thee, and in a day of salvation I have helped thee' (Isa. 49:7–8). Particularly memorable is that hauntingly beautiful passage in Isa. 63:8–9, 'Surely, they are my people, children that will not lie: so he was their Saviour. In all their affliction he was afflicted, and the angel of his presence saved them; in his love and in his pity he redeemed them, and he bare them, and carried them all the days of old.' What a rich complex of associated concepts we have here! God is their Saviour and Redeemer, he suffers with his people, his presence is in their midst; their salvation issues from his love and pity which constitutes them as his people, the 'children' whom he protects and safeguards. But in addition to all this, it is impossible to miss the hint of costliness of their redemption to God. He identified himself with their situation, in order to rescue them from it.[17]

Almighty God, Father, Redeemer and Saviour, this passage shines like a diamond, revealing so many glistening facets of your character. These words reflect your great mercy towards your wayward children. You are my God. Such meditations are indeed 'hauntingly beautiful'.

The words I have spoken to you – they are full of the Spirit.
(John 6:63)

When Saul disobeys God, and is rejected as king over Israel, we read, 'You have rejected the word of the LORD', and consequently, in judgment, 'the Spirit of the LORD departed from Saul' (1 Sam. 15:26; 16:14). Bishop John Taylor, in his moving and perceptive book *The Go-Between God*, has pointed out the importance of this link between the Spirit, with all his undifferentiated power, and the Word, with all its particularity of meaning. By distinguishing too sharply between the divine Word and the divine Spirit the Church has lost a most important biblical perspective. Certainly that link is strong and clear in the Old Testament Scriptures.[18]

Thank you, Heavenly Father, for presenting me with this important distinction. I pray for your help in understanding it. I enjoy this thought, Lord, of Word and Spirit in perfect harmony. That makes good theological sense, for it speaks reassuringly of divine balance and unity in the courts of heaven. Help me also, though, to spot and suspect anything contrary to such ordained concord.

14 February

My grace is sufficient for you, for my power is made perfect in weakness.
(2 Corinthians 12:9)

For all its rapid spread, the centrality of the cross of Jesus is very remarkable and surprising. After all, there is nothing specially Christian about the cross. Almost every culture from stone age times onward has made use of the symbol. It is found widely from China to Egypt. It has a variety of forms, including the swastika, as used in India and China. Why should this particular cross of Jesus have had such enormous impact and made it such a universal emblem? After all, one could scarcely have chosen anything more offensive to Roman, Greek and Jew alike, than a cross.

As we have seen, the Romans regarded the cross with loathing – though they continued using it! It was not a death designed for Roman citizens; only for subject peoples, as a vicious and exemplary deterrent. It spoke of shame, of guilt, of pain, but above all of failure. If a man ended up on a cross he was an undoubted failure.[19]

God of paradox, God of counter-culture, whereas this world values and promotes might and ruthless power, your victory was achieved through apparent 'undoubted failure'. Your ways run contrary to so much of our logic, Lord: the dying man bleeding out on a filthy cross hoisted on some kind of rubbish tip is in fact King of the world. Stay with me as I ponder this seeming contradiction and its implications.

15 February

I am not ashamed of the gospel, because it is the power of God that brings salvation to everyone who believes: first to the Jew, then to the Gentile. (Romans 1:16)

This new faith was a Jewish offshoot, and that made it [the cross] instantly unsavoury. One has only to read the Latin authors of the first century AD to see how very unpopular the Jews were; for their financial success, for their strange beliefs, for their mutilation of the body in circumcision, for their political and social inscrutability and for their special privileges. A faith from Judaea was not a good recommendation. And thirdly, the presentation of a central figure in this new religion who had been put to death on a cross as a failed pretender after kingship – why, this was the kiss of death. And yet the faith of an empty cross spread fast in Rome and eventually captured the Empire.

It was no less unattractive to Greek ears. As Paul remarks in 1 Corinthians, 'the Greeks seek wisdom, but we preach Christ crucified' (1:22). It was very plain to civilised Greeks, the sophisticated élite of the ancient world, that wisdom resided in universals; beauty, truth, goodness, freedom and the like. These had universal validity and applicability. But here were these followers of Jesus maintaining that the wisdom of God was to be found in a particular; and a very disgusting particular at that, the mangled body of a crucified man. What an unlikely message to capture the heart of leading individuals.[20]

An unsophisticated Saviour! A deity prepared to be regarded as 'a very disgusting particular'. I can but thank you, Lord Jesus, for your incarnate willingness to inhabit 'the mangled body of a crucified man' all for my sake. I can but thank you.

16 February

The cheerful heart has a continual feast.
(Proverbs 15:15)

Some protest that [Jesus] used violence in kicking crooked traders and cheapjacks out of the Temple when they had 'turned my Father's house into a den of robbers' (Matthew 21:13). I am not sure that I would have thought it wrong if he had used that thing of cords he had in his hands! But we are not told that he did. He just turfed them out.

[Another] moan is that he lost his temper with the fig tree and cursed it unreasonably. Not a bit of it. His cursing of the fig tree was an acted parable. The fig tree had for centuries been a symbol of the Jewish nation. Jesus had come to Jerusalem and found that they rejected him. He had found no fruit on the fig tree of Israel. He pronounced on it the judgment of God, and that judgment awaits us all, so we had better not be too high and mighty about it . . .

The third complaint I have heard against Jesus' character is that he had no sense of humour. I find that hilarious! How can anyone with a perfectly straight face tell his very smug and pious hearers that they must remove a whacking great plank from their own eye before they can see clearly to pull the tiniest speck out of their brother's eye? Can you imagine him sitting as solemn as a lord while he ticked the Pharisees off for their punctilious care in straining out any unclean thing, like a gnat, from their wine – whilst not realising that they were swallowing the biggest unclean beast in the book, a camel? Don't tell me Jesus hadn't got a sense of humour. Read the gospels and see.[21]

Wonderful! A deity with a sense of humour! A deity whose humanity chimes so beautifully with mine. Lord Jesus, you came as one of us; the divine and human natures combined in such a marvellous way. You know the human lot, full well, and that brings me great reassurance. Your interest in my life is not merely academic or distant, but rooted in reality. I like this kind of God!

17 February

You were bought at a price.
(1 Corinthians 6:20)

Go'el primarily means to act the part of a kinsman. It is a family word. The kinsman vindicates his relative . . . Whenever this word was used it carried with it the idea of effort on the part of the redeemer in the cause of the relative; effort, and often the payment of a ransom, too.

Frequently God is spoken of as the *go'el*, the great kinsman of his people, in particular when reference is made to his deliverance of Israel from Egypt. 'Thou art the God that doest wonders. Thou hast made known thy strength among the peoples. Thou hast with thine arm redeemed thy people' (Ps. 77:14–15); 'I will redeem you with a stretched out arm' (Ex. 6:6). Or again, 'Their redeemer is strong; the LORD of hosts is his name: he shall thoroughly plead their cause' (Jer. 50:34). This word is applied to God with great frequency in the latter part of Isaiah. He is seen as the Redeemer from Egypt, the Redeemer from Babylon (Isa. 41:14; 43:14; 44:6,24; 47:4, etc.) and the Redeemer from sin (Isa. 44:21–3, cf. 63:9). Now in what sense can God be a redeemer or kinsman in this way? Has the idea of payment been entirely lost, and does the word mean no more in Deutero-Isaiah than 'deliver'? This is often said. Indeed, Snaith in his *Distinctive Ideas of the Old Testament* regards Isa. 52.3 as regulative for the ideas of *go'el* when applied to God, 'Ye shall be redeemed without money.' Certainly no crude concept of a ransom price must be applied to God's redeeming work, or we shall find ourselves asking with Origen, to whom God paid the ransom, and wherein it consisted. But nevertheless the idea of the costliness of deliverance is not so lightly to be dismissed.[22]

Heavenly Father, I wonder if I will ever know just how much it cost to see my sin upon the cross. It's possible I shan't ever fully realize. Redeeming God, my vindication is owed entirely to the price that was paid on Calvary. It seems I can barely begin to thank you for the 'effort made on the part of the redeemer'. Nevertheless, I want to do so, and I offer what thanks I can.

18 February

Who has a claim against me that I must pay?
Everything under heaven belongs to me.
(Job 41:11)

Surely B.F. Westcott has caught the right nuance of the word when applied to God, 'It cannot be said that God paid to the Egyptian oppressor any price for the redemption of his people. On the other hand the idea of the exertion of a mighty force, the idea that "redemption" cost much, is everywhere present. The force may be represented by divine might, or love, or self-sacrifice which became finally identical.'[23] Certainly the *go'el* metaphor was ascribed to God to stress his kinship with his people Israel and his gracious love to them. But it also emphasizes[24] that the carrying out of the kinsman's function by the Lord cost him as dear as it did the human kinsman who had to pay a ransom price.[25]

Almighty God, you are no one's debtor, yet you paid a ransom to love which cost you very dear: 'his gracious love to them' indeed. My kinsman-redeemer.

**Be perfect, therefore, as your heavenly Father is perfect.
(Matthew 5:48)**

Jesus had no vices. Jesus never did anything wrong. The gospels never praise him; but they never give a single example of anything for which he had to say 'My mistake' or 'So sorry'. Those sorts of incidents did not take place. He told his disciples to say 'Forgive us our trespasses' each time they said the Lord's Prayer, but that was the prayer the Lord taught them – not the one he used himself. His claim was, 'I do always those things which please him' (John 8:29). He seems to have been conscious of no cloud between him and his heavenly Father. Remarkable, and all the more remarkable in one who was so quick to spot hypocrisy in the prayers of the religious, showmanship in the donations of the 'generous', lustful, murderous thoughts lurking under respectable exteriors which were very ready to condemn adultery and murder in others. How could a man as perceptive as this not have apologised to God in his prayers. The only answer I can see is this. He did not say 'Sorry' for his misdeeds, because *he did not have any.*[26]

A perfect man. A man perfectly filled with the Holy Spirit. A perfect God in whom no fault is found. To be like Jesus: this is my creed, my hope, my aim. So help me, God.

20 February

**This is eternal life: that they know you, the only true God,
and Jesus Christ, whom you have sent.
(John 17:3)**

Just as the will of God cannot be known without the revelation of the Spirit, so the service of God cannot be carried through without the equipment of that same Spirit. It is only through God's revelation that we can know him. It is only through his power that we can service him.[27]

First, Lord: to know you. Then, to serve you. Finally, to see you as you are. Sweet will of God, draw me ever-closer until I am wholly lost in this sequence.

**Do not cast me from your presence
or take your Holy Spirit from me.
(Psalm 51:11)**

Jesus strikingly fulfilled one of the main strands of Old Testament teaching about the Spirit. God had given his Spirit to his anointed king in order to equip him for his leadership of the people. Saul is the classic example. Samuel anoints him king: he is promised, and receives, the power of the Spirit of God upon him (1 Sam. 10:1,6). Subsequently, he disobeys God disastrously, and has to be set aside as king in favour of David. Samuel anoints David, and we read that 'the Spirit of the LORD came mightily (literally "leaped") upon David from that day forward' (1 Sam. 16:13). What happened to Saul, then? 'The Spirit of the LORD departed from Saul', and from now on we read that an evil or distressed *ruach elohim* troubled him. The Spirit of the Lord, the *ruach adonai* passes to David to equip him for his princely service. The profane word *elohim* (which need not necessarily refer to Yahweh) is now used to describe Saul's fits of mania and ecstasy.[28]

Heavenly Father, I find this a desperately sad reading. My heart goes out to Saul, even though he sinned 'disastrously'. It is not for me to judge. I simply pray that you will not take your Holy Spirit away from me, even though I too am a sinner. Guest of the soul, make your abode in me. Have mercy.

22 February

The Lord your God will raise up for you a prophet like me from among you, from your fellow Israelites. You must listen to him.
(Deuteronomy 18:15)

The cross of Jesus was so special because of the one who was suffering there. On any showing this was the best and greatest life the world has ever witnessed. He should never have been put on that terrible cross. More, he was the fulfilment of the hopes of the Old Testament. Here was the 'prophet like Moses'. Here was 'Elijah returned'. Here was the Son of David's line. Here was the Son of man whom Daniel had predicted. Here was Isaiah's Suffering Servant. Never in all history had all these threads from centuries ago converged into a single knot: and that knot was Jesus Christ on the cross. Here was the fulfilment of the prophetic, priestly and kingly expectations of the Old Testament. This is indeed why the name 'Christ' was applied to him, and why it stuck to him so closely that within a few years it acted as surname. It means 'Anointed One' and Jesus was seen as fulfilling the three figures in Old Testament days who received anointing – the prophet, priest and king.[29]

Anointed, though, with blood and spit and sweat, and crowned with splintered thorns: such is your love and such is your grace, Lord Jesus; Christ of the cross.

23 February

I know him because I am from him.
(John 7:29)

One of the striking differences between Christianity and the other religions is that the others all start with the assumption that God is known. Christianity does not. Jesus says that nobody knows God in the personal sense of Father except himself; and he alone can bring people into that intimate relationship (Matthew 11:27f). He then follows that up with one of the most marvellous offers that have ever passed the lips of man: 'Come to me, all you who labour and are heavy laden, and I will give you rest' (Matthew 11:28, RSV).

What a fantastic offer. I find three or four heavy laden ones an enormous burden to cope with. Jesus invites all! And, in many ways, that is the heart of his teaching. It is not primarily demand, though demand is there. It is primarily offer, free offer. We have got a bit cynical about free offers, because so often they aren't free at all; there's a catch in them somehow. But the very fact that the free offer business is so widespread in the supermarkets reminds us that a genuine free gift is one of the most attractive things in the world. That is what the religion of Jesus is all about.

'See here,' he says. 'You do not know God, although a lot of you are very religious. You are strangers to him. You are, frankly, lost. Well, listen to me. God cares about that, I know, because I know him in a way none of you do. He is my heavenly Father. I talk to him in the same family way as you chat to your dad.' His special word for the Father, 'Abba', means 'dear Dad'.[30]

Lost, but found. Lost, but invited home. Thank you, Lord Jesus. Allow me to take a moment to pray for anyone known to me personally who is looking for you by looking at other faiths. I respect their search, of course, but at the same time I pray that you will make them aware of your 'fantastic offer'.

24 February

The LORD is with you when you are with him.
If you seek him, he will be found by you.
(2 Chronicles 15:2)

The Jew knew full well that God had acted for him in the past. How could he ever forget it? At every Passover his mind was graphically taken back to the great deliverance from Egypt; the very existence of his nation was grounded in that dramatic rescue. 'I brought your armies out of the land of Egypt; therefore ye shall observe this day in your generations by an ordinance for ever' (Ex. 12:17). This Passover ordinance was not seen as a bare memorial of what had once happened in the past. In some way it actualized the past for the worshippers. It is interesting to notice, e.g. in Deut. 26:2–10 and in the later Passover *haggadah*,[31] how these salvation-events of long ago are represented as affecting not just our forefathers but *us* . . . The logic of this was inescapable. For God was not dead. He who had saved them once would save them still. How can he scrap what is precious to him, what he has made his own at great cost?[32]

> **Faithful God, your covenanted love is infinite. You are utterly consistent in your commitment to save, rescue, pardon and restore; from generation to generation. Despite our every provocation, despite our fickle ways, 'The Lord is with you'. You are not dead, and neither, therefore, is your redeeming grace.**

25 February

The ransom for a life is costly.
(Psalm 49:8)

[The word *padah*] means 'to acquire by giving something in exchange'. It is mainly applied to the redemption of a life by the surrender of another life to die in its stead. Thus 'Every firstling of an ass thou shalt redeem with a lamb; and if thou wilt not redeem it, then thou shalt break his neck: and all the firstborn of man among thy children shalt thou redeem' (Ex. 13:13). It was a permanent reminder of the deliverance from Egypt, when the firstborn were all killed by the angel of destruction, except those Hebrews who obeyed the divine instruction to sacrifice a lamb in the place of the firstborn; then the destroying angel passed over that household (Ex. 13:14–15). The word is essentially substitutionary . . . But God is also made the subject of this verb. Clearly, the idea of substitutionary death requires some modification when applied to him. 'When it is a question of God ransoming his people, there is no exchange conceivable; God acts purely from grace and requires nothing in return. It is thus that he saved his people from their bondage in Egypt (Deut. 7:8)'[33] . . .

Deliverance is costly to God.[34] This point is made very clear by the way in which the LXX[35] translators almost translated it by *lutroō*, 'to ransom'.[36] As with *go'el*,[37] the biblical writers seem deliberately to have chosen a word which expressed the costliness of deliverance, even though they might leave themselves open to some misunderstanding.[38]

Whence to me this waste of love?
Ask my Advocate above![39]

26 February

Since the creation of the world God's invisible qualities –
his eternal power and divine nature – have been clearly seen,
being understood from what has been made.
(Romans 1:20)

Jesus thought in pictures. So do most of us – which is why we find the bureau-cratic government forms so difficult to fill in.[40]

This is a lovely little statement, Lord. Thank you for all the word-pictures you created in order to describe your kingdom. I ask today, that you will alert my senses to catch glimpses of 'kingdom images' as I go about my business, or even just look out of my window; reflections of heaven on earth.

27 February

**There is surely a future hope for you,
and your hope will not be cut off.
(Proverbs 23:18)**

The kings of Israel were a pretty disappointing lot, and most of them showed little sign of the presence of the Lord the Spirit in their lives and reigns. However the link was not lost, and the hope grew in Israel that one day God would raise up a prince of the Davidic line for whom the Spirit would be no passing enduement, to be bestowed and withdrawn as he joined his predecessors in disobedience. Instead, the Spirit of the Lord would rest and remain on such a man. Hence the idyllic dream of Isaiah 11:1ff:

> There shall forth a shoot from the stump of Jesse,
> And a branch shall grow out of his roots.
> And the Spirit of the Lord shall rest upon him,
> The Spirit of wisdom and understanding,
> The Spirit of counsel and might,
> The Spirit of knowledge and the fear of the Lord.[41]

Lord, I thank you for the gift of hope. When all seems lost – through sin, through disobedience, or through circumstance – you offer hope, according to your steadfast love. I pray today for those who feel hope-less. God of hope, draw near.

28 February

If God is for us, who can be against us?
(Romans 8:31)

A mother might die for her child; a man might die for his friend. But who would die for his enemy? Yet that is what Jesus did. 'God shows his love for us in that while we were yet sinners Christ died for us. While we were enemies we were reconciled to God by the death of his Son' (Rom. 5:8,10). Many have done something like it since, in the power that the crucified and risen Jesus gives. Father Damien, giving his life to a leper colony for Jesus' sake, and eventually contracting leprosy and dying; Toyohiko Kagawa, a Japanese college student, who identified himself with the lowest and neediest of his own people in the degraded slums of Shinkawa. Men like these have given embodiment, in their day and generation, to the infectious love of Jesus who gave himself for sinners. But men have not learned it from anyone else. His love was unprecedented. It was for those who opposed him, had no time for him; and hated him. That is what makes Calvary so special. It shows us that God is not alienated by the mess we have got the world into; he is not against us. Rather, he loves us so much that there is nothing, literally nothing he will not endure for us. God so loved the world, that he gave his only Son. On Calvary we see it, and it nerves the heart to face whatever comes, in the confidence that nothing can separate us from a God who loves that much. [42]

Lord, this statement of truth 'nerves the heart' and bolsters the mind. Thank you for this injection of confidence as the varied way of life I journey. Teach me, I pray, whenever I am tempted to look at my sin, to look at Calvary instead. If the spiritual outlook doesn't look too bright, remind me, Lord, to try the 'up-look' and see you there, in your great fullness; the God who died for me.

1 March

Rich and poor have this in common:
The LORD is the Maker of them all.
(Proverbs 22:2)

On the whole, you had to be someone rather special in the Old Testament days to have the Spirit of God. A prophet, a national leader, a king, perhaps some specially wise man (Prov. 1:23) or artistic person (Exod. 31:3) – in which case you would be beautifying the Lord's Tent of Meeting, or enunciating the Lord's wisdom. But the Spirit of God was not for every Tom, Dick and Harry. To be sure, there were promises in a very general sense that 'My Spirit abides with you: fear not' (Hag. 2:5), but this was an assurance to the people as a whole, not a promise to the individual. The gift of God's Spirit was on the whole to special people for special tasks. It was not generally available, nor was it necessarily permanent.

Many a godly Jew must have felt what a wonderful thing it would be if Moses' longing could be fulfilled, 'Would that all the Lord's people were prophets, that the Lord would put his Spirit upon them' (Num. 11:29): and that is just what the prophets were led by God to foretell for the last days.

> And it shall come to pass afterwards,
> That I will pour out my Spirit upon all flesh;
> Your sons and your daughters shall prophesy,
> Your old men shall dream dreams,
> And your young men shall see visions.
> Even upon the menservants and maidservants
> In those days I will pour out my Spirit.
> (Joel 2:28ff.)[1]

All-encompassing God, you speak warmly of inclusivity: 'I will pour out my Spirit on all flesh'. You invite and welcome rich and poor, young and old, 'menservants and maidservants'. May my life reflect this, without prejudice or favour.

2 March

The kingdom of heaven is like a merchant looking for fine pearls. When he found one of great value, he went away and sold everything he had and bought it.
(Matthew 13:45–6)

Entering God's Kingdom is like finding treasure, like discovering the pearl that puts all other pearls in the shade. Did you realise that? Probably not. Like me, you may have thought it was a matter of trying hard and doing good things and going to church and all manner of dull and dreary occupations. That just shows how effective the propaganda from His Infernal Eminence has been. Because the life that is shared with Jesus Christ is the most joyful and rewarding and full life anyone can possibly live. Did he not say, 'I am come that you might have life, and have it in all its fullness' (John 10:10)? Yes, entering the Kingdom is infinitely satisfying. You may come upon it all of a sudden while slogging along the road of life, feeling that everything is a bit jaded and dull and a bore. You may have been seeking it for years as you tested a variety of philosophies, religions or drug trips. People come upon it by either path. Once they see what is offered, the shrewd ones realise it is the most important thing in the world. They are willing for any sacrifice, in order to possess it.[2]

A very straightforward prayer today, Lord, but heartfelt, for all that: I bring before you anyone known to me – friends, family, colleagues, neighbours – who is 'slogging along the road of life' and finding the going heavy. I pray for them, Lord, that you would visit their lives and impress upon them a better way. By your Spirit, touch their thinking and speak to their hearts. Save them from slogging.

3 March

'He saved others,' they said, 'but he can't save himself! He's the king of Israel! Let him come down now from the cross, and we will believe in him.'
(Matthew 27:42)

[Jesus] could have walked out of Pilate's courtroom as he had walked through a murderous mob (John 8:59). He could have asked the Father and been given twelve legions of angels (Matt. 26:53). He could have done as his enemies taunted and come down from the cross at any moment during that appalling Good Friday. Unlike any sufferer before or since, Jesus' suffering remained entirely voluntary for every moment it lasted.[3]

He could have – but he didn't. He could have saved his own skin, but he chose to save my soul instead. He could have run to safety, but he opted to run the course of my salvation. He could have chosen compromise, but he considered the cross and counted me worthy. His name is Jesus: Saviour of the world.

4 March

He who began a good work in you will carry it on to completion until the day of Christ Jesus.
(Philippians 1:6)

Is there no future element in God's salvation? Indeed there is. And increasingly the prophets laid emphasis upon it. It was the corollary of their conviction that God is the Lord of history. He could not rest content with this constant alternation of rebellion and repentance. He would surely one day complete the salvation of which he had so often given them the foretaste . . .

It is important to notice, with Knight,[4] the rich variety of imagery in which God's final purpose for mankind is expressed in different parts of the Old Testament; themes such as the Son of David, the Branch, the Royal Psalms, the Ideal Priest, the Holy City, the Bride of Yahweh, the Prophet like Moses, the Servant, the New Covenant, the Outpouring of the Spirit and many others mark the varying conceptions of the 'Day of the Lord'.[5]

Heavenly Father, you are not a God of loose ends. You are not a God of half-done pieces of work. There is nothing shoddy about the way you operate. This gives me extra confidence in your dealings with me, that you will not relent or retire until your purposes have been accomplished. Thank you.

5 March

**Though they dig down to the depths below,
from there my hand will take them.
(Amos 9:2)**

The hope of life after death has never been entirely absent from the religion of Israel, but the prospect, as assumed by popular mythology, was not particularly comforting.

The Sheol of popular religion had much in common with the Homeric hades, as a shadowy abode of the dead, almost a land of non-being. Almost all the sixty-five references to Sheol in the Old Testament come in poetic contexts, where the popular view is alluded to without being taught as part of the religion of Yahwism. 'The grave cannot praise thee, death cannot celebrate thee; they that go down into the pit cannot hope for thy truth' was Hezekiah's feeling about it (Isa. 38:18). And the psalmist cries to 'the God of his salvation' and pours out his fears, 'I am counted with them that go down into the pit; I am as a man that hath no strength, free among the dead like the slain that lie in the grave, whom thou rememberest no more, and they are cut off from thy hand' (Ps. 88:1,3–5).

Nevertheless, the very existence of Sheol, even in its most shadowy form, bears testimony to their conviction that death did not mean annihilation. Furthermore, the conviction grew in Israel that Yahweh is Lord even of Sheol. It is within the realm of his sovereignty (Job 26:6; Prov. 15:11).[6]

This is not easy or pleasant reading, Heavenly Father. Nevertheless, there is nothing here that is not in the Bible. These are scary concepts, to be honest, so I pray for your help in understanding them, within the context of your great love. I thank you, Lord, that Jesus died for me, to rescue me from the grave. Help me to share that message: there is a Saviour.

6 March

When they came together in Galilee, he said to them, 'The Son of Man is going to be delivered into the hands of men. They will kill him, and on the third day he will be raised to life.'
(Matthew 17:22–3)

We find [Jesus] teaching that his death is inevitable. It *must* be so. Early in Mark's Gospel he says that he, the Bridegroom, will be taken away from the party (Mark 2:19–20). In the next chapter we find him seeing to the heart of the Pharisees, who were complaining at his healing on the Sabbath. He asked them, 'Is it lawful on the Sabbath day to save life or to kill?' And immediately a plot was hatched to kill him (3:6). No sooner does Peter confess him as the Messiah than Jesus tells him 'the Son of Man must suffer many things and be rejected by the elders and the chief priests and the scribes, and be killed, and after three days rise again' (Mark 8:31). That statement is remarkable for identifying the Son of Man, that most glorious figure (to whom was given dominion, glory and kingdom and whose destiny was to ascend to the Ancient of Days, cf. Daniel 7:14) with the fate of the Suffering Servant of Isaiah 53 . . .

He knew he had to die. And the theme is repeated time and again in the central portion of the oldest Gospel. He gives the prediction of his fate in almost the same words in Mark 9:31 and 10:33, culminating in the ransom saying of 10:45.[7]

How much more impressive it is, Lord Jesus, in the light of this comment, that you kept going. You continued to love and to share and to bless and to help, all the while knowing full well that the shadow of your impending death was hanging over you. This places your earthly life and ministry in the most wonderful context. Even in the face of assassination, you loved.

7 March

**The kingdom of God is not a matter of eating and drinking,
but of righteousness, peace and joy in the Holy Spirit.
(Romans 14:17)**

God is not going to have proud people ruining his Kingdom. We enter it as forgiven people, forgiven by him at his expense and irrespective of our merits – or we do not enter at all.

Such is the amazing teaching of Jesus. Free forgiveness, free membership of his family – the God I have neglected, and snubbed, and pretended did not exist. And that life of love and peace and joy and good relationships is a party, a real banquet. It cost him everything to prepare. It costs me nothing to accept – except my pride. For I have to take it as a gift, not dream I can earn it by trying a bit harder, going to church more often, or subscribing to the Fund for Disabled Dogs.[8]

I am made the honoured guest at a party! Invited with an invitation gilt-edged in grace. And all I need to do is arrive with a blood-stained passport in my hand.

8 March

He is not here; he has risen!
(Luke 24:6)

Is it true? Did [Jesus] leave the tomb on the first Easter Day? It is, at first sight, most unlikely. Dead men are not in the habit of leaving their graves. But wait a moment. Any dead men we know about have all succumbed to the human disease of sin and failure. We do not know what would happen when a perfect example of the species died. There haven't been any, apart from Jesus! We are in no position to say that he could not have broken the bands of death.[9]

Don't ask me how, for I can't say, how Jesus rose on Easter Day,
How, stabbed and butchered, left for dead,
Crimson bandage round his head, he fled his armed-guard tomb.
Was there a trapdoor? Chimney pot? Sneaky accomplices paid a lot?
Muscled men to roll the stone? Grappling hooks through window thrown,
To holy carcass free?
No! I don't think so! Faith says 'No!'
Don't ask me yet, I still don't know,
But something deep within me cries that conjured tricks and wizard lies
Were not his repertoire.
A greater power worked that dawn, when Mary strolled across the lawn
And said 'Hello' to Jesus there: thought him the gardener!
(didn't stare):
The power of life o'er death.
But that's not all! The point is proved, that coffin lids can still be moved,
And though these powers be unapproved (in hell and places such):
Those dead in Christ shall rise![10]

9 March

Do your best to present yourself to God as one approved, a worker who does not need to be ashamed and who correctly handles the word of truth.
(2 Timothy 2:15)

The Spirit of God . . . is hardly ever connected with creation. This is all the more significant when one thinks of the nature mysticism that was so common in every variety of ancient paganism. There was no hint of it in the religion of Israel, which maintained such a clear emphasis on the otherness, the transcendence of the Creator God. Indeed, in the Old Testament, language about the Spirit is restricted almost exclusively to the area of relationship between God and *man*.

Despite this, whole theologies have been erected on the theme of the Creator Spirit. It is moving to think of the Spirit of God being involved in the continuous and on-going process of creation. It is fascinating to follow John Taylor's poetic imagination in attributing to the Spirit of God the 'inner awareness of the unattained', 'the stimulation of initiative and choice', and the 'principle of sacrifice' inherent in the creative development of our world (*The Go-Between God*, chapter 2). But the roots for all this in the Old Testament are rather shaky . . .

The Old Testament *may* give . . . few hints of a Creator Spirit, and certainly this thought is found in the intertestamental period – where the parallelism between Wisdom, Word and Spirit is important – but the paucity of instances that can be adduced, and the plausibility of taking them in another sense, does make one very cautious of building up a great doctrine of co-operating with the Holy Spirit in his on-going works of creation. The Spirit of God breathes his life into man; he revives the dry bones; he infuses vitality into inert matter, but the evidence that he is involved in the work of creating the world is very slim indeed in the Old Testament and non-existent in the New. We would be wise not to build too high a building on such a flimsy foundation.[11]

Thank you, Lord, for this hint to exercise reasonable caution and wisdom when reading my Bible. Help me, I pray, to resist the temptation to read into the Scriptures that which isn't actually there! Holy Spirit, speak to me as I ponder these things, whenever I settle down to read my Bible. Guide me, Divine Interpreter.

10 March

He has shown you, O mortal, what is good.
And what does the LORD require of you?
To act justly and to love mercy
and to walk humbly with your God.
(Micah 6:8)

You will not need a larger size in hats the longer you go on with Christ. Quite the reverse. The more time you spend in his company the more you will see yourself in your true colours, and the more you will realise that any progress is to be credited to him not you. Simon Peter learnt that from painful personal experience. The man who thought he could never fall away from Jesus denied him three times the night when Jesus was arrested. He writes later, with feeling, 'Clothe yourselves, all of you, with humility toward one another, for "God opposes the proud, but gives grace to the humble." Humble yourselves therefore under the mighty hand of God, that in due time he may exalt you' (1 Peter 5:5f).[12]

Remind me often, Lord, to check my hat size.

11 March

Jesus, the pioneer and perfecter of faith.
(Hebrews 12:2)

[Jesus'] death was necessary in order to fulfil the scriptures. Jesus clearly believed that the scriptures had much to say about himself, and that they predicted his death. All the evangelists mention this. Luke represents Jesus after the resurrection as saying:

> O fools, and slow of heart to believe all that the prophets have spoken! Was it not necessary that the Christ should suffer these things and enter into his glory? And beginning at Moses and all the prophets he interpreted to them in all the scriptures the things concerning himself. (Luke 24:25f)

That is the most comprehensive passage, but in Mark 9:12 we find Jesus musing on the fate of Elijah, 'Is Elijah to come first to restore all things? Then how is it written of the Son of God that he should suffer many things and be treated with contempt?' As the passion drew near we find Jesus saying 'I tell you that this scripture must be fulfilled in me "And he was reckoned with transgressors"; for what is written about me has its fulfilment' (Luke 22:37). In St John's account of the end of Jesus' life, the theme of the fulfilment of scripture is a major one: the betrayal by Judas, the loss of Judas, the thirst of Jesus and his final cry, are all in fulfilment of scripture.[13]

Lord Jesus, it seems you were born to die. It seems, too, that your death was the great crimson thread running all through the scriptures. As you would have studied those scriptures for yourself, Lord, and as you would have concluded that you were indeed the main protagonist in the stories, I can but marvel at your commitment to their fulfilment. Knowing what you did, you nevertheless ventured towards Golgotha, setting your face (and heart) like flint, all for love's sake.

12 March

Give account to him who is ready to judge the living and the dead.
(1 Peter 4:5)

The Jews had realized at an early date, even if by implication only, that God's sovereign power extends over the voracious monster of this shadowy underworld (Isa. 5:14). But in the last two or three centuries BC the hope took on clearer outlines. This may have been partly due to the breakdown of national and ethnic groups under the vast conquests of Alexander the Great, and the increasing sense of personal responsibility and personal destiny throughout the ancient world which resulted from these conquests. It was partly due, too, to the destruction of thousands of martyrs in the Maccabean wars . . . who had demonstrated their election by Yahweh in their faithfulness to him unto death. How could God's final word to them be one of rejection? There *must* be a differentiation in the after-life: 'At that time thy people shall be delivered, every one that shall be found written in thy book' (Dan. 12:1). He is speaking, of course, of the last day and final salvation, and he continues, 'And many of them that sleep in the dust of the earth shall awake, some to everlasting life, and some to shame and everlasting contempt.' How could it be otherwise if God is just? There *must* be a day of reckoning.[14]

Other refuge have I none
Hangs my helpless soul on thee.
Leave, ah! Leave me not alone,
Still support and comfort me.
All my trust on thee is stayed,
All my help from thee I bring;
Cover my defenceless head
With the shadow of thy wing.[15]

13 March

I, the Lord your God, am holy.
(Leviticus 19:2)

Pagan Greek literature does not have the phrase [*Holy* Spirit] at all, and only twice do we find it in the Old Testament. In Isaiah 63:10–11 we read that the people on whom God had set his love 'rebelled and grieved his Holy Spirit', although he had put his Holy Spirit in the midst of them when he rescued them from Egypt. In Psalm 51:11 the writer prays to God in penitence;

> Create in me a clean heart O God,
> And put a new and right spirit within me.
> Cast me not away from thy presence,
> And take not thy Holy Spirit from me.

In both cases the writers are very conscious of the moral and ethical aspect of God's *ruach*.[16] The nation of Isaiah 63 had grieved this Holy One to whom they were dedicated. The individual of Psalm 51 had done the same. The holiness of the Spirit of the Lord stands in sharp contrast to the unholiness of his fallible servants, and perhaps this is why the Spirit is here called Holy.[17]

What a marvellous thing it is, Holy Spirit, that you should want to inhabit my life; even better, that you desire to make me holy, as you are holy, by your indwelling presence and influence. Given that I have no other hope of holiness, that is a lovely option. Make your abode in me, gracious Holy Spirit.

14 March

Salvation comes from the Lord.
(Jonah 2:9)

We have hitherto said very little about salvation from sin. This is not the ruling concept in the Old Testament doctrine of salvation, but it is by no means absent, especially in the Psalms and Deutero-Isaiah. In Ps. 119, which speaks much of salvation, it is said to be 'far from the wicked who seek not God's statutes' (Ps. 119:155). In contrast, the psalmist calls to God for his tender mercies and his life-giving power (119:156). Again in Ps. 116 it is hard to escape the conclusion that the 'cup of salvation' (116:13), which the psalmist takes from God's hand in adoring faith, at least includes this interior and profound sense of personal salvation, in view of verse 8, 'Thou hast delivered my soul from death, my eyes from tears, and my feet from falling.' It is a significant insight into the inability of man to help himself which drives the writer to answer his rhetorical question, 'What shall I *render* to the Lord for all his benefits?' with the reply, 'I will *take* the cup of salvation.' Rather similar is the understanding of salvation as a garment made by God to clothe the men of his choice (Ps. 132:13–18. Cf. 2 Chron. 6:41). Much the same thought underlies Isa. 61:10, an important verse in view of New Testament developments, 'I will greatly rejoice in the Lord, my soul shall be joyful in my God; for he hath clothed me with the garments of salvation, he hath covered me with the robe of righteousness.'[18]

A robe of white, no less, and a crown of gold, furthermore. There is very little – if anything at all – I can 'render' you, Lord, in exchange for my salvation. In fact, there is nothing at all, except faith, by which I hold out my empty hands in order to gratefully receive my new garments. I simply 'take' and thereby receive my salvation from sin. I therefore 'rejoice greatly in the Lord'; the Lord who freely gives.

15 March

Every day they continued to meet together in the temple courts. They broke bread in their homes and ate together.
(Acts 2:46)

Christianity is not a solo trip. It has to be done as a team. God is not interested in changing individuals alone. He wants to show what he can do in a community who trust him.[19]

God of community, I pray for those who are feeling somewhat 'displaced' today, at least in terms of church membership. I pray for those who feel as though they don't quite belong. Guide them, I pray, to a place of belonging, either afresh within their own church fellowship or anew within another one.

16 March

Jesus replied, 'You are in error because you do not know the Scriptures or the power of God.'
(Matthew 22:29)

When you broach the question of religion, and a fellow replies, 'Oh, but all religions lead to God', ten to one he knows almost nothing about his own religious background, still less about any other. When he says, 'I'm not the religious sort', you can be fairly confident that he has made no investigation whatever into whether or not there is a religious sort, and, if there is, what it is like. When he says, 'Jesus was just a marvellous teacher but no more', it is unusual to find that he has ever examined the claims Jesus made, or the evidence supporting those claims. When you hear a person say, 'I do my best – no man can do more', of one thing you can be certain: he does not do his best (which of us does?) but he hasn't the honesty to admit as such. So do you see why I am not all that impressed by these parrot cries which come up, as regular as clockwork, whenever I begin to talk about God? They are so shallow. They simply show that people, on the whole, are content not to *think* about the really important matters of life and death.[20]

God of love, I pray, once again, for people I know personally who come up with 'parrot cries' such as these. Grant me, I pray, wisdom, sensitivity and grace in terms of my own responses. Above all, Lord, lead those individuals to faith; move them away from excuses to belief. Have mercy. Lord, hear my prayer.

17 March

**You, Lord, are with these people.
(Numbers 14:14)**

In it [his death] he [Jesus] identifies with sinners. This was totally unlike any rabbi, who despised the 'people of the land' as sinners who could never attain to the law of God. But Jesus received such; he ate with them. And at the very outset of his ministry he unambiguously asserted his identity with them. John the Baptist was baptising 'a baptism of repentance for the remission of sins' (Mark 1:4), and men and women who felt the burden of their sins came to be baptised by him. So did Jesus, though his relationship with his Father was unclouded by any awareness of sin. But he wanted to throw in his lot with sinners (Matt. 3:14ff).[21]

A God who chooses to 'throw in his lot with sinners'! Lord Jesus, this fact alone places you head and shoulders above every other so-called deity. You really are a hands-on God. This is remarkable theology and wonderful love.

18 March

They all alike began to make excuses.
(Luke 14:18)

I am not impressed by the common responses about religion which I meet everywhere I go. They are not only shallow, betraying an absence of thought: they are also evasive, betraying an unwillingness to face up to the evidence . . .

And the trouble is that they are not only shallow but dishonest. The man who says, 'It doesn't matter what you believe as long as you are sincere', would never dream of applying that motto to any area of life other than religion. He may think he's being straightforward when he comes out with a statement like this, but he isn't really. What he means is that he is not going to take the trouble to investigate the truth of Christianity or of any other religion – maybe because he doesn't think it important enough, maybe because he fears he would get exposed, or challenged, or involved. Although he sounds so fine and liberal-minded, he is likely to be an escapist at heart.

You see, then, why I am not satisfied to find such widespread agreement about fundamental beliefs? The agreement is unthinking and escapist. It is an agnosticism which does not want to know in case the answer should prove costly or inconvenient.[22]

Lord, it really is a wonder you stay with any of us as you do! We are prone to excuse-making, yet you persist in loving us and working with us. Thank you for that. Help me, this day, to avoid making excuses. Help me to walk in the light and to play with a straight bat in all my dealings. And I pray for anyone known to me who is inclined to prevaricate or procrastinate in matters of faith. By your sovereign power and grace, convert escapist hearts to believing hearts.

19 March

'You are my witnesses,' declares the LORD.
(Isaiah 43:10)

'No, Vicar, go and talk to someone else. I'm afraid I'm not the religious sort.' That is very often said, and I have a lot of sympathy with it. There is something creepy and sanctimonious, something effeminate and wet about that phrase 'the religious sort'. I think of business men in black ties at the funeral of one of their companions trying to imitate 'the religious sort' for half an hour, and then emerging breathless from the funeral to the open air in order to light up a cigarette and return to normality. I think of a country church with six people in it along with the vicar, not to mention a bat or two, while the men of the village meet across the green in the pub for a cheerful evening in each other's company. Church? Not for them, thank you; they're not the religious sort.[23]

From these kinds of preconceptions and misconceptions, Good Lord, deliver us. And while you are delivering us, show us why people so often think these kinds of things about your people and about church in general. Then, help us to address that.

20 March

The anointing you received from him remains in you.
(1 John 2:27)

The one in whom the Spirit had a permanent dwelling [Jesus] amazed men by the sinlessness of his life. Such was the character produced in human life by the Spirit of Yahweh once he was given full control. Such, therefore, should be the character in the followers of Jesus, called as they were to be 'holy' or 'separated to God' as his special possession (1 Pet. 1:15f; 2:9) . . .

Ezekiel and Jeremiah expected God to change men in the days of the New Covenant by putting his Spirit within them, so that they should walk in his ways and keep his commandments: after Pentecost the Holy Spirit begins to produce holiness in God's people. This does not mean separation from sinners, in a sense of isolation and self-satisfaction like the monks of Qumran; instead, it means involvement with needy, fallen, spoiled humanity, following the example and endued with the Spirit of him who was a friend of tax gatherers and sinners.[24]

Holy Spirit, if you expect me to change, as you are entitled to, then I pray for your help in meeting that expectation. It is only by your 'permanent dwelling' within my heart and mind that I can anticipate any hope of spiritual progress. Thankfully, though, I may do so!

21 March

The Spirit came into me and raised me to my feet.
(Ezekiel 2:2)

In the Old Testament the Spirit does not appear as a divine being. He is rather seen as God's personal presence and intervention. The point is well made in a verse like Isaiah 31:3

> The Egyptians are men, and not God;
> And their horses are flesh and not spirit.

In those words, Isaiah is not contrasting flesh and spirit in the way we might, as the exterior and the interior of the same being. No. He is grouping flesh and men together, and God and Spirit together. The Spirit is on God's side of reality; quite different from our side. And when the Spirit of the Lord is present with men, it means the gracious and personal intervention of God himself . . .

The Spirit is the personal expression of God himself, and can be grieved: he is holy, not only the divine power but the moral character of God: he is God in action for the benefit of his people . . . the Spirit is equated with the 'arm' of Yahweh, that is to say his saving activity. The Spirit is no less than the personal, moral, active power of the Lord God, and for the further revelation of his nature we must await Act Two, the coming of Jesus.[25]

'The gracious and personal intervention of God himself' – what a beautifully reassuring sentence that is; loaded with love, goodwill and intention. Thank you for being this sort of God.

22 March

**Yours, Lord, is the greatness and the power
and the glory and the majesty and the splendour,
for everything in heaven and earth is yours.
Yours, Lord, is the kingdom;
you are exalted as head over all.
(1 Chronicles 29:11)**

Salvation from sin is unquestionably Israel's greatest need, according to Ezekiel. They need, of course, to be brought from among the heathen to their own land (36:24), but even more they need God to save them from all their uncleanness (36:29). When they remember their own evil ways and their doings that were not good, and loathe themselves in their own sight for their iniquities, then God will cleanse them from their iniquities and cause them to dwell in their cities, and the wastes shall be built (36:31–4). Once again we meet the characteristic Hebrew recognition that this salvation both from physical and spiritual ill was not due to their own righteousness but for God's own glory. Once again we find universalist overtones in the wonder of the heathen round about, who shall see all this, 'and they shall know that I am the Lord'.[26]

**A God who:
Delivers
Saves
Cleanses
Rehomes
Rebuilds
Heals.
This is my God. To God be the glory.**

23 March

The heart is deceitful above all things.
(Jeremiah 17:9)

In Isaiah's day back in the eighth century BC men were offering God all manner of sacrifices, but their hearts were far from him. In Jesus' day the scribes and the Pharisees gained the reputation for being hypocrites. Many of them must have been absolutely genuine. Some, however, were seen to make long prayers in order to impress; to give ostentatiously so that everyone should think how generous they were; to make a great show of their biblical knowledge in order to shame others. Piety outside and corruption inside is a revolting mixture. Jesus had to accuse some of his hearers of being just like that: they reminded him of the white sepulchres which were such a common sight on the hills set against the deep blue of the Sea of Galilee. They looked marvellous from the outside: but inside they were foul and full of corruption and dead men's bones.[27]

Lord Jesus, I guess my prayer today is a pretty obvious one: for holy authenticity inside and out. This might sound like a straightforward prayer, but I know only too well how complex we human beings can be. Nevertheless, I pray, asking you to straighten this out within my life; that I may be a Christian through and through.

24 March

Righteousness exalts a nation.
(Proverbs 14:34)

The link between religion and hypocrisy did not die in the first century. Think of the hypocrisy in those very religious days of the Victorian era: the immorality that flourished, the exploitation that went on alongside meticulous religious observance. And, rightly or wrongly, there are many who suspect hypocrisy in the high churchgoing figures among the whites in Rhodesia and South Africa, and among the middle class in America. Could this be a sort of insurance policy to preserve the regimes against the inroads of black power and Communism? I do not know. But what I do know is that many people assert very forcefully that they are not the religious sort because they hate hypocrisy, and they feel that somehow it is tied up with religion.[28]

These are hard-hitting words today, Lord. There is nothing comfortable or easily palatable about them. However, if they cause me to stop and think, then I receive them like medicine; it might not taste great, but it will do me good. So, my prayers today are for regimes and empires that are founded on hypocritical statutes and which implement injustice under the external guise of Christian behaviour. I pray for change in nations where this is so. I pray for leaders, asking you to raise up people of religious conviction whose leadership will improve matters.

25 March

This gospel of the kingdom will be preached in the whole world as a testimony to all nations.
(Matthew 24:14)

[St Mark] begins his Gospel with the story of the baptism of Jesus. The crowds who flocked to listen to John's preaching of repentance were baptised by him in the Jordan in penitent expectation of the age of fulfilment which he proclaimed. But when Jesus was baptised, Mark makes it plain that the age of fulfilment *has already dawned*. A voice was heard from heaven. Now there had been a great shortage of messages from heaven for a very long time. The writings of the rabbis repeatedly maintain that the Holy Spirit departed from Israel after the last of the prophets, Haggai, Zechariah and Malachi . . . What is more, the Spirit of God, and the *shekinah*, or glory of God, were not to be found in the Second Temple . . .

Men cherished a tremendous sense of nostalgia for the departed glories of the previous temple, and for the Spirit of Yahweh which used in Old Testament days to be displayed in mighty deliverers and inspired prophets.[29]

Lord of times and seasons, God of aeons, controller of centuries, this reflection today causes me to pray for some kind of revival – a fresh visitation, perhaps – within my own nation. It really does seem, in some countries around the world, as though there has 'been a great shortage of messages from heaven for a very long time'. I think of secular Europe, for example. Nostalgia has its place, of course, and the past is to be honoured, but I also want to pray for the future of world evangelism. Hear my prayers.

26 March

Blessed are you when people insult you, persecute you and falsely say all kinds of evil against you because of me. Rejoice and be glad, because great is your reward in heaven, for in the same way they persecuted the prophets who were before you.
(Matthew 5:11–12)

[Jesus'] death [was] God's judgment on the world. Jesus makes this plain in direct statements like the following: 'Now is the judgment of this world . . . and I, when I am lifted up from the earth, will draw all men to myself . . . This he said to show by what death he was to die' (John 12:31ff). The theme recurs many times in St John, but it also comes in more pictorial ways in other Gospels. One of the starkest is the parable of the wicked husbandman (Mark 12:1–9), based as that is upon the famous parable of Isaiah about the vineyard of God's people Israel (Isa. 5:1–7). God, like the vineyard owner, looks for some return from his tenants, but gets none. He sends one servant after another for the fruit, but they get misused or killed. Last of all he decides to send 'his beloved son, saying, "They will respect my son". But those tenants said "This is the heir; come, let us kill him and the inheritance will be ours". And they took him and killed him and cast him out of the vineyard. What will the owner of the vineyard do? He will come and destroy the tenants'. And to rub in the theme of judgment Jesus puns on the word *ben* 'son' and *eben* 'stone' and continues, 'Have you not read this scripture "The very stone which the builders rejected has become the head of the corner; this was the Lord's doing, and it is marvellous in our eyes"?' The Jews saw the point, were furious, and tried ineffectually to arrest him. His time had not yet come, but he had made very plain that one purpose of his death was to demonstrate God's judgment on the sinfulness of a rebel world.[30]

A dying God; lover of 'a rebel world'. Knowing that you would be killed, Lord Jesus, you came – you still came. This divine judgement is ultra-severe and serious, yet, even so, tinged with remarkable love and mercy.

**They are to perform duties for him and for the whole community.
(Numbers 3:7)**

The Spirit of God is offered to Israel to equip them for . . . service to the un-
reached multitudes of the heathen. 'Behold, my Servant, whom I uphold; mine
elect in whom my soul delighteth; I have put my spirit upon him; he shall bring
forth judgment to the Gentiles.'

But Israel as a whole declined this call ([Isaiah] 42:19). She saw her election by
God as a privilege to treasure, to hold on to, to boast about; not as a responsibility
to be shared with the Gentiles.[31]

**This is a valuable reminder, Lord – a lesson, perhaps – of Christian
duty, privilege and responsibility. I am saved to save, and saved to
serve. Let me never forget the latter half of that deal. A charge to keep
have I.**

John saw Jesus coming toward him and said, 'Look, the Lamb of God, who takes away the sin of the world!'
(John 1:29)

Jesus saw his death as a sacrifice. This is very plain from the Last Supper, a meal laden with Passover imagery. Instead of referring to the lamb or the 'bread of affliction' eaten by their forefathers in the Exodus, Jesus says 'This is my body' and 'This is my blood of the covenant'. As Jeremias has demonstrated so conclusively in *The Eucharistic Words of Jesus*, body broken and blood poured out could only mean one thing: violent death. And Jesus foresees that death of his as fulfilling the pattern of the Exodus when the blood of the lamb sprinkled on the doorpost spelt safety for the Israelites, while its body brought them nourishment for the journey into the promised land.[32]

Lion and Lamb. Saviour and Sustainer. Mediator and meat. Blood and bread. Your death means that you are all of these things to me, Lord Jesus.

29 March

**Seek first his kingdom and his righteousness,
and all these things will be given to you as well.
(Matthew 6:33)**

None of us like seeing beggars. It makes us feel uncomfortable; indeed, we feel 'got at'. But organised religion bears the image of the beggar. How many churches do you pass with a notice outside inviting you to save this ancient building? How many cathedrals do you go into with a notice inside telling you how much per minute it costs to run the place? Then there are the fêtes, the whist drives, the door to door collections, the stewardship campaigns and all the other money raising gimmicks. The churches always seem after your cash . . .

On the money-grabbing issue, I think the church has deserved its appalling image. It does give the impression that it is always out for money. It should rather proclaim that it has found great treasure in Jesus Christ, and that unlike most treasures, this one is for free. Jesus was always impressing upon people that entry into the Kingdom of God, or the Great Supper or friendship with himself (all three add up to the same thing) was absolutely free, for black and white, Jew and Gentile, prostitute and Pharisee alike. Free. But he also made it plain that life within the kingdom was costly. It might cost you all you have, just as it cost him all he had. So the church is right to say to its members that they owe Christ a proportion of their time as well as their money and their talents. The church is wrong to ask those who are not its committed members to act as if they were . . .

Jesus is the one we are concerned with. And he never went round taking collections from folk who dropped in for the odd funeral. He never put a collecting box outside the Nazareth synagogue begging non-members to prop it up. If the church does not follow his example, so much the worse for the church.[33]

Wow! This is quite some challenge to the church, Lord. Perhaps we need to learn afresh the value of dependency upon you alone. If so, teach us what that might entail, all the more so if anything we are doing is off-putting to people who might otherwise wish to know more about faith.

30 March

'I will send my messenger, who will prepare the way before me. Then suddenly the Lord you are seeking will come to his temple; the messenger of
the covenant, whom you desire, will come,' says the LORD Almighty.
(Malachi 3:1)

In John the Baptist's ministry you find the fulfilment of the prophecies made long
ago that a messenger would come to prepare the way of the Lord. That is precisely
what the Baptist was doing. And Mark immediately introduces Jesus on to the
scene: the messenger has indeed prepared the way of the Lord. Daring words
those, for in the prophet Malachi they clearly referred to Yahweh himself. Mark is
quietly claiming that in Jesus we have to do with none other than Yahweh, who
had come to our world in the man Jesus.[34]

I believe that God the Father is seen in God the Son: prophesied One,
to whom all the prophets gave witness. As I read these words today, I
ask you to help me assimilate them, for they are so deeply profound;
and in assimilating, to worship.

31 March

See what God has done!
(Numbers 23:23)

Jesus himself speaks about . . . the uncanny darkness which fell on the world during the crucifixion, out of which came that terrible cry of dereliction 'My God, my God, why hast thou forsaken me?' (Mark 15:34). Nobody has pierced to the full depths of that cry, drawn from Psalm 22. It has been pointed out that the psalm, on which Jesus was perhaps meditating as he hung on the cross, ends in confidence and victory ('men shall tell of the Lord to the coming generation, and proclaim his deliverance to a people yet unborn, that he has wrought it').[35]

Christus Victor!

For Christ, whom God the Father raised from the dead, is Victor . . . and he is our righteousness.[36]

Today, Lord Jesus, I continue to worship.

1 April

They cried out in a loud voice:
'Salvation belongs to our God,
who sits on the throne,
and to the Lamb.'
(Revelation 7:10)

It is God who saves, whether it be a matter of saving a small Semitic tribe from the onslaughts of its neighbours, or of saving God's elect with an everlasting salvation in the 'Day of the Lord'. The understanding of what salvation meant deepened and became more spiritual throughout the centuries, but its broad outlines remained constant during the whole Old Testament period. Salvation does not depend on man's goodness, but on God's faithfulness (Ps. 40:10). And thus we find the psalmist, conscience-stricken, after grievous sin, praying not that God would restore to him his salvation, but rather, the joy of it. 'Restore unto me the joy of thy salvation' (Ps. 51:12). He could never have prayed like that had he deemed salvation to depend on human effort and attainment. The author, knew, however, that human sin does not abrogate the covenant mercies of God. He had not lost his salvation by the terrible sins he had committed; only deliberate apostasy can cut the link between God and his people. He had not lost his relationship with the Saviour God, but he had lost his joy in it. Wrongdoing always spoils fellowship with God (cf. 1 Jn. 1:7–9), until it is repented of and put away; but it is never said in Scripture to annul the relationship with him.[1]

'Human sin does not abrogate the covenant mercies of God'. What a statement this is! Truly, in this life and the next, 'all my hope on God is founded'.[2]

2 April

The LORD upholds all who fall.
(Psalm 145:14)

In both covenants [Old and New] God takes bad men, and in sheer grace treats them with a magnanimity which they could never deserve, a generosity which liberates them from themselves and makes new men of them. This is the salvation which redounds to his eternal credit as he shows what he can do with fallen, sinful men, once they make him the God of their salvation.

Thus Nathan can say to David after the Bathsheba affair, 'The LORD hath put away thy sin; thou shalt not die' (2 Sam. 12:13), and the worshipper of Ps. 51 knows that nothing but the sheer forgiveness of God can cleanse him from his defilement; the same is true of Ps. 32.[3]

Gracious God, you are not too proud to stoop, in order to lift (and carry) the fallen. You are not too angry to pardon, in order to turn bad into good. You are not too miserly to give (freely) of your salvation and further assistance. You are not too resentful to put away our sins, in order that we might repent.

3 April

When the centurion, who stood there in front of Jesus, saw how he died, he said, 'Surely this man was the Son of God!'
(Mark 15:39)

[Mark] knows that Calvary brought terrible darkness and separation into the heart of Jesus, and yet the achievement of his death was sufficient to bring his executioner to admit that Jesus was the Son of God. Whatever the centurion meant by it, his words very soon became an important part of the Christian baptismal confession, and Mark's readers would not be slow to catch the allusion. For the most tremendous thing had happened. The 'veil of the temple', a great curtain keeping people out of the Holy of Holies in the temple, was split from top to bottom when Jesus died, Mark tells us, as if God were showing that the way into his holy presence was no longer confined to one high priest, once a year, after due sacrifice for his own sins and those of the people. No, the way into God's presence was now available for all who would confess Jesus as the Son of God: even for the most brutal of murderers, even for the person who nailed him to the cross![4]

The vilest offender who truly believes,
That moment from Jesus a pardon receives.[5]

4 April

You are a people holy to the Lord your God. The Lord your God has chosen you out of all the peoples on the face of the earth to be his people, his treasured possession.
(Deuteronomy 7:6)

Within the land of Israel the people of God had to put up with invasion after invasion; Antiochus, Pompey, Herod, followed by direct Roman rule through the Procurators after AD 6, were a hard succession of evils to bear.

Life was no easier for the many Jews who had to live outside Palestine, in Rome, for instance, or Alexandria. They always seemed to spark off riots, as the pagan populace jibbed at their peculiar dress and appearance, their refusal to work on the Sabbath and their unwillingness to recognize any of the customary gods. They seemed a very curious people to the ancient world, and they were usually met with a good deal of unpleasantness, even when they were not involved in a pogrom, which was often enough. Both inside Palestine and without, the Jew had to be on the defensive against attitudes ranging from suspicion and dislike to active persecution.[6]

Heavenly Father, my prayers today are with your beloved chosen people, whose history is scarred with persecution after persecution. It seems that almost anywhere they tread, they are unwanted, and hounded. I pray that you will bring many to know their Messiah, and I pray too for individuals and organizations whose specific ministry is to share the love of Jeshua with Jews. Bring them home.

5 April

**All those the Father gives me will come to me,
and whoever comes to me I will never drive away.
(John 6:37)**

Can you honestly say there is a religious sort? Don't pretend it is comprised of the effeminate, the retired and the addle-headed. I think round some of the people in our own parish church: a leading gynaecologist, a factory worker, a librarian, a horticulturist, a garage owner, a builder, an architect, an engineer, a man who has been finding God in prison, a lawyer, an atomic scientist, a university teacher, a man on the dole, literally hundreds of students, the majority of whom are studying scientific subjects, members from Iran and India, Sri Lanka and Rhodesia, South Africa (black and white) and U.S.A., Canada and Sweden, Germany and Hong Kong, Japan and Australia, Kenya and Uganda, Sudan and Nigeria and so on. The diversity of their attitudes, their backgrounds, their educational attainments, their temperaments, their ages, their *everything*, is so vast that it would be ridiculous to class them all as the religious type. These Christians are not just one type: they are all types – extrovert and introvert, tough and weak, old and young, black and white. Their diversity has only one unifying factor, but that factor is strong as steel: Jesus Christ.[7]

Father of all, I thank you for this lovely reminder of the fact that your love reaches out, in equal measure, to one and all. Your love has no boundaries of the type we so often construct. Assist me to remember this, I pray, in my prayers and my personal evangelism (whatever that looks like): that your grace, that 'one unifying factor' is amply sufficient, and that no one need come to you and leave disappointed. Let that be my inspiration and encouragement in witnessing.

6 April

**The stone the builders rejected
has become the cornerstone.
(Psalm 118:22)**

I had a letter . . . from a correspondent working with *Time Magazine*. He was converted in 1966 largely through conviction of the Holy Spirit's presence in the life of my predecessor as Rector of St Aldate's. He is deeply involved in the work of the church in Hong Kong at present, and is not only experiencing a deepening maturity in his own life but is also leading numerous other people to the Christ he used to reject but who is now his living Lord.[8]

Lord, you are gracious to forgive and redeem. Help me to bear that in mind as and when I share my faith; that it is always your will to pardon and restore. Let that truth, too, be my inspiration and encouragement. I pray for my own church leader(s), that 'the Holy Spirit's presence' in their lives may similarly influence others. I pray for the worship, work and witness of my church in general.

7 April

**Trust in the LORD with all your heart
and lean not on your own understanding.
(Proverbs 3:5)**

The Sadducees . . . did not believe in any life after death worthy of the name; they seem to have clung to the earliest Hebrew belief in the shadowy, tenuous half-life of Sheol, and rejected the more recent belief, current among the Pharisees, in a future life where men are rewarded or punished according to their behaviour in this life (Matt. 22:23). They were an aristocratic party of noble priestly and land-owning families, comprising most of the wealthy men in Palestine.[9] They generally seem to have had a majority in the Sanhedrin under the Herods and the Romans. They were the hard-headed practical men of affairs, stubborn in their ways and conservative in their temperament – characteristics not unknown among aristocrats and ecclesiastics! So devoted were they to the ritual of the Temple that they disappeared as a party with its destruction in AD 70. So involved were they with maintaining the status quo (with the retention of political influence in their own hands) that they inevitably cooperated with the Gentile overlords of their country, and so earned general odium as quislings. They were great believers in free-will and self-determination, and had little time for those who waited wistfully for God to intervene on their behalf.[10] [11]

Ah! The folly and hubris of so-called self-made people. The reliance (and over-reliance) on one's own resources and political nous. Forgive us, Lord, if we fall into such traps, forgetting our dependence on your grace. Forgive us too, Lord, when we manoeuvre and manipulate in order to save our own skins, and bring us back to a place of humility and faith.

**Whether you turn to the right or to the left, your ears will hear a voice
behind you, saying, 'This is the way; walk in it.'
(Isaiah 30:21)**

Had we asked a Sadducee how Israel was to be saved, he might have answered us something like this, 'Salvation for Israel lies in cooperation with the ruling powers. You may not like the Romans, but it is folly to oppose them. Politics is the art of the possible. And as long as we hold power in Israel we shall endeavour to keep her from the madness of revolt which those hot-headed zealots are always urging. If the Pharisees like to dream up hopes of an after-life where the tables are turned and all the righteous saved, good luck to them. We are concerned with the harsh realities of life as it is.' It is hardly surprising that this blend of spiritual deadness and political dependence made little appeal to the common people, and had little lasting effect upon the beliefs and behaviour of Judaism. Indeed, something of the scorn and hatred with which they came to be regarded is preserved in the Mishnah. 'The daughters of the Sadducees, if they follow after the ways of their fathers, are deemed like the women of the Samaritans.'[12]

Lord of life, we read here of the cold hand of death upon one's reputation as the price of political expediency and compromise. As I ponder this thought, help me to examine my own life in order to live according to conscience and your guidance. May my heart reflect what my ears hear.

9 April

Jesus healed many who had various diseases. He also drove out many demons, but he would not let the demons speak because they knew who he was.
(Mark 1:34)

Time and again we find [Jesus] casting out unclean spirits from afflicted people: it is one of the well-known characteristics of Mark's Gospel, which on the whole contains little teaching, but a great deal of action by Jesus. This action includes many miracles of healing, the most important being the curing of people who were possessed. The meaning is clear. Jesus is the conqueror of demonic forces through the power of the Spirit. He is the victor over Satan, and he tells a gem of a story to drive the point home. 'No one can enter a strong man's house and plunder his goods unless he first binds the strong man; then indeed he may plunder his house.' The context in Mark 3:20–30 makes it abundantly clear that by his cures and exorcisms Jesus is driving out the demons. The man endued with the Holy Spirit is more than a match for the unclean spirits which are such a feature in Mark's account. Jesus is the conqueror. And men are amazed. They see in the presence and power of Jesus a cameo of the final victor over the forces of evil. 'With authority he commands even the unclean spirits and they obey him' (1:27).[13]

Lord, grant your church and its people confidence, authority and courage in matters of spiritual conflict. Grant wisdom too. We don't want to see demons around every corner, but neither do we wish to proceed in ignorance, fear and trembling. Teach us to study the Scriptures and to adopt a stance that is sturdy and God-glorifying.

10 April

**The law was our guardian until Christ came that
we might be justified by faith.
(Galatians 3:24)**

Paul makes the largest contribution of any writer in the New Testament to our understanding of the cross and resurrection. His range of imagery is amazing. Perhaps his best known picture is that of the law court, where we all have to plead guilty before God; and, by an astonishing act of grace, God is able to declare us 'justified', acquitted, on account of what Jesus achieved on Calvary. Though 'all have sinned and come short of the glory of God' they are 'justified by his grace as a gift, through the redemption that is in Christ Jesus' (Rom. 3:23f). It is universally agreed nowadays that 'justify' does not mean 'to make righteous' as used to be argued by Roman Catholic theologians; it is almost certainly a forensic term, and means 'to account righteous'. Possibly it may have the overtones, as T.W. Manson has suggested, not so much of the law court as the throne room, where the sovereign can say to the commoner 'Arise, Sir John' and that word not only *declares* something but *does* something. Thereafter he is not merely accounted a knight; he *is* one. And God does not merely account us in the right with him; he makes us so. And how does he do that? Through what Jesus achieved by his death on the cross and resurrection. For 'he was delivered to death for our offences, and was raised for our justification' (Rom. 4:25).[14]

And what a glorious 'throne room' yours is, Heavenly Father: a place of grace where we are declared innocent on account of 'what Jesus achieved on Calvary'. I thank you, Lord, for this promise of eternal security, and I pray that you will grant me fruitful opportunities to share this news with others, so that they too may stand alongside me in that lovely venue.

11 April

Everyone born of God overcomes the world. This is the victory that has overcome the world, even our faith. Who is it that overcomes the world? Only the one who believes that Jesus is the Son of God.
(1 John 5:4–5)

It is not only through his healings and exorcisms that Jesus shows himself as the bearer of the Spirit: he claims it explicitly in the controversy with the scribes about Beelzebul (apparently another name for Satan, conceived of as 'lord of the house'). In response to their charge (Mark 3:22) that it is through demonic power that he casts out demons, he replies that no divided house can stand: if Satan casts out Satan, his empire is doomed. And he makes that terrifying statement about the sin against the Holy Spirit, over which many people have needlessly tortured themselves.

'All sins will be forgiven the sons of men, and whatever blasphemies they utter; but whoever blasphemes against the Holy Spirit never has forgiveness . . . for they said, "He has an unclean spirit."' More light is shed on this verse by the form in which it occurs in the 'Q' material (sayings of Jesus preserved in Matthew and Luke independently of Mark). 'Whoever says a word against the Son of Man, it shall be forgiven him. But the man who blasphemes against the Holy Spirit will not be forgiven' (Luke 12:10). It is one thing to mistake and misrepresent Jesus, clothed in all his humility as Son of Man; it is one thing to misread his parabolic teaching, coming as it does in riddles. But it is quite another thing to see the truth clearly and wilfully to reject it; quite another thing to ascribe the power of the Holy Spirit to the devil – which is what the scribes were doing. If men firmly reject the saving work of God in Jesus, they forfeit the very possibility of rescue, not because God will not have them, but because they say, like Satan in *Paradise Lost*, 'Darkness, be thou my light.'[15]

Lord Jesus, there are indeed elements of this excerpt that are 'terrifying' – not least the thought that some will choose eternal darkness instead of light. Hear my prayers today for any of my relatives and friends who persist in travelling in this direction. In your mercy, touch their lives in a powerful way – nothing less.

12 April

The Sadducees say that there is no resurrection, and that there are neither angels nor spirits, but the Pharisees believe all these things.
(Acts 23:8)

Unlike the Sadducees, the Pharisees were coming to hold clear views on the subject of salvation. They were a democratic party, and they had the ear of the people. They were, furthermore, a progressive party, and were not afraid either to apply the Law to new circumstances by authoritative pronouncements,[16] or to open their minds to new ideas. For instance, there is reason to believe that their doctrine of the after-life with rewards and punishments, of angels and demons, may well have been influenced by Persian thought. They believed passionately that God was in control of history, and they speculated a great deal about the Deliverer who they felt would surely come . . .

They looked for an anointed one, a Messiah . . . of Davidic stock.[17]

As I continue to walk with you, Lord, please keep my mind open to new ideas if those ideas deepen and strengthen my faith. Prevent my mind from becoming stodgy and prejudiced, lest I miss some aspects of truth of which I am not yet aware. Bless my thinking and my attitudes with freshness and receptivity. Grant me a holy curiosity.

13 April

God will bring every deed into judgment,
including every hidden thing,
whether it is good or evil.
(Ecclesiastes 12:14)

While God's salvation tarried, how was the pious Jew to achieve the personal salvation which was a natural corollary of the Pharisaic doctrine of the judgement and separation of the righteous and unrighteous dead?[18] How was he to be sure of the favourable verdict on the great day? One would expect it to be through living a good life. And so it is. As early as Ben Sirach[19] it is stated that those who fulfil their filial duty in honouring their parents will be saved (3:1ff.). Indeed, it goes on to say that 'he that honoureth his father maketh atonement for sins'. Again, 'benevolence to a father shall not be blotted out, and as a substitute for sin it shall be firmly planted' (3:14). We have here the beginning of the Jewish doctrine of merit, the idea that if you kept the Law, you could put God in your debt. This doctrine develops as the keeping of the Law becomes increasingly the main concern of the Jew. Thus in *Pirqe Aboth* 2:8 it is said, 'He that getteth to himself words of Torah has gotten to himself the life of the world to come', and in 6:7, 'Great is Torah which gives life to those who practise it, both in this life and in the world to come.' Good works are taught as the way of salvation equally explicitly in 4 Ezra,[20] a composite work of the first century AD. 'The righteous who have many works laid up with thee shall out of their own deeds receive their reward' in contrast to 'those who have no works of righteousness' (8:3–9).[21]

Heavenly Father, I know full well that my salvation depends entirely upon the blood of Christ; his death and resurrection. I have no other argument. Nevertheless, I owe you my good works, by way of gratitude and devotion. Let me not overlook the place of my 'own deeds' in the context of Christian commitment. They do not represent my atonement, but they certainly constitute my reasonable response to saving grace.

14 April

I no longer call you servants, because a servant does not know his master's business. Instead, I have called you friends.
(John 15:15)

The German martyr, Dietrich Bonhoeffer, was not playing with words when he coined the phrase 'religionless Christianity'. That is precisely what Christianity is. It is not an attempt by good-living men to please God and win a place in heaven. It is God coming in his love and generosity to seek folk who would never seek him, holding out his arms to them on a cross, and saying 'Come to me, and let us share life together'. Not a religion, but a rescue. That is why the earliest Christians were so keen to stress that they had no temple, no altars, no priests. They had no religion in the normally accepted sense of the term: hence the Romans called them 'atheists'. Instead they had a Person, who knew them, loved them, and never left them. Nothing could separate them from his loving presence. So prayer became not a ritual but converse with a Friend. Worship was not a ceremony for Sundays but the natural outpouring of love and adoration to the Saviour by his people when they met together. They needed no churches, for where two or three were gathered together in his name, he was in their midst. They needed no priests, for Jesus had opened immediate, equal access to God's presence for every one of them. Christianity, properly understood, is the most earthy of faiths: it does not separate the secular from the sacred, but keeps the two firmly together. The Lord is as interested in what I do at eleven o'clock on Monday in my daily work as he is in what I do at eleven o'clock on Sunday in a church service.[22]

Lord Jesus: King of kings, Lord of lords, Friend of sinners. This is grace. I pray for this sense of divine friendship to flow through my heart, through my life, through my church, and through my relationships. May this define my 'religion'.

15 April

I am going to send you what my Father has promised; but stay in the city until you have been clothed with power from on high.
(Luke 24:49)

Luke has a lot to say about the Holy Spirit, both in the Gospel and the Acts . . .

He makes a very special point of emphasising the presence and activity of the Spirit in the birth stories of John and Jesus, and in underlining the new outbreak of prophecy, which had been silent so long, but as we have seen, was confidently expected afresh in the Age to Come. Right at the start of the gospel story we find the Spirit active in full vigour. The new age had dawned, and the signs of its presence were experienced . . . Luke could hardly go to greater lengths in stressing that the Age to Come dawned with Jesus' birth. The Spirit, active in an upsurge of prophecy, active in the birth of John and Jesus, rests upon Jesus and in its power he carries out his mighty works and after the resurrection imparts that same Spirit to his disciples. From Bethlehem at the beginning of his Gospel to Rome at the end of Acts it is the one Spirit active throughout: first showing us the nature of that messianic salvation brought by Jesus, and then showing us how it was spread.

Luke lays even more stress on the Spirit activating the whole life and ministry of Jesus than any other evangelist.[23]

This point about 'the Age to Come' is fascinating, Lord, for it speaks to me of sovereign sequence and order. I may not understand how such timescales are organized or counted in the courts of heaven, but I am, nonetheless, reassured that the ages of humanity are well within your control and supervision. Thank you for this, Lord: the knowledge that as my own days come and go, and pass, they are not outwith your attention.

My times are in your hand;
My God, I wish them there![24]

16 April

As in Adam all die, so in Christ all will be made alive.
(1 Corinthians 15:22)

Christ, the one who repairs the ruin Adam wrought, involves us in his risen life, having first dealt with our accusing past (Rom. 5:21). No wonder Paul exclaims in wonder at the victory which Jesus achieved on Calvary, and in which we share. 'He disarmed the principalities and powers and made a public example of them in him' (or, more probably 'in it' – the cross, Col. 2:15). And therefore 'thanks be to God who always leads us in triumph' (2 Cor. 2:14). Not even death itself will be able to take that victory away from him and those who are 'in him'. Is he not the risen one? Therefore 'I am persuaded that neither death nor life . . . nor anything else in all creation, will be able to separate us from the love of God in Christ Jesus our Lord' (Rom. 8:39).[25]

Let me carry these thoughts around with me today, Lord. You are the God who:

Repairs,
Involves,
Resurrects,
Triumphs,
Conquers and
Vanquishes.
You are the God from whose love I cannot be separated.
Let these be my meditations this day.

17 April

Day after day every priest stands and performs his religious duties; again and again he offers the same sacrifices, which can never take away sins. But when this priest had offered for all time one sacrifice for sins, he sat down at the right hand of God, and since that time he waits for his enemies to be made his footstool. For by one sacrifice he has made perfect forever those who are being made holy.
(Hebrews 10:11–14)

Old Testament sacrifices could not actually atone for sins; they merely acted as a painful reminder of them (Hebrews 10:1–4). The blood of bulls and goats could never remove sin: they, too, acted as a *praeparatio evangelica*, and pointed toward the fully voluntary and fully personal offering of Jesus the ultimate sacrifice. We have been sanctified by the offering of the body of Christ once for all. Where there is forgiveness of sin, there no longer needs to be any offering for sin (10:11–18) . . .

The old covenant was ineffective because man failed to keep his part of it. But the Old Testament itself had looked for the day when God would give a new covenant, which would include a personal knowledge of God, an interiorising of his commands and the forgiveness of sins. This is what he has brought about through the death and resurrection of Jesus (chs. 8, 9 and 10). The ambivalence of the Greek word *diathēkē* allows the writer to make a further point. It can mean either 'covenant' or 'will'. Now no will is effective without the death of the testator. But that is precisely what has happened on Calvary. So in Christ crucified and risen, we have the ultimate sacrifice, the ultimate priest and the ultimate covenant between God and man.[26]

An ultimate God. Herein is the great Christian hope: you are not the God of jobs half-done, but of completeness, thoroughness and perfection. There need be no anxious thought in my mind that you might have missed a detail, because you haven't. The outworking of your plan of redemption is gloriously ultimate.

18 April

**May your hearts be fully committed to the LORD our God,
to live by his decrees and obey his commands.
(1 Kings 8:61)**

Christianity is for non-religious people. It is not going too far to say that if you insist on being religious you will find Christianity hard, almost impossible. You will find it almost impossible to *become* a Christian, because your 'religion' will get in the way: you will feel that somehow you are better and more pleasing to God than your irreligious neighbour, and that is just what the Pharisees felt – and what kept them away from Jesus. And you will find it almost impossible to *be* a Christian: because once again your 'religion' will get in the way: you will feel that the Christian life depends on your religious observances, and not on the Lord. You will be inclined to keep a little religious corner in your life for God and not allow him to have the whole thing. You will definitely find it harder to become and to be a Christian than the man who is not 'the religious sort'.[27]

Food for thought here, Lord, not least the (daily) challenge of surrendering 'the whole thing' to your will and way. Furthermore, the challenge of letting that surrender be something joyous and maybe even fruitful – some kind of blessed relief – rather than anything reluctant. Lead me in these ways, Holy Spirit.

19 April

**The Lord is not slow in keeping his promise, as some understand slowness.
Instead he is patient with you, not wanting anyone to perish,
but everyone to come to repentance.
(2 Peter 3:9)**

If you really believe in a doctrine of merit to win God's favourable verdict on the day of judgement, you must recognize that, in all probability, there will be few enough who pass the test! There is reason to believe that the question, 'Are there few that can be saved?' (Lk. 13:23) was debated with interest in rabbinic circles. The more rigid your doctrine of merit, the gloomier became your estimate of the number of the saved. So while the *Apocalypse of Baruch*,[28] a book which is, at any rate in places, marked by a generous and genial tone, asserts that 'not a few will be saved' (21:11), 4 Ezra, which belongs to much the same date, but has a very much stricter doctrine of merit, is in no doubt that the saved will be few. 'Many have been created, but few shall be saved' (8:3). This view, of course, involves the corollary, which the writer does not shrink from drawing, of a ghastly doctrine of God. 'Ezra' represents him as saying, 'I will rejoice over the few that shall be saved' (7:60), and 'I will not concern myself about the creation of those who have sinned, or their death, judgement or perdition. But I will rejoice, rather, over the creation of the righteous, over their pilgrimage also and their salvation and their reward' (8:38–9). And that, of course, is the logical – though intolerable – outcome of the doctrine of merit. You can only gain a credible doctrine of salvation at the expense of an ethical doctrine of God.[29]

Thank you, Lord, for the clear truth of 2 Peter 3:9. That is so very reassuring, and a great encouragement in evangelism. It speaks well of your heart for the lost. Lord, lay some soul upon my heart, and bless that soul through my life and witness. Work in ways that demonstrate and validate your word.

I will ask the Father, and he will give you another advocate to help you and be with you for ever – the Spirit of truth.
(John 14:16–17)

The Spirit of God which appeared fitfully, in a variety of forms, and prophetically in the Old Testament days shone steadily, personally, and fully in the Man of Nazareth. No longer is the Holy Spirit encountered as naked power; he is clothed with the personality and character of Jesus. If you like, Jesus is the tunnel through whom the Spirit becomes available to men. Jesus transposes the Spirit into a fully personal key. Jesus is the prism through whom the diffused and fitful light of the Spirit is concentrated. Jesus is *the* prophet (Luke 7:16; Acts 3:22; 7:37) – the long-awaited prophet of the end-time, through whom the prophetic Spirit, so active in the Old Testament, gave full and final revelation . . .

Jesus gave this Spirit to his disciples in virtue of, and subsequent to, his death and resurrection. What follows is that the Spirit is for ever afterwards marked with the character of Jesus. Indeed, he can be called 'the Spirit of Jesus' (Acts 16:7).

This is the common teaching of the New Testament, but no writer brings it into sharper focus than St John. In the fourth Gospel Jesus tells his followers, heart-broken because he is going to leave them, that it is better for them that he should do so:

I tell you the truth: it is to your advantage that I go away; for if I do not go away, the Paraclete will not come to you; but if I go, I will send him to you (John 16:7).[30]

I give thanks that at the moment of my (heart-broken?) weakness, when my need for power is evident, your Spirit is with me 'for ever'. Thank you, Lord, for this divine arrangement and promise, whereby I am never abandoned. Thank you for this lovely plan, whereby your presence is always with me. Thank you that when my own strength is exhausted, yet again, I can whisper a prayer and find you there.

21 April

Salvation has come to this house.
(Luke 19:9)

At the time of Jesus's birth, there was a deep longing for salvation throughout the length and breadth of the ancient world. The politician, the thinker, the man of religion, the man in the street, and supremely the Jew, all alike were looking for 'salvation'.[31]

As indeed, Lord, so many still are! God whose salvation is freely available to the politician, the philosopher, the religious, the ordinary everyday men and women going about their business, and the Jew, visit lives today, I pray. Bless those who are, in one way or another, 'looking for salvation'. God whose love is all-encompassing, visit hearts and homes where salvation is sought and pondered, and where questions of eternity are discussed from time to time, albeit without any commitment or decision. Come, long-expected Jesus, as you did to Bethlehem, and to all who met you there, into the lives of people whose eyes are not yet opened.

22 April

God was reconciling the world to himself in Christ.
(2 Corinthians 5:19)

Jesus Christ united people, and brings harmony where once there was discord: and that spells fulfilment at the deepest level of all.

I think of a painfully shy student who found a living faith in Christ his first weekend at university. Within six weeks he had opened up like a flower and was relating with far greater freedom to others. I think of a couple whose marriage was on the point of breaking up, when both partners were brought to faith in Jesus. The new relationship with Christ brought them closer together than ever before, and their marriage is now strong and happy. I think of a soldier, loathed for his big-headedness and rudeness, whose whole attitude to others changed radically when he allowed Jesus Christ to take control of him. I think of two schoolboys who could not stick each other, until both of them found Christ in the same summer holidays: thereafter relationships were on a completely new plane (I should know, for I was one of the boys). This same Jesus draws together those whom every pressure in the world is driving apart. He does it in Northern Ireland, as genuine believers (as opposed to the 'religious sort', be they Protestant or Catholic) meet across the border at nights and pray for one another, support each other's widows and tend each other's wounded. He does it in the Middle East as he brings together in one Christian fellowship the political irreconcilables, Jews and Arabs. He does it in South Africa . . . I have seen it time and again with my own eyes. But I know no force on earth that can do the same. Jesus is treasure indeed: for he brings fulfilment to all our relationships, once we allow him to repair our relationship to God.[32]

God and sinners reconciled![33]

God of reconciliation, God of healing and harmony, God of unity, my prayers this day reach out to family, friends, loved ones and colleagues whose lives and relationships are splintered, fragmented and falling apart. Come to them as only you can, Lord Jesus, and do for them what you did for the people in this account. I name them in prayer before you now.

23 April

God is spirit, and his worshippers must worship in the Spirit and in truth.
(John 4:24)

The idea of God has been so abused in the past that we tend to shy away from it. God has been portrayed as the man in the sky with the big stick. We have been told to be good and to do the right thing because God would judge us if we offended. God's will has been found a very useful tool for keeping people in their place:

> The rich man in his castle,
> The poor man at his gate;
> God made them high and lowly,
> And ordered their estate.

A whole system of social and racial oppression has been founded on that view of God (a verse from the hymn 'All things bright and beautiful', now generally omitted). Indeed, God's will is something which certain people in certain ages have claimed to be so sure about that they have engaged in religious wars, like the Crusades, or religious persecutions, like the Inquisition, to press their point. God has, furthermore, been used as a sort of plug to fill gaps in scientific knowledge: even Newton postulated God to keep the universe and its laws going.[34]

Loving God, forgive us (me) when we (I) have used/abused you for our own ends, and for when you have, therefore, been misrepresented. Forgive us for inserting your name into a conversation or a debate in order to shore up our ignorance or prejudice, rather than thinking things through. We ask your pardon, and at the same time, pray that you would help us to present you to a watching world considerably more carefully, with humility and restraint. Preserve us from thinking we need to know all the answers, so that our witness to your reality might be all the more charming and efficacious, in both spirit and truth.

When he comes, he will prove the world to be in the wrong about sin and righteousness and judgment.
(John 16:8)

Not only was the Spirit to universalise the person of Jesus to future believers, he was to do the same to the unbelieving world. One of the prime purposes of his coming was to nerve the disciples themselves to witness to Jesus in the face of a hostile or apathetic society . . . 'He will bear witness to me . . . and you will also bear witness'. Through the witness of the disciples which he will apply to the hearts of the hearers, the Spirit will convict men of being in the wrong . . .

Through the witness of the apostles and the witness of the Spirit (now seen as Accuser), men are shown that they are wrong with their moralistic ideas of sin: sin is essentially the refusal to commit themselves to Jesus. They are wrong in their views of righteousness, supposing Jesus to be a sinner like themselves – and worse, because he ended up in the place of cursing on a cross (cf. Deut. 21:23): his sinlessness had been vindicated by the resurrection ('I go to the Father'). And they are wrong in thinking that the judgement lay entirely in the future: the decisive battle which dethroned Satan had been won on the cross, and from now on he was a defeated foe, and believers were ransacking his empire.[35]

Help me, Lord, to be ever-ready to accept the fact that I might be wrong, on any given subject. Give me the grace to apologize if and when that is the case, and to rethink my stance. Give me, likewise, the humility to learn from my mistakes. Help me like this in my daily routines, but perhaps especially in terms of theology and spiritual understanding. May I never stand above contradiction, especially when it comes to my witnessing for Jesus.

25 April

**May the grace of the Lord Jesus Christ, and the love of God,
and the fellowship of the Holy Spirit be with you.
(2 Corinthians 13:14)**

[The Spirit] is sent to replace Jesus among the disciples and to do for them what Jesus has done on earth. More, he is to equip them for their mission just as he had equipped Jesus for his. Yet there is no complete autonomy for the Spirit, just as there had been none for Jesus. He had lived his life in dependence on his heavenly Father: if he was to give a true representation in human terms of the nature of Yahweh, then he needed to live, as man, in constant obedience to Yahweh both as his anointed Ruler and as his obedient Servant. And if the Spirit was truly to represent Jesus, he had to remain bound to the person and character of Jesus. Jesus was God's Last Word to man; and the function of the Spirit was not to give some new revelation of his own, but to bear witness to Jesus, to draw out the implications of God's Last Word.[36]

God in three persons! A mystery indeed, yet also a marvellous truth. Thank you, Blessed Trinity, for this account of divine interaction and interdependence: Father, Son and Spirit, coequal in power and glory. Teach me more, I pray.

**What I received I passed on to you as of first importance:
that Christ died for our sins according to the Scriptures.
(1 Corinthians 15:3)**

Peter is deeply gripped by the example of Jesus, the innocent sufferer, and the call to discipleship which that imposes (1 Pet. 2:18–25; 3:17–22; 4:14–19). He sees the death of Jesus on the cross as vividly as if it had happened but yesterday: for ever it is etched on his mind. 'He himself bore our sins in his body on the tree,' writes the one who describes himself as 'witness of the sufferings of Christ as well as partaker in the glory that is to be revealed' (2:24; 5:1). The death is a fulfilment of Old Testament prophecies (1:11), particularly the ones concerning the Suffering Servant: there are at least five references to Isaiah 53 in 1 Peter 2:21–5. Jesus in his death was the fulfilment of the death of the Passover lamb, which spelt freedom and life for the beleaguered Israelites who lay under threat of death in Egypt (1:18–19). His death was planned from all eternity: there was no accident about it (1:20). Essentially, the meaning of the cross is very simple and clear. 'For Christ died for sins once for all, the righteous for the unrighteous, that he might bring us to God, being put to death in the flesh but made alive in the Spirit' (3:18). That death was the harrowing of hell: it proclaimed his cosmic victory to the most notorious of sinners in Jewish thought, the men of Genesis 6:1–8 (1 Pet. 3:19). It was accompanied by the glorious resurrection that Peter had witnessed, and that made a new man of him (5:1; 1:3). It was the pledge of glory (5:4), and the assurance of final salvation (1:4–9).[37]

Heavenly Father, thank you for deeply gripping Peter's mind and heart with this analysis of the death and resurrection of Jesus. Thank you, moreover, that there are patently so many glorious facets to this subject, each one resonating with love. Grip my mind and heart too, I pray, that I may ponder your grace and generosity.

27 April

Every word of God is flawless.
(Proverbs 30:5)

Why is there so little about the Holy Spirit in the Gospels? We know that the early Church was intoxicated with the experience of the Spirit, and the comparative silence of the Gospels about him is a great credit to their historical trustworthiness in not reading back the conditions of their post-resurrection situation into the days of Jesus' life. This in itself is highly significant, particularly since many New Testament scholars seem to believe that the early Christians had no sense of historical propriety and would be perfectly happy to dream up some saying and attribute it to Jesus, or to listen to a message from one of the Christian prophets in the congregation, and then put that into the mouth of the historical Jesus. It is a staggering compliment to their historical reliability that we find almost nothing of the major concerns which engaged the primitive Church written back into the Gospels. How easily they could have tried to solve their problems about law keeping, Spirit possession, circumcision, law and grace by inventing 'words of Jesus' to settle the matters in question.[38]

A reliable God. A reliable Saviour. A reliable Bible. Thank you.

28 April

In the beginning God created
(Genesis 1:1)

Doesn't evolution rule out the possibility of a Creator? Far from it. The theory of evolution sets out to explain how varied forms of life have developed from more simple forms over millions of years. Belief in a Creator sets out to explain the great Mind behind all matter. There is no contradiction between the two. Interestingly enough, the Bible account of God's creation tells us something of the One who created, and something of why he did it. But it does not set out to tell us how. The world may have originated in a big bang or in a steady state; our first parents may have been developed from a collateral stock with monkeys or they may not. This is not a matter on which the Bible has anything to say. What it does say is that behind the creature lies the Creator, and that we are not only 'of the dust of the ground', and part of the physical universe, but are also in some sense infused with the 'breath of life' and made in the Creator's image. No discoveries in the realm of how life developed can repudiate that claim. If man discovers how to create life in a laboratory that would not put God out of business. It would simply show that when brilliant minds take matter (with real living matter to copy, incidentally) and arrange it in a very special way, a living particle may come into existence. In other words, matter arranged by intelligent minds can produce life. Exactly what Christians have always claimed for God. If we discover the secret of life, we shall merely be thinking the Creator's thoughts after him.[39]

Creator God, I worship you this day. I confess my ignorance of so many things, yet, thanks entirely to your grace, I have come to know you, and, furthermore, to know that you love me. That is a thought of staggering proportions, that the Creator, Sustainer and Governor of the universe should know me, the created, by name. Yet, I believe it to be completely true. Many are the things I cannot understand, but your loving interest in me is not in doubt. All around me, mystery I see, yet your gift of grace shines through every complexity.

I reserve seven thousand in Israel – all whose knees have not bowed down to Baal and whose mouths have not kissed him.
(1 Kings 19:18)

[It is well to differentiate] between *religio* and *superstitio* in Roman eyes. *Religio* was the state religion. It stemmed from an agreement between the king of the gods, Jupiter, and the first king of Rome, Numa. It was, in fact, a contract between the state and the gods, whereby the gods undertook to protect and further the nation provided its peoples observed them, and offered regular sacrifices to them. On the proper performance of the cult depended the *salus populi Romani*, 'the salvation of the people of Rome'. It did not matter whether or not one happened to believe in the pantheon of the gods. As a matter of fact, most educated Romans of the first century had ceased to believe in them, and had adopted a scepticism which we meet among the Greeks as early as the fifth century BC in men like Xenophanes, Euripides and Plato. Belief was unimportant; it was the state religious ceremonial that mattered. Once leave off those sacrifices, and disaster could overtake you . . .

The Roman Empire was very broadminded and tolerant in religious matters. She was continually enlarging the boundaries of her pantheon to accommodate the deities of captured races. But what she would not brook was an exclusive religion which precluded its devotees from worshipping the traditional gods of the state. This was seen not only as an affront to whatever gods there be, but as an act of sinister political disloyalty to the empire.[40]

A few important things here, Lord:
The futility of superstition, even (especially, perhaps) in religious practices:
Guard my heart from its intimidations.
The folly of pseudo-religion, which leads to nowhere:
Thank you for the truth of the good news of Jesus.
The plight of those whose Christian stance, even nowadays,
puts them at serious odds with authorities and regimes:
Strengthen their resolve and honour their witness.

He will testify about me.
(John 15:26)

Why is there nothing said in the New Testament about the Holy Spirit disclosing himself in other faiths, in the struggles of men to find God, and in the ethical endeavours of decent people? In our day . . . we are sometimes told that the efforts of our statesmen, the voting procedures of our councils, the ethical advances of our humanitarians, are being directed by the Holy Spirit. We go further, and it is often said that God has revealed his Spirit as much in Buddhism and Hinduism as in Christianity; indeed, as much in atheism as in theism.

In these days when inter-faith dialogue can easily slip into syncretism, and when man's search for God can easily supplant all idea of God's self-disclosure to man, it is most important to remember the emphatic union which the New Testament asserts between the Holy Spirit and Jesus. If God really has disclosed himself in a Son; and if that Son was characterised by his possession of the Holy Spirit which he has passed onto his followers, then we cannot without denying Christ maintain that God has revealed himself as much in Buddhism as in Christianity; we cannot make an amalgam of religions as if we were all honest seekers after a God who hides himself. I think it is of the utmost significance that the New Testament writers do not assign to the inspiration of the Holy Spirit the noble elements in pagan ethics or in other religions. For the task of the Spirit is to bear witness to Jesus. He is the Spirit of Christ.[41]

Thank you for this insight, Lord. It is most helpful as I go about my way in a multicultural, multiethnic world. Grant me your assistance, I pray, to witness well in the 'supermarket of religions' that is out there. I want to respect the faith choices of others, but I also want to present Jesus as clearly as possible. I'll need all the help you can give me, please.

1 May

All my longings lie open before you, Lord;
my sighing is not hidden from you.
(Psalm 38:9)

There's the ghastly problem of suffering. Not that it is greater than ever before, but it seems greater. It is brought into the living room every night on TV. How can there be a God if he allows all this pain and anguish in his world?

I do not want to minimise this problem for one moment. It is by far the strongest argument against the existence of God. But suppose for a minute that the problem of pain drives you to reject God's existence and to imagine that either some monster rules our destinies or that the stars are in charge of our fortunes, how does that help? You may have got rid of the problem of evil and pain (though you still have to live with them) but you have replaced them with a much bigger problem; how you get kindness and humanity, love and unselfishness, gentleness and goodness in a world that is governed by a horrid monster or uncaring stars. No, that way does not help.

As a matter of fact the Christian has a greater insight into the insoluble problem of suffering (and it remains insoluble, whatever philosophy of life you take up) than anyone else. For the Scriptures teach us that God is no stranger to pain. He did not start the world off and leave it callously to its own devices. He does not willingly afflict us, and take delight in torturing us. The very reverse. He cares so much about the agony and pain of this struggling world of his that he has got involved in it personally. He came as a man among men. He lived in squalor and suffering; he knew thirst and hunger, flogging and heartbreak, fear and despair. He ended his life in one of the most excruciating ways known to man. Let nobody tell me that God doesn't care! Let nobody claim that the boss doesn't know what life is like on the shop floor![1]

God who knows my every weakness; God who knows my every care.
God who knows the lot of humanity; God who trod where I now tread.
What a relief to know that you know: you know how it is; you know
the very road.

2 May

Create in me a pure heart, O God,
and renew a steadfast spirit within me.
(Psalm 51:10)

The man who does not respond to the divine initiative by growing in discipleship 'is blind and shortsighted and has forgotten that he was cleansed from his old sins' (2 Peter 1:9). Cleansing and purchasing: two central aspects of the atonement.[2]

Divine Optician, work hard on my spiritual eyesight, I pray, lest I carelessly fall into blindness or shortsightedness. Be near me, Lord Jesus. I ask you to stay. I, likewise, pray for those whose cleansing is beginning to wear off a little; those who feel the grime of this old world but no longer care to wash. Help me and help them. Come with renewal.

3 May

Through Christ Jesus the law of the Spirit who gives life has set you free.
(Romans 8:2)

[In the tenets of other faiths] there is much that is true, alongside much that is not. It does not mean that God has failed to give any indication of his person through 'the moral law within and the starry heaven above'.[3] It does not mean that the Holy Spirit cannot work on men of other faiths and draw their inner longings to Christ. John Taylor, in *The Go-Between God*, says rightly, 'The eternal Spirit has been at work in all ages and all cultures making men aware and evoking their response, and always the one to whom he was pointing and bearing witness was the Logos, the Lamb slain before the foundation of the world. Every religion has been a tradition of response to him, however darkly it groped towards him, however anxiously it shied away from him.' He goes on to give a splendid example of the thing he has in mind, when an old Muslim tribesman went on urging a drug-addicted English hippy to 'pray to Jesus the Messiah', until he was converted and delivered. The old man explained his view on the matters afterwards to a Christian friend, 'For an ordinary man in normal circumstances it is enough that he believe faithfully in God. But when anyone is beset by such evil power as this, nothing can save him but Jesus Christ: this I firmly believe.'[4]

What a marvellous work you do, Holy Spirit! You lead, nudge, persuade and point people to Christ the Liberator, and you do so powerfully yet gently, urgently yet patiently. My prayers today are for those like the man in the story who are trapped in addiction (of any kind). May they know your liberating power, Lord, as he did. I pray too for churches, agencies and groups whose caring ministry and expertise is shared on behalf of those struggling with addictions.

He has also set eternity in the human heart.
(Ecclesiastes 3:11)

[In the culture of the Roman Empire] alongside your *religio* . . . which for most men was a mere formality devoid of what we could call religious content, you were free to hold what private beliefs you liked. These, if not Roman, were called *superstitiones*, and there were many of them, all competing with one another to capture that basic religious instinct in man which the formal state religion did little to satisfy. Their astonishing success is due to the hunger in men's hearts for wholeness, emotional release, security, in a word for salvation in this world and the next. This salvation is what the *superstitiones* offered. Indeed, the very instability of the times helped to make men conscious of their needs and ready for a religion that would save them from the emptiness and insecurity of life.

The directions in which they turned were, broadly speaking, two. Salvation was sought either through cultus, or else through knowledge. The first method comprised magic, astrology, mystery cults, and appealed particularly to the ignorant masses; the second comprised philosophy and Gnosticism, and appealed to the more sophisticated.[5]

How gracious you are, Lord, in that you wait patiently for us stumbling people to eventually find our way to Calvary. You do not quit on us, even though we may take ourselves down ever so many spiritual rabbit holes and even though we opt for quick pseudo-fixes to our deepest longings. Thank you for being a patient God. Thank you for your willingness to lead us through one maze after another, without giving up.

5 May

You have heard that it was said, 'Love your neighbour and hate your enemy.'
But I tell you, love your enemies and pray for those who persecute you.
(Matthew 5:43–4)

Take a long hard look at the cross. Through that cross God is saying to you that he does care about pain. He cares passionately and selflessly. He cares so much that he came to share it. He is for ever the Suffering God. The cross tells me that God loves me even in the midst of pain and suffering; when everything looked at its blackest Jesus was still the supreme object of his Heavenly Father's love. More, through that cross I can vaguely discern another truth: that God uses pain. He turns evil into good. For it was evil, real evil, that crucified Jesus. And yet by the way he took it he overcame evil; he turned hatred to love in some at least of his persecutors. He gave an example of innocent, uncomplaining suffering which has inspired men ever since, and enabled men like Bishop Wilson[6] to win the hearts of some of the men who tortured him in a Japanese prison camp in the Second World War by means of his courage and spirit.[7]

Help me, Lord, to learn how to be like Jesus; to be like Bishop Wilson.
I have little or no resource to manage this in my own strength, which
is precisely why I am making this prayer today. And, Lord, not only
my 'enemies' per se, but those who annoy me and irritate me, whom I
don't even like very much, never mind actually love.

6 May

You must be born again.
(John 3:7)

The mystery religions of the first century . . . grew out of the age-old fertility cult and nature worship. Men were fascinated by the successive rise, flowering, fall and rebirth of the seasons of the year. Renewal of life was at the heart of the mystery religions. And as sex is intimately connected with regeneration, many revolting obscenities became part of the mystery religions. But this was incidental to the main object of the worshipper, which was to seek for divine aid to intensify and enrich his life here and now, and to assure him of immortality hereafter. All the mysteries, therefore, held out to their initiates the hope of salvation. And salvation meant primarily deliverance from the tyranny of an oppressive and capricious Fate which could quench life at a moment's notice; it meant the promise of a better life beyond the grace – and this was singularly attractive to the slaves, the maimed and the unfortunate who had an unsatisfactory present existence. Many of the cults initiated their worshippers into this experience of salvation through a sacramental ritual by which they were said to die and to be born again. A man who has been through the *taurobolium* of Mithras and thus achieved salvation is described in the inscriptions as *renatus in aeternum*, 'born again to eternal life'. Salvation, in fact, was secured, as Cumont says, 'by the exact performance of sacred ceremonies'.[8] Dionysus, chief god of the Orphic cult, together with Serapis, Mithras and other cult deities were given the title of Lord and Saviour, and the worshippers sought union with their god through sacramental acts, including baptism in water and a sacred meal! This notion of salvation, of course, was for the most part irrational and non-ethical. There was no theology, no rationale in this supposed salvation. Nobody attempted to show *how* the death of a bull, or castration, or the Bacchic frenzy of Orphism could make a man sure of salvation. Nobody expected the worshipper to live a better life as a result.[9]

Lord, I have little idea how you actually bring about the changes you do in the lives of those you manage, but there is evidence galore of your transforming power. I pray to you afresh today for more of the same in my life, and I pray too for those whom I would love to see living better lives as a result of your loving governance.

7 May

The Father himself loves you.
(John 16:27)

There were several words for 'love' in Greek, among them *storgē*, *erōs* and *philia*. The New Testament uses none of them. They are all determined by the worthiness of the recipient. But that is not so with the love of God. It is something entirely different, so the New Testament writers are driven to an entirely new word which is almost unknown in classical writers. The word is *agapē*, and it is not qualified and determined by the worthiness of the recipients but by the nature of the donor. God loves us for the simple reason that he is like that. He is the supremely generous giver, even though it costs him everything. 'God so loved that he gave'. And the only way we know God is like that is because Jesus Christ his Son went to the cross for us. There was nothing he would not do to prove to us that God loves us passionately, unworthy though we are. There are modern theologians who say 'God loves, and therefore he can dispense with atonement.' The apostles say 'God is love, and therefore he provides the atonement.' That is the difference. There is nothing shallow or soft about the love of God. He is light as well as love. He can by no means clear the guilty, for his is a moral universe. But such is his love that there is nothing to prevent his standing in for the guilty at their place of greatest need.[10]

'That is the difference.' Indeed. Amen.

8 May

**The seventy-two returned with joy and said,
'Lord, even the demons submit to us in your name.'
(Luke 10:17)**

Christ reigning from the tree (strongly hinted at in St John's Gospel) became a favourite theme of the writers of the second century. As I have observed in *I Believe in Satan's Downfall*, the ancient world, both Jewish and Greek, was hag-ridden with the sense of demonic forces gripping and ruining men's lives. The Gospels, particularly Mark, show Jesus taking on the forces of evil and winning all along the line particularly in the final victory of the cross . . . 'Christ has delivered us from ten thousand demons' exulted Tatian (*Orat.*, 29). The cross was the place where the power of the demonic forces was broken for ever.[11]

**Jesus, the name high over all,
In hell, or earth, or sky:
Angels and men before it fall,
And devils fear and fly.[12]
Hallelujah!**

9 May

**The wind blows wherever it pleases.
You hear its sound, but you cannot tell where it comes from
or where it is going.
So it is with everyone born of the Spirit.
(John 3:8)**

The first missionaries to preach in the Muslim north of Nigeria were greeted by a handful of people who were already believers in Jesus and claimed to follow him. They were the disciples of one Malam Ibrahim, a teacher of the Koran whose studies had slowly convinced him that the Jesus of whom he read in its pages was the mediator through whom the prayers of the faithful are offered up to the All-Merciful. So he gathered around him a group who began to pray regularly in the name of Is Masih, Jesus the Messiah. When the Islamic authorities discovered this, he was charged with heresy, refused to recant, and was crucified in Kano market place thirty years before a Christian missionary arrived in the country.[13]

Sovereign Spirit, blow in the direction of Muslims today, would you? Blow towards my local mosque with winds of truth and revelation. I pray specifically today for anyone known to me who follows the faith of Islam.

They came to Philip, who was from Bethsaida in Galilee, with a request. 'Sir,' they said, 'we would like to see Jesus.'
(John 12:21)

It is thoroughly in line with the teaching of the New Testament to ascribe such leanings among non-Christians [like the one mentioned on the previous page] to the agency of the Holy Spirit. Is it not his task to convince the world of sin, righteousness and judgment? Is it not through his agency that anyone makes the Christian confession 'Jesus is Lord' (1 Cor. 12:3) and is born again (John 3:5)? After all, it is the role of the Paraclete to bear witness to Jesus, and he does it with and without our testimony, to men of any faith or none.

But that is a very different matter from the exegetically unjustified expedient adopted by some modern students of mission, of divorcing the Spirit from Jesus, evading the scandal of his particularity, and attributing to the Spirit's agency whenever what seems to them to be admirable in the beliefs and practice of other faiths. If we wish to claim the leading of the Spirit of God with any assurance, we shall find that the leading is always towards Jesus.[14]

'The leading is always towards Jesus'. Thank you, Lord, for that useful compass bearing. I'll try to keep it in mind. Help me to think of that principle – that truth – whenever I am unsure about something spiritual or theological: does this lead me to Jesus? If it does, I will take it as your leading. If it doesn't, I'll leave it be.

11 May

**You are neither cold nor hot. I wish you were either one or the other!
(Revelation 3:15)**

[The religion of the Roman] was a cold unemotional affair; a matter of respect to his household gods and ancestors, a matter of ceremonial observances which were designed to securing various practical benefits – a safe journey, a good crop, and so forth. But despite this brave façade, there must have been a hunger for something more lurking in many a Roman breast. Otherwise the Romans would not have fallen so easy a prey to every foreign cult which offered salvation, not to the diluted Platonism which, now more a religion than a philosophy, was concerned with much the same thing.[15]

**Good Lord, preserve me from:
Lukewarmness of heart and decision
Ulterior motives
and
Any personal denial, or neglect, of my spiritual hunger.**

12 May

My heart began to despair over all my toilsome labour under the sun.
(Ecclesiastes 2:20)

Never before in the history of mankind has there been such a widespread belief that in the end nothing matters; we came from nothing and we go to nothing. No values are implanted in us because there is no God to implant them; no part of the human frame survives death, because there is no eternity. Meaning has disappeared from life. More money, more leisure, yes: but don't talk to us about meaning in life, because there isn't any. A leading modern painter, Francis Bacon writes:

> Man now realises that he is an accident, that he is a completely futile being, that he has to play out the game without reason. Earlier artists were still conditioned by certain types of religious possibilities, which man now, you could say, has had cancelled out for him. Man can only now attempt to beguile himself for a time by prolonging his life – by buying a kind of immortality through the doctors . . . The artist must really deepen the game to be any good at all, so that he can make life a bit more exciting.

What in fact the artist has done is to bring home this meaningless to every level of society. It comes through the films and the pop music. It is everywhere.[16]

God of life in all its richest fullness, my prayers today reach out to those whose lives are full only of despair. I pray for them. I pray especially for anyone who just can't see the point of it all, even to the point of contemplating suicide. For those whose lives are empty and hollow, and for those who feel that everything is pretty much futile, I ask your gracious touch.

13 May

**In the name of the Father and of the Son and of the Holy Spirit.
(Matthew 28:19)**

In contrast to a few years ago, when one would rarely hear any teaching on the
Holy Spirit, it seems that some people can speak of nothing else these days. There
is a cult of the Holy Spirit, and often it has precious little to say about Jesus or
God the Father. It was very apt of Tom Smail to write a book entitled *The Forgotten Father*. Now in view of the past neglect, this is understandable enough. But
it is none the less dangerous. The Holy Spirit does not draw attention to himself.
He is sent by the Father to glorify Jesus, to show Jesus' attractiveness, and not to
take the centre of the stage. One of the wisest criteria we can apply to any of the
claims made for the Holy Spirit and any of the teaching about the Spirit which is
being advanced from all sides today is this: does it glorify Christ? It is the characteristic of the Paraclete to bear witness to Jesus, to glorify Jesus, to take the things
of Jesus and declare them to us (John 15:26; 16:31f). In contrast to this emphasis
of the New Testament writers, much of the stress on the Spirit today dishonours
Jesus, tends to squeeze him out of the picture, and infers that allegiance to Jesus
is only the lower reaches of the Christian life, the heights of which belong to the
Holy Spirit. Imbalance of this sort is only to be expected; for we are very human
and our understanding is limited and our perspectives often determined by what
has particularly struck us. But it is a salutary reminder that nothing less than a
fully Trinitarian Christianity can stand.[17]

**Help me, Lord, to keep my balance. Keep my heart and mind from
unwise prejudice, however sincere that might be.**

Trust in the LORD with all your heart
and lean not on your own understanding;
in all your ways submit to him,
and he will make your paths straight.
(Proverbs 3:5–6)

The Jew recognized the transcendence of God, his holiness; to the Greeks and Romans 'the divine' was not far away from any one of us, but rather congenial to us.[18] The Jew was impressed by the creatureliness of man, his sinfulness and inability to save himself. The Greek or Roman was impressed by the dignity and ability of man; he was, for the most part, unconscious of or indifferent to the ravages of sin within. If saviour were needed, he would be his own saviour by means of his magic, his knowledge, his philosophy.[19]

Self-made people! Self-made salvation? The first concept, Lord, undoubtedly leads to the other, and both are unacceptable in your sight. Forgive us, Lord, when we fail to heed the advice of Proverbs 3, especially if it leads to us thinking we can be our own saviours. Such a path is not only futile, but deadly. Draw close to those known to me personally; family, loved ones and friends, that they may come to know the one and only Saviour.

15 May

As for God, his way is perfect.
(Psalm 18:30)

'When the fullness of time was come, God sent forth his Son . . . to redeem' (Gal. 4:4). So Paul sums up the situation; and subsequent ages have only been able to admit that he was right. For Jesus was born at the one time in history when all civilized nations in the world were united within a single empire, linked by excellent communications, divided by no customs barriers. A single peace, the *Pax Augusta*, reigned from France to the Euphrates; a single language, Greek, could be understood throughout practically all the diverse nations which together made up the Roman Empire. There was . . . a widespread longing for saviours; there was a growing movement towards monotheism. Such was the world into which Jesus made his obscure entry, probably in the year 7 BC. 'The Incarnation of the Desire of all nations,' wrote S. Angus[20] . . . Jesus was the answer to that inchoate longing for salvation; Jesus came to seek and to save the lost (Lk. 19:10). He was rightly given the ancient name Jesus ('God the Saviour'); for he was to save his people from their sins (Matt. 1:21).[21]

Gracious God, I thank you for the timing of the incarnation. It was nothing less than a miracle. Grant me grace, Heavenly Father, to trust your timing in my life, and to take this example as my confidence. Help me especially, I pray, when it seems that you might have missed a deadline. Teach me to know, deep down, that you won't have done any such thing. Nor will you.

**Having disarmed the powers and authorities,
he made a public spectacle of them, triumphing over them by the cross.
(Colossians 2:15)**

[Jesus'] descent to Hades robbed even death of its powers. Cyril puts it power-fully: 'Death was struck with dismay on beholding a new visitant descended into Hades, not bound with the chains of that place' (*Catechetical Lectures*, 14.19), and there is an emotive passage in the apocryphal *Gospel of Nicodemus* (6.22) where the legions in Hades cry out 'We are overcome. Woe to us!' It was not only his life, his death, and descent into Hades which wrought this total victory over the forces of evil. Origen sees the force of the resurrection too. 'Through his res-urrection he destroyed the kingdom of death' (*Comm. in Rom.*, 5.1.). This is, of course, a powerful New Testament theme, notably in such passages as Colossians 2:15 and 1 John 3:8; 4:4. The Fathers got themselves into many problems work-ing this theory out in terms of how the devil was tricked, and robbed of his prey. But their central theme of the victory of Christ through the cross and resurrection became the main way of understanding the cross for nine hundred years. It is not the whole truth, but it is a very important aspect of it.[22]

Up from the grave you rose, Lord Jesus, with a mighty triumph over your foes. Death could not hold you prey, Jesus my Saviour.

17 May

Without faith it is impossible to please God, because anyone who comes to him must believe that he exists and that he rewards those who earnestly seek him.
(Hebrews 11:6)

'You can't prove God,' they say. Perfectly true. You can't. But you can't prove that your mother loves you, either. In fact, there are precious few things that you can prove, and they are by no means the most interesting things in life. To prove a thing really means to show that it could not be otherwise, a very final form of certainty. You cannot prove that the sun will rise tomorrow. You cannot prove that you are alive. You cannot prove the link between cause and effect which runs through every action we do. You cannot prove that you are the same man you were ten years ago. The philosopher, David Hume, attempted to prove the link between cause and effect and between himself as he then was and himself ten years previously, and he failed. Failed utterly. Proof is only applicable to very rarefied areas of philosophy and mathematics and even here there is debate. For the most part we are driven to acting on good evidence, without the luxury of proof. There is good evidence of the link between cause and effect. There is good evidence that the sun will rise tomorrow. There is good evidence to believe that I am the same man as I was ten years ago. There is good reason to suppose that my mother really loves me and is not just fattening me up for the moment when she will pop arsenic into my tea. And there is good reason to believe in God. Very good reason. Not conclusive proof, but very good reason just the same.[23]

'For I do not seek to understand in order that I may believe, but I believe in order to understand. For this also I believe – that unless I believe I shall not understand.'[24]

Help me, Lord, I pray, to share this message of faith with others. Bless them as I pray for them here and now; friends of mine who might respond to this point of view.

18 May

Seek the LORD while he may be found.
(Isaiah 55:6)

If we are to believe St Luke, and scholars are increasingly recognizing the primitive nature of his birth stories, John grew up in a house impregnated with the hope of salvation as understood by the end of the Old Testament. In contrast to the pessimism of contemporary paganism[25] . . . godly priests like Zacharias were quietly trusting that God would remember his mercy, and deliver his people Israel. They were looking for salvation. Simeon was one such man; he was 'waiting for the consolation of Israel' (Lk. 2:25).[26] So was the prophetess Anna, who served God so assiduously (2:36). When she saw the child Jesus, she gave thanks to God and told all those who were waiting for redemption in Jerusalem (2:38) of her conviction that the promised redeemer had come.[27]

God of promise, keep my eyes open, my ears alert, and my heart awake to all that you are doing. Impregnate the house of my being with 'the hope of salvation' so that I don't inadvertently miss anything. I want to be like the people mentioned here.

19 May

**Jesus said to Jairus, 'Don't be afraid; just believe.'
(Luke 8:50)**

It is not particularly easy to approach the teachings of Jesus on any subject, because of the diversities of opinion on the extent to which the Gospel material gives us a reliable account of his words. Estimates vary . . .

It is universally recognized today that however far you penetrate back into the oral stage that preceded the writing of our Gospels, you cannot find the non-supernatural Jesus so long and so fruitlessly sought by Liberal scholarship. Wherever we probe, it is a supernatural Jesus that we find, a Jesus who works miracles, a Jesus who makes claims that would be madness if not true. The Gospels, of course, were the products of a believing community. They are not *disinterested* history (some theologians talk as if such a thing were possible). They were written by believers to give evidence on the strength of which others might come to faith in the One they had found to be the Saviour of the world (Jn. 20:32). But that does not mean that they are *dishonest* history. Because they selected the events which would be useful in the church situation, this does not mean that it had no place in the life of Jesus, but that they made it up instead! Indeed, it is interesting to notice down the history of Gospel criticism that the most conservative estimates of its reliability are taken by the *historians*[28] and the most sceptical estimates are made by those *theologians* who sit loose to history because of Hegelian or existentialist presuppositions.[29]

Lord Jesus, preserve my heart from a lazy faith that casually takes things for granted, but preserve it, too, from unhealthy scepticism. Grant me a confidence in the Bible that is reasonable and well-maintained, and which grows ever stronger. Shield me from the disease of scepticism, especially if I too am to 'give evidence' so that others might come to faith in the Saviour.

20 May

To the person who pleases him,
God gives wisdom, knowledge and happiness.
(Ecclesiastes 2:26)

If remembering that the Spirit is the Spirit of Jesus keeps doctrinal formulation authentic, the same may be said for experience. There is real danger in prizing, let us say, speaking in tongues (which I believe can be a real gift of the Holy Spirit) so highly that those who lack it are regarded as second-class Christians if Christians at all. So far as we know, Jesus never spoke in tongues. And the Spirit is the Spirit of Jesus. It cannot, therefore, be a *Christian* insight to urge that speaking in tongues is an indispensable mark of life in the Spirit of Christ; whereas it is an undeniably Christian insight to insist that love and holiness, so manifest in the life of the incarnate One, should mark those who claim to have his Spirit. The Spirit of Jesus points us back to Jesus. If we want to understand and possess the Spirit in his fullness, we need to keep our eyes firmly on Christ himself, for it is to him that all the Spirit's authentic witness is directed. If we do this we shall not claim as the teaching of the Spirit what does not relate to Jesus. And we shall not claim as experience of the Spirit what cannot be shown to flow from Jesus . . .

If the Spirit of Jesus is the gift bestowed on his followers, we shall expect to find the same characteristics marking authentic Christian life in the Spirit. And that is very much what we do find in the pages of the New Testament.[30]

If, Lord, my life is meant to signpost others to you, and to your love and salvation (as I believe it to be), then, really, my only hope of that happening is for my initial commitment to be bathed in your Spirit's presence and power. Grant me that privilege and honour, I pray, so that my life may tell. Give me your living self within.

21 May

**He predestined us for adoption to sonship through Jesus Christ,
in accordance with his pleasure and will.
(Ephesians 1:5)**

There is a very obvious difference between us and Jesus. He was born by the express agency of the Holy Spirit: we are not. He was the Son of God by right: we are sons only by adoption. Nevertheless it was the possession of the Spirit that set Jesus apart as the messianic Son of God, and brought the voice from heaven at his baptism 'Thou art my Son'. As Son, Jesus coined a new word for God. He called him 'Abba' (Mark 14:36). Jeremias has shown in *The Central Message of the New Testament* that nowhere in pre-Christian literature does anyone dare to call God by this intimate, family word which could be better translated as 'Daddy' or 'Dear Father'. It was a word for the intimacies of the family, not for the worship of God. Jesus, the one set apart by the Spirit as the Son of God, dares to call God by this name. He alone has the right to, for he alone enjoys the intimate relation of sonship with God the Father.

Unto this sonship he installs us. He enables us to pray the Lord's Prayer, which, in the form known to Luke, begins simply 'Abba', 'Father'. It is the Spirit who adopts us alongside Christ into this sonship, and who enables us to cry the 'Abba' of little children in the family of God. 'You have received the Spirit which makes you sons', exults the apostle Paul.[31]

God, my Father. This is an incredible thought: three words saturated with meaning. Trying to understand this concept – this actual reality – is something akin to attempting to pour the contents of an ocean into a cup. It is a very great deal to take in, yet everything within me knows it to be wonderfully true. God, my Father!

**In him we have redemption through his blood, the forgiveness of sins,
in accordance with the riches of God's grace.
(Ephesians 1:7)**

Why do we need forgiveness? Because we are sinners. Every single man, woman and child who has ever lived has done things wrong: wrong words, wrong thoughts, wrong actions, wrong attitudes, resulting in warped character. 'The heart of man is deceitful above all things, and desperately wicked' (Jer. 17:9). 'There is no difference, for all have sinned and come short of the glory of God' (Rom. 3:23). 'From within, out of the heart of man' said Jesus, the great physician of the soul, 'proceed evil thoughts, fornication, theft, murder, adultery, coveting, wickedness, deceit, licentiousness, envy, slander, pride, foolishness. All these evil things come from within, and they defile a man' (Mark 7:21ff). The heart of the problem is the human heart. All over the world, it is 'very far gone from original righteousness'.[32] We have broken God's laws, we have come short of his standards, we have rejected his love, we have kept him out of our lives, we have put all our idols before him. And then we have the front to wonder why we need forgiveness![33]

Hard words today, Lord – yet good words, in their way, for this direct teaching sets the context for your great rescue act. Help me, Lord, to ponder these things in my heart, because they will keep me grounded. They will also remind me of the great price you paid, on Calvary – and why. This, Lord, in a sense, is where my experience of pardon and redemption begins. These are helpful reminders, and I thank you for them. These are the crucial building blocks of my pilgrimage.

23 May

God has made this Jesus . . . both Lord and Messiah.
(Acts 2:36)

John the Baptist . . . was the last of the prophets and the greatest of them all, because of his unique and immediate relation to Jesus (Matt. 11:10–11). Jesus went to great pains to stress his solidarity with the Baptist. He was baptized by him: he came preaching exactly the same message (Matt. 3:3; 4:17); and he made his own authority coordinate with that of John (Mk. 11:27–33). It would not therefore, be surprising if his doctrine of salvation were an extension of his forerunner's. But to our surprise we find that it is not so. John had looked for what we might call a unitary eschatological crisis. The Coming One would save and would destroy; he would gather his wheat and burn his chaff. His coming would be final and victorious.

But it did not turn out like that. In the early days when Jesus joined John in preaching repentance in view of the coming kingdom, and when his disciples joined in the work of baptizing (Jn. 4:1–2), the Baptist will have felt that all was proceeding according to plan. Particularly will this have been the case if the chronology of the Fourth Gospel is correct in placing the cleansing of the Temple at the outset of the Ministry. This would have seemed right and desirable to John. The messenger of the covenant comes to his Temple to judge and to refine, just as Malachi had said he would (Mal. 3:1,2). John from his prison would have no grounds, as yet, for doubting the correctness of his unified eschatology. But then the days and months pass and, instead of judgement, he hears that Jesus offers men mercy and forgiveness, and is meek and gentle. He begins to doubt whether this can possibly be the one to whom he had been led to point (Lk. 7:18–23; Matt. 11:2–6).[34]

Lord, this is a salutary reminder for me never to make you in my own image. I realize, Lord, that I cannot possibly shape you to fit my own preferences or even expectations. Nor can I hope to keep you in my pocket. You are God, and it is up to me to accept that, to respect that, and to submit to that. Help me to trust and obey, even when, like John the Baptist, I don't quite understand what's going on.

24 May

You alone are the LORD. You made the heavens, even the highest heavens, and all their starry host, the earth and all that is on it, the seas and all that is in them. You give life to everything, and the multitudes of heaven worship you.
(Nehemiah 9:6)

Look at the fact of the world. So far as we know at present, this planet is the only part of the universe where there is life. What accounts for this world of ours? Whether we go for the 'Big Bang' theory or the 'Steady State' theory, we are driven to ask *why* it should be so. The world must have come from somewhere. It will not do to reply 'It is just one of those things.' It will not do to assign the whole thing to chance. If the world is due to chance, how is it that cause and effect are built into that world at every turn? It isn't very rational to suppose that chance gives birth to cause and effect! And it isn't very rational to argue that the world which is based on cause and effect is itself uncaused. Huxley once said, 'The link between cause and effect is the chief article in the scientist's creed.' If you think hard enough, science itself drives you back to believe in a Creator.[35]

Creator: Lover of my soul. What a God this is!

25 May

**If you forgive other people when they sin against you,
your heavenly Father will also forgive you.
(Matthew 6:14)**

Why cannot God simply forgive us everything? Because he is the moral ruler of the universe. God is not a private person who could pat us on the head and assure us that it does not matter. That is what you can do to me if I offend you. But there would be an outcry if any judge acted like that. The consistent teaching of the Bible is that God is the king of the whole earth. He is the supreme judge, the lawgiver, the ruler of all. His laws are not arbitrary. They are truth. They spring from his own being. To disobey them is not like committing some offence against the property laws of the state: it is self-destructive, because evil is always like that. In rebelling against God the sinner rebels against his own highest interests, and those of others. You only have to universalise failings like lying, stealing and immorality to see what a chaotic world it would be if everyone acted like that – and yet we make excuses for ourselves when we do. For God just to forgive without any cost to anyone would be sheer indifferentism. It would obliterate any distinction between right and wrong. It would say that right does not matter, and that evil is a matter of indifference.

How can that be before a holy God? All such views regard forgiveness as God's job (*c'est son métier*). It is not his job. It is never anyone's job when they have been wronged. Forgiveness is always a matter of sheer generosity on the part of the wronged party. It can never be demanded as a right. And how much less in God's case.[36]

Forgive me, Heavenly Father, for those times I have failed to forgive others; those sticky grudges that somehow cause me to forget all about the vast quantities of mercy I have received. Pardon my blindness, Lord, and help me to bear that in mind today. Place within me a heart that is able to forgive; a heart that is willing to forgive, mindful of my own dependence upon daily mercies.

26 May

I want to know Christ – yes, to know the power of his resurrection and participation in his sufferings, becoming like him in his death. (Philippians 3:10)

Authentic Christian experience is stamped with the mark of the Servant. In the enthusiasm of the renewed emphasis on the Spirit these days he is sometimes presented as the pathway to power in the Christian life, the secret of success in personal living and in service. There is truth in this, but it is only a half truth. The other side of the coin is the agonising trust in the dark, the utter obedience when all our inclinations go the other way, and the willingness to suffer which marked our Lord. It is when they first suffer for Christ that the earliest apostles return to their friends, pray (not for safety but for boldness), and find the place shaken by the Holy Spirit (Acts 4:29–31). It is the Spirit who not only convinces Paul that 'imprisonment and afflictions' await him if he goes to Jerusalem, but constrains him to accept that destiny (Acts 20:22–3). Peter, too, stresses that the Spirit calls us into the experience of suffering which Christ underwent. He calls on his persecuted readers to rejoice when they suffer as Christians and so share Christ's sufferings, for 'the Spirit of glory and of God rests upon you' (1 Pet. 4:13–16).[37]

Holy and emboldening Spirit, I pray especially for my Christian brothers and sisters around the world who are locked up, tortured and even murdered (martyred) for their Christian faith. May they know you closely beside them. Likewise, their families and loved ones. I pray for churches whose ministers have been imprisoned. Dispatch ministering angels to support them, I pray. Reach out to those in need of great courage. Theirs is a glorious calling, but not an enviable one.

When the men came to Jesus, they said, 'John the Baptist sent us to you to ask, "Are you the one who is to come, or should we expect someone else?"' (Luke 7:20)

Jesus' reply to [the] honest doubts of John takes the Baptist back to the prophecies Isaiah had given of the messianic age. He alludes to Isa. 35:4–5, 'God will come and save you. Then the eyes of the blind shall be opened, and the ears of the deaf shall be unstopped. Then shall the lame man leap as an hart, and the tongue of the dumb shall sing', and 61:1, 'The Spirit of the LORD God is upon me; because he hath anointed me to preach good tidings unto the meek; he hath sent me to bind up the brokenhearted, to proclaim liberty to the captives, and the opening of the prison to them that are bound; to proclaim the acceptable year of the Lord.' Jesus points out, in effect, that he is indeed fulfilling the prophetic picture of the Coming One.[38]

Teach me, Lord, to rely upon the promises I have received from you in the past, and to trust in their reliability for the present and the future. If I'm honest, Lord, I too sometimes have 'honest doubts'. At such moments, bring words of reassurance. Grant me that particular grace.

28 May

**Your kingdom come,
your will be done.
(Matthew 6:10)**

The kingdom [of God] drew near in the preaching of John the Baptist (Matt. 3:2). It dawned in the person of Jesus, and it was proclaimed as a present reality in his preaching. He tells us that the kingdom has been eagerly besieged by throngs of people since John's preaching awoke them to the realities of the situation (Lk. 16:16).[39] A scribe is told that he is not far from it (Mk. 12:34). The disciples already have the kingdom among (or 'in') them (Lk. 17:21). Discussion has often centred on whether the incarnation, the atonement, or the coming of the Spirit should be thought of as the inauguration of the kingdom. But surely the question is wrongly put. God has never abdicated his kingly rule, and there have always been those who accepted it.[40]

This is, in one important sense, Lord, a question of acceptance. Your kingdom is not in question, and neither is your divine right of kingship. Whether or not those points are acknowledged and embraced, though, is another matter. To that end, I repeat my prayers for those known to me personally who have not yet received their gift of citizenship. Draw close to them in mercy and great love.

29 May

In Christ Jesus you are all children of God through faith.
(Galatians 3:26)

God is not a private person like an earthly Father, He is the source and upholder of the moral universe in which human beings live. And we would never have any idea that he might be called Father were it not for Jesus who gave him the unprecedented title of 'Abba' and in the Lord's Prayer instructed his disciples to do likewise. But if it is Jesus who introduces us to the concept of God as Father, we must pay attention to what he says. And nowhere in the Gospels does he indicate that all men are children of God. Far from it. He says that even punctiliously religious Pharisees are a 'viper's brood' (Matt. 12:34), that they belong to 'their father the devil' and are by no means children of God (John 8:41–4). He did indeed attribute sonship of God to his followers: the words 'your Father' in the Gospels are invariably directed to disciples. It is clear from his teaching that there is only one Son of God in the full sense of the word himself but that it is possible for us to *become* sons of God by 'believing in' him or 'receiving' him (1:12) . . .

We are not children of God unless we have come to Jesus, the Son of God, for adoption and grace.[41]

Plenty of good food for thought today, Lord – thank you. Stay with me, please, as I digest this, and help me to get these things straight in my understanding. While I ponder and examine the rest of what's here, I thank you for the marvellous gesture of adoption; for the establishment of that heavenly adoption agency whereby my name is listed and the invitation is extended. Thank you, too, Heavenly Father, that you are always looking to enlarge your family.

30 May

**I am the Lord your God;
consecrate yourselves and be holy, because I am holy.
(Leviticus 11:44)**

The holiness of God is a major theme in the teaching of Jesus, alongside his readiness to welcome the penitent sinner . . . But there is no suggestion in Jesus' teaching that God's love modifies his justice. Here is one among many remarkable passages in the Gospels which highlights the separate action of God's love and holiness:

And when he drew near and saw the city, he wept over it saying 'Would that even today you knew the things that make for peace! But now they are hid from your eyes. For the days shall come upon you when your enemies shall cast up a bank about you and surround you, and hem you in on every side, and dash you to the ground, you and your children within you, and they will not leave one stone upon another in you; because you did not know the time of your visitation.' (Luke 19:41ff)

Here we have the passionate love of Jesus for Jerusalem. But Jerusalem is adamant against him. What is to be done? Love can only weep while judgment acts. And act it did, with ferocious intensity in the destruction of Jerusalem in AD 70. Love does not override either the holiness of God or the free will of men.[42]

For your service, make me holy. Consecrate each moment fully. Teach my heart to rest quietly before you today, even though the world rushes on. And then, within that quietness, explain holiness to my unholy mind. There are, to be perfectly candid, Lord, times when I feel anything but holy, yet I pray, nevertheless, for 'the holiness of God' to somehow become 'a major theme' in my life. This is my desire, and I pray that you will graciously bestow this specific blessing.

31 May

Teach me to do your will,
for you are my God;
may your good Spirit lead me.
(Psalm 143:10)

It is the Spirit who inspires Peter to withstand the rulers of Israel (Acts 4:8ff) and proclaim to them the Messiahship of Jesus. The Spirit marks out Stephen as a special vehicle of God when he refuses to remain restricted to the static categories of the temple and moves into broader pastures (6:3,5,10; 7:55).

It is the Holy Spirit who so signally lays his mark of blessing upon the preaching of the good news to those untouchables (from the traditional Jewish viewpoint) the Samaritans in the first half of Acts chapter 8, and the eunuch in the second part of that chapter. For it was the Spirit who called Philip from his successful mission in Samaria to reach the Ethiopian eunuch with the gospel (8:29 and probably 26), and led him on his further preaching tour as far as the very Hellenised city of Caesarea.[43]

'It is the Spirit'! A simple prayer today, Lord: may that statement loom large over the life and mission of my own church. May it form the foundation and fabric of all that my church undertakes in worship, work and witness. Come, Holy Spirit, as I pray Psalm 143:10 for my church fellowship today.

1 June

**I praise you because I am fearfully and wonderfully made;
your works are wonderful,
I know that full well.
(Psalm 139:14)**

Look at the fact of personality. It is one of the most remarkable phenomena in the world. The difference between a person and a thing, between a live person and a dead one, is fundamental. When Sartre . . . denied that the world was created by Intelligence, he was not only insulting his Maker but his own power of reasoning. He was saying, in effect, that there was no reason to believe what he was saying![1] The fact is that we are not mere robots; there is more to us than that – human personality. Some thinkers are so reluctant to believe this that they have advanced the improbable creed of materialism, seeking to reduce everything in life to what can be measured scientifically. In other words, other people are mere blobs of protoplasm: so am I. I have no future, no real existence. I think I am a conscious, rational being who can mix with others like me. But no, Science knows nothing of rationality and consciousness, of personality and sociability. It deals only with molecules and magnetism, elements and electricity, things which can be counted and measured. I have no place in such language, and if that is the ultimate language of reality, then I cannot describe myself, and am driven to the conclusion that I do not exist. Not very plausible.[2]

Lord Jesus, you came to give us life in all its fullness: so much more to it than being a mere 'blob of protoplasm' or 'a little puddle of water'! Help me, therefore, to get the most out of that gift, before it's time to call it a day. You who grant life, teach me life.

2 June

Sent on their way by the Holy Spirit.
(Acts 13:4)

It is one of the remarkable indications of the balance of St Luke that he manages to stress the initiative of the Spirit in ever-expanding circles of evangelism with the reminder that the mission is one. The Paul who receives his mission to the Gentiles does so in a trance in the temple at Jerusalem (Acts 22:17ff). The apostle who brings the Acts to an end by preaching unhindered in the capital of the pagan world is also shown as arguing all day with the leaders of the Jews 'declaring to them the kingdom of God' and 'persuading them about Jesus' by appeal to the law and the prophets (28:16–31). To the Jew first and also to the Greek, the Spirit of the Messiah is available through the preaching of the good news of what the Messiah has done. There is neither Jewish nor Gentile bias in this chronicler of the Holy Spirit's initiative in mission throughout the world, though his application of the famous 'blinding' passage of Isaiah 6 to Jewish leaders who refused to receive their Messiah, and his assertion, 'Be it known to you that this salvation of God has been sent to the Gentiles: *they will listen*' (28:25–8), is suggestive of the direction in which the Christian mission would, for the most part, go.[3]

So what happens next, international God? Lead us, show us, guide us; that your ever-unfolding mission might continue. We await your impulse and your light upon our pilgrim way.

3 June

The wicked go down to the realm of the dead,
all the nations that forget God.
(Psalm 9:17)

People sometimes ask how a loving God can send even an Adolf Hitler to hell. The love of God, with arms extended on a cross, bars the way to hell. But if that love is ignored, rejected and finally refused, there comes a time when love can only weep while man pushes past into the self-chosen alienation which Christ went to the cross to avert. God sends nobody to hell. But it takes two to make a friendship. If man firmly and repeatedly refuses the proffered hand of God, God will honour and ratify that man's decision to live to himself and die by himself. God respects our free will even in the hell of our own choosing.[4]

Lord of the breakthrough: Baal-Perazim, hear my prayers for those dear to me who show no sign of responding to your grace. Have mercy on me and hear my prayer. Have mercy on them and visit with your salvation. My prayers are marked 'urgent'.

4 June

**He anointed us, set his seal of ownership on us, and put his
Spirit in our hearts
as a deposit, guaranteeing what is to come.
(2 Corinthians 1:21–2)**

Salvation is both present and future in the teaching of Jesus. It means submitting to the kingly rule of, and, indeed, sharing in the very life of, God who is both immanent and transcendent. It is entered on here and now as men enter (Mk. 9:47), or receive (Lk. 8:17), or inherit (Matt. 25:34) the kingdom. It is to be fulfilled hereafter (Lk. 20:34–6). And for the meantime, life in the kingdom is characterized by humility (Lk. 6:20), the assurance of answered prayer (Matt. 7:7), the confidence of forgiven sins (Matt. 6:10–12), the experience of God's power (Lk. 11:20), the understanding of God's plan (Lk. 8:10), single-hearted obedience to God's will (Matt. 6:23–4) and an implicit trust in his protection (Matt. 6:31–4). It is a foretaste of the life of heaven.

[Jesus] shifted the ultimate crisis in man's destiny from death to conversion, from concern over the future life to commitment here and now to God's messenger of the kingdom. Salvation had become a present reality in the light of Jesus's teaching about the kingdom of God.[5]

'From death to conversion'! Teach me, Lord, the skill and joy of living a kingdom life in this world, whilst simultaneously anticipating a kingdom life in the world to come. Thank you for 'kingdom deposits' that will help me to navigate – and enjoy – my time here on earth, and thank you, too, for all that is yet to be: present blessings and future promises; all that has been, is, and is yet to be.

5 June

Just as one trespass resulted in condemnation for all people,
so also one righteous act resulted in justification and life for all people.
(Romans 5:18)

Salvation is achieved by the Son of Man.

It is clear from the most cursory glance at the Gospels, that this was Jesus's favourite name for himself. A closer look reveals two interesting points. Nowhere in the Gospels does anyone else refer to Jesus in this way, and it was not a title used to describe him in the early church.[6] This, incidentally, argues strongly for the reliability of the evangelists. They knew that while they did not refer to Jesus in this way, he himself had done so.

Now the Son of Man is unambiguously linked with salvation in the teaching of Jesus, notably in Lk. 19:10, a verse which seemed to be of such importance to the early Christians that it was introduced in two other places in the Gospels.[7] It is important, then, to discover what Jesus meant when he spoke of the Son of Man coming to seek and to save the lost. The antecedents of the Son of Man doctrine lie far back in the Old Testament.[8]

They probably go back, indeed, to the original man, man as he was intended to be, subordinate to God, but in authority over God's world. This is how the phrase Son of Man is used in Ps. 8:3–8, where it is a synonym for *man* and clearly refers to Adam. Adam, of course, failed in his twofold function. Was Jesus quietly suggesting, by the use of this title, that he came as the second Adam to fulfil the proper destiny of man? Indeed, in Ps. 80:17–19, God's salvation is expressly associated with the man of God's right hand, 'the Son of Man whom thou madest so strong for thyself'. This could well supply part of the background for the term in the teaching of Jesus.[9]

O loving wisdom of our God!
When all was sin and shame,
A second Adam to the fight
And to the rescue came.[10]

Thank you, Son of Man, for coming to the rescue.

6 June

This is the word of the LORD to Zerubbabel:
'Not by might nor by power, but by my Spirit,' says the LORD Almighty.
(Zechariah 4:6)

The sovereignty of the Spirit is worth dwelling on. It humbles us, as God intended it to do, to find that there is no tidy doctrine of the Spirit to be found in Acts or, for that matter, in the whole of the New Testament. He always retains that unpredictable, mysterious otherness of the *ruach Adonai*.[11] Utterly unmediated in his coming on the day of Pentecost, and on what has been called 'Gentile Pentecost' to Cornelius and his entourage, the Spirit works in many varied ways. He leads through a committee at the Council of Jerusalem (15:28), through a prophet in 11:28, through a trance in 10:19. In 13:2 he reveals his will to the community gathered at worship. Sometimes it is through a mysterious inner constraint that he makes his presence felt, as when he guided Paul's evangelistic direction away from the province of Asia in 16:6–7 and towards the hardships and opposition he realised he would have to face if he went up for that last journey to Jerusalem (Acts 20:22–3). It is impossible to get the Holy Spirit taped, to fit his movements in the Acts into any tidy ecclesiastical or doctrinal pattern. He remains the sovereign Spirit, but always the Spirit who is bent on leading the people of Jesus out into mission.[12]

'It is impossible to get the Holy Spirit taped'. Wonderful! Sovereign Spirit, reign in me. I make that prayer afresh today. An untaped God!

7 June

**In him we have redemption through his blood, the forgiveness of sins,
in accordance with the riches of God's grace.
(Ephesians 1:7)**

I remember Bishop Stephen Neill, a Christian deeply versed in other faiths, describing the uniqueness of Christian forgiveness with moving simplicity. He explained how in Hinduism the principle of *karma* prevails everywhere: the Hindu doctrine of retribution. Your actions incur indebtedness in a multitude of ways. These debts have to be worked off in a further reincarnation. If you do well, your next life will be on a higher level. If not, it will be on a lower level. But always *karma* drives you on. There is no possibility of forgiveness. Indeed it would be immoral, for you must pay your debts. The iron hand of *karma* rules all. The ethical structure of the world is parallel to the physical. The law of *karma* is as omnipresent as the law of gravity. And it says to the Hindu 'You sin . . . and you pay.'

What a contrast Christianity presents! Grace instead of retribution. Forgiveness instead of endless working-off of debts. Eternal life instead of countless reincarnations culminating in a sea of non-being. Because of what Christ did on Calvary the message of God to the believer is totally different to the Hindu concept. It says 'You sin . . . I pay.'

This makes no sense in commerce: it makes excellent sense in personal relationships. It happens every time we forgive.

How do I know that God is like this? Calvary is the answer.[13]

Gracious God, my prayers today are extended to anyone I know who is following the faith-path of reincarnation in hopes of, one day, achieving a much better life than anything they have known previously. I pray, Lord, that (somehow) you will open their eyes to Calvary and 'forgiveness instead of endless working-off of debts'. I pray too for Christian missions, organizations and churches whose specific outreach is towards communities and individuals where Hinduism holds sway.

8 June

**I am the Alpha and the Omega,
the First and the Last, the Beginning and the End.
(Revelation 22:13)**

A common [objection] is to ask how the death of Christ 2,000 years ago could avail for all men everywhere down the ages. The answer lies partly in the relativity of time: 'a thousand years with the Lord are as one day, and one day as a thousand years' (Ps. 90:4; 2 Pet. 3:8), for the death of Christ was 'foreordained before the foundation of the world' (1 Pet. 1:20). The Lord who is above and outside time entered time for us. 'In the beginning was the Word, and the Word was with God and the Word was God . . . the Word became flesh and dwelt among us' (John 1:1,14). Isaiah's instinct had been right when he said of the Suffering Servant: 'The LORD has laid (or, caused to meet) on him the iniquity of us all' (Isa. 53:6). It was as if Christ died at the mid-point of time, and his death availed retrospectively as well as prospectively. Abraham and the saints of the Old Testament were justified because of what Christ *would* one day do at Calvary: men in generations since by what he *has* done. God has been forgiving penitent sinners from time immemorial: only the ground of that forgiveness had not been made plain. Since Calvary it has been made abundantly plain.[14]

The weight of eternity bearing down in favour of my forgiveness! A plan of pardon that is carefully administered on behalf of sinful humankind. Thank you, Lord. Help and enable me to share the news of this saving mercy as and when I can.

**I have become all things to all people
so that by all possible means I might save some.
(1 Corinthians 9:22)**

The agents in [the] mission inaugurated by the Spirit are, of course, the disciples of Jesus. But this role is by no means confined to the Twelve. 'The great mission of Christianity was in reality accomplished by means of informal missionaries', wrote Harnack long ago (*The Mission and Expansion of Christianity* p. 368). He was right. As early as Acts 6 we find the apostles seeking deputies to manage the administration of the church, while they give themselves to prayer and the ministry of the Word. The Seven, sometimes improperly called deacons, are accordingly appointed. But the next thing we find is one of these administrators, Stephen, preaching his heart out! As soon as he has been liquidated, another of the Seven, Philip, takes over. And he has four daughters with the gift of prophecy: doubtless they engaged in the mission too. That same eighth chapter of Acts records the spread of the gospel by informal missionaries, men and women evicted from Jerusalem by the persecution which followed Stephen's death. Their message is clear. All disciples are expected to bear their testimony to Jesus. That is what the Holy Spirit is given them for.

The word 'witness' is significant. Its root figures over thirty times in the Acts, in one form or another. The apostles, the folk who had known Jesus in the old days in Galilee, Stephen, Paul; all are 'witnesses of these things; and so is the Holy Spirit whom God had given to those who obey him' (Acts 5:32). The witness attests his own experience: he does not necessarily preach.[15]

Show me, Lord, how I can best witness today. I may not have any opportunity to preach as such, but I ask to be sensitive to your guidance, so that my witness may tell, in one way or another and in one place or another. Let that witnessing be according to your prompting and empowering.

10 June

'Isn't this the carpenter's son? Isn't his mother's name Mary, and aren't his brothers James, Joseph, Simon and Judas?'
(Matthew 13:55)

[The] emphasis on testimony is one of the great strengths of the present Pentecostal revival in South America. You are scarcely accounted a Christian in Chile until you have got up in the street and given testimony to Jesus. This is not necessarily the best way of passing on the good news, but it does stir the passers-by to find not the paid priests but the cobbler, the miner, the man who sells meat fritters telling them about Jesus. In his book, *Haven of the Masses* (p. 47), Dr. d'Epinay describes the impact of such witness. It offends the élite, of course. 'These men', said a teacher, 'do not even speak in Castilian, but in slang; sometimes they don't even know how to write, and can hardly read. And they quote epistles of St Paul so difficult that the theologians, who have been working on them for two thousand years, have not got to the bottom of them. By what authority do they teach?' That is just the reaction provoked by Jesus and by the informal missionaries in the Acts (Mark 1:27; Acts 4:13). The élite were offended, but the common people loved it. If the language is slang, what does it matter so long as the preachers are radiant with the experience they speak of, and live in the midst of the same social situation, with all its problems and difficulties, as the listeners?[16]

Grant me grace, Lord, to receive consecrated slang in the same way as I would an articulate sermon, if the message is the same and if it is ablaze with conviction. Help me not to be a gospel snob, but to see the bigger picture of souls saved and lives turned from darkness to light. Convert my sensibilities, Lord!

11 June

The large crowd listened to him with delight.
(Mark 12:37)

Salvation centres on forgiveness of sins.

What had been peripheral to the Old Testament doctrine of salvation becomes crucial to the New. Forgiveness is a primary part of salvation to the New Testament writers, and in this they clearly follow Jesus himself, who came, not to call the righteous, but sinners (Mk. 2:17).

This spelt revolution in Judaism. There had been nothing like it since the individualism of the psalmists, and their patient trust in God to save them despite their sins. No rabbi in Israel addressed himself to the common people, the 'Am-ha'arets.[17] They were *ex hypothesi*, beyond the pale, not only because of the moral and social odium accorded respectively to the harlots and the tax-gatherers, but because righteousness in later Judaism was beyond the reach of the poor and the ignorant.[18] How could the poor afford the sacrifices and the elaborate ritual that was proper for the 'righteous'? How could the ignorant masses acquire that knowledge of the Law which led to 'righteousness'? . . . The attitude of the Pharisees in the time of Christ is doubtless fairly reflected in Jn. 7:49, 'This multitude which knoweth not the Law is accursed.'[19] [20]

What a dreadful, shocking prospect, Lord, that such elitism should have any place at all in the life of the church. Rid us of all such societal injustices, I pray. Root them out of my heart, if you find them there. And, Lord, I pray for anyone whose access to the gospel is hindered by illiteracy and/or poverty. Grant your blessing to those individuals and agencies whose ministry is within those spheres of influence.

12 June

**Be wise in the way you act toward outsiders;
make the most of every opportunity.
(Colossians 4:5)**

Look at the fact of values. We all have them, but they are very hard to understand if there is no God. After all, you don't expect to find values knocking around in molecules! Matter does not give rise to morals. So modern Godless man is confused about where his values fit in . . . We value life – but why should we if life really springs from chance? We value truth – but why should we if there is no ultimate reality? We value goodness – but what is that doing in a world derived from plankton? We revel in beauty – but there is nothing in it, since it too springs from the chaos in which our world originated. We value communication – but the universe is silent. Yes, we have our values, and they do not accord very well with the atheist's picture of the world, sprung merely from chance, matter, and millions of years to allow for extensive development. I do not find much basis for value judgments there.[21]

Your truth is logical, Lord. These points make sense. Help me, therefore, to bear witness in likewise manner, logically and sensibly. May I witness with humility, but never to the extent that I am intimidated by atheism.

The master told his servant, 'Go out to the roads and country lanes and compel them to come in, so that my house will be full.'
(Luke 14:23)

When ordinary men and women are fired by the Spirit to bear witness to 'a Lord who pardons and loves, a Lord who is just as powerful as the landowners, the mine-managers or the trade union secretaries, because he is God, a God who desires to be called Father, and who treats the most wretched of men as his son' (d'Epinay) then people will sit up and take notice. They did in the first century, and they do still when Christians come out of their ghettos and chatter the good news in the streets.[22]

'So that the house will be full' – what a marvellous prospect, Heavenly Father; I would love to see my own church full every week. Full of people, full of converts, full of seekers, full of people sitting up and taking notice. Full of God. May it be so, in your mercy. I pray for the household of faith that is my church.

14 June

There is still room.
(Luke 14:22)

How, it may be asked, could a few hours' suffering of Christ on the cross avail to rescue the whole world from eternal loss? In so far as that question is open for mortal men to discuss, it would seem that the key to it is the person of the sufferer. Christ is *qualitatively* distinct from the whole mass of mankind. There is no question of qualitative equivalence in what Christ suffered and what men alienated from God might suffer. The one who hangs there brings totally different considerations to bear. We should be more distressed by the pain of a child for an hour than by the death of hundreds and thousands of mice, because we know there is something qualitatively different. So it is when the Son of God tastes death for every man.

It has sometimes been a problem to the tidy-minded that they have thought of the death of Christ in quantitative terms, precisely equated with the number of the elect. It would be important, on such a view, to ensure that there be no waste in the saving work of Christ. Thus some of the more stringent of the Calvinist theologians have argued the theory of limited atonement. Christ, on this view, did not die for the world but only for the elect. Thus there is no waste, so to speak, incurred by people refusing to respond to his sacrifice. Such a theory verges on the blasphemous, and it totally contradicts 1 John 2:2 where the writer assures us that 'he is the expiation for our sins, and not for ours only, but for the sins of the whole world'. There is a glorious prodigality of grace in God. There is no parsimonious precision and precise equating of the work of Christ with those who will in due course respond. Think of such parables of the Great Supper, overflowing with generosity and grace.[23]

You are a God whose heart is 'overflowing with generosity and grace'. You are a God about whom there is nothing remotely parsimonious. Even if for these reasons alone, I offer you my worship today. You are my God.

The word of God is alive and active. Sharper than any double-edged sword, it penetrates even to dividing soul and spirit, joints and marrow; it judges the thoughts and attitudes of the heart.
(Hebrews 4:12)

'The Word' is as common in the Acts as 'The Spirit', and they belong very closely together. One of the great merits of C.K. Barrett's book, *Luke the Historian in Recent Study* is the weight he gives to the Word as the prime agency through which the Spirit extends the good news of Christ. It is expressed in a number of ways: 'The Word of God', 'the Word of salvation', 'the Word of the gospel' or quite simply 'the Word'. It means the message about Jesus. Wherever the early Christians went, it was the Word they carried (Acts 8:4). When Paul was encouraged at Corinth by the fellowship of Priscilla and Aquila we read that he became gripped by the Word (18:5). During the two years and more of his mission in Ephesus 'all the residents of Asia heard the Word of the Lord' (19:10). When Luke wants to indicate the success of evangelistic work, he can say that 'the Word of the Lord grew and prevailed'. So it was in Judea (6:7), Samaria (8:4–7,14), on the first missionary journey (13:49) and in Asia (19:10). The Word makes its own impact on Theophilus (Luke 1:1; Acts 1:1), Cornelius (10:44), the proconsul of Cyprus (13:7), and on the citizens of Antioch (13:44). No wonder the Twelve made it their priority, and the nameless missionaries of 8:4 took it as their great weapon. For if a man believes, it is because the Word brings faith (4:4). If a man receives the Spirit, it is because he has responded to the Word (10:44). It is no exaggeration to say that the Word is the prime tool used by the Spirit of God in advancing the Christian mission.[24]

Thank you, Lord, for this note of encouragement. In a day and age when secular forces seem to be on the march, I appreciate this reminder that the Bible is as true and as powerful and as vibrant as it ever was. Living Word, speak to me as I read the Scriptures, so that my faith is bolstered and my witness strengthened. These are timeless truths, reliable for all eternity.

16 June

My Father's house has many rooms.
(John 14:2)

Some are not able to respond [to the gospel]. Small children, those who die young, the infirm in mind. Did Christ not die for them, too? Did he not die for the masses of heathen who have never heard his name? Of course he did, and there may well be in heaven many of all races who knew nothing of Christ but somehow trusted in God to accept them though they knew themselves to be unacceptable. That is how David and Abraham, Isaac and Jacob were accepted. They had no idea how it could be. But they entrusted themselves to God, and he accepted them, knowing the atonement that was to be made. There is generosity enough and to spare in the Father's house. All who call on his name, however ignorantly and tentatively, will not be disappointed. On that matter he has given his solemn pledge (Rom. 10:11–13).[25]

'There is generosity enough and to spare in the Father's house'. What a line! What a house! What a Saviour! What a promise! What love!

17 June

**If it is possible, as far as it depends on you, live at peace with everyone.
(Romans 12:18)**

If I steal twenty pounds from you I have contracted a liability to the criminal law, and I can be judged for that: I have defrauded you and wronged you; and I have done something evil in the sight of God, something which builds yet higher the wall of alienation between him and me. Clearly the cross of Christ cannot affect my guilt before the law. I may well be prosecuted, and if convicted I shall have to shoulder my punishment. Neither can the cross of Christ affect the fact that I have wronged you. I need to make reparation for that.[26]

This day, Lord, prompt me in terms of reparation. If there is someone I need to speak to, then bring them to mind. If I need to make amends, then convict me of that. I pray for grace and courage to follow your Spirit's leadings in these ways.

18 June

**The one and only Son, who came from the Father, full of grace and truth.
(John 1:14)**

In [Jesus] the divine antinomy of wrath and mercy is revealed. He both vigorously asserts and vicariously bears the judgement of God upon sin. The heavenly Judge is the Suffering Servant. The lost are indeed judged in righteousness, but called in grace. The judge of human hearts will be one who has shared our nature, one who bore our sin. He is not wholly other than ourselves; the Son of Man is one with us, both to judge and to save.[27]

I welcome this news of a perfect balance, Lord Jesus: this lovely combination of so many crucial elements pertaining to salvation. Thank you, Lord, that your decision-making is perfect, rooted in divine empathy, love and justice. You are a fair God.

**They came to Philip, who was from Bethsaida in Galilee, with a request.
'Sir,' they said, 'we would like to see Jesus.'
(John 12:21)**

'The whole have no need of a physician,' [Jesus] pointed out, 'but the sick' (Mk. 2:17). Accordingly, it was with the morally and socially sick that he constantly mingled, to the chagrin of the Pharisees. They complained that he ate with tax-gatherers and sinners (Mk. 2:16), or that he was friends with them (Luke 7:34). In their pride they adopted an attitude of superiority which made it impossible for Jesus to help them. In their shallow and external view of sin,[28] they failed to see that hypocrisy, pride, envy, uncharitableness and so forth are every bit as bad as crude and flagrant vice.[29] They were in precisely the same need of forgiveness as the notorious evil-doers whom they despised. It is a sad commentary on a paradoxical situation that when Jesus goes to his death, a death engineered by these self-righteous men who despised sinners,[30] he says, 'The Son of Man is betrayed into the hands of sinners' (Matt. 26:45; Mk. 14:41; Lk. 24:7). St John's way of bringing out the same truth is the drama of Ch. 9. Jesus has healed the blind man. The Pharisees say he could not possibly have done so. Since he had not been to one of the scribal schools of theology he was by definition an *Am-ha'arets* (quite apart from the fact that he had done this reputed cure on the Sabbath). God does not hear sinners; therefore he could not have heard Jesus, and healed in answer to his prayer. Q.E.D.! A superb example of the aphorism, 'The dogma must conquer history.' Jesus concluded the incident by telling the Pharisees that if they were blind (i.e. to spiritual truth), they would not be accounted as sinners: but because they said, 'We see', therefore their sin remained (9:41).[31]

What a desperately sad account this is, Lord, of unrequited and unwanted love. Divine Optician, keep my spiritual eyesight sparklingly clear, I pray, lest I too fall into the traps of 'hypocrisy, pride, envy, uncharitableness and so forth'. In your mercy, let no such tragedy infect my life. By the same token, hear my prayers for those I know who are trapped by spiritual blindness. We all need to see Jesus.

20 June

How beautiful are the feet of those who bring good news!
(Romans 10:15)

Guilt has little to do with guilt feelings. These, as modern psychiatry has shown, are often prompted by a variety of sources unconnected with the supposed offence. Christianity is not about guilt feelings. But Christianity has a lot to do with objective guilt. It has a message of complete and free acceptance for the man who knows he is most unacceptable. And that makes a new man of him. It is in this sense that Christ took our guilt. He stood in for us at the point of our total inability to face God. As man, he went to that bitter cross, that place of guilt and shame. As God, the sacrifice he made there is eternally valid. As the head of the new humanity, he shouldered our responsibility towards God. The weight of it spelt a cross. In that sense he did indeed bear our guilt (though the New Testament writers prefer to speak of him bearing our sins). In the simplest of language, we sinned and he accepted responsibility . . .

There remains the nagging doubt in many minds whether the offering of Christ in our place could be fair. The answer is an unequivocal No. For the cross of Christ far transcends any conception of justice we could ever entertain. If we are looking for justice we can have it. 'The wages of sin is death.' However, as Romans 6:23 goes on to say 'but the gracious gift (*charisma*) of God is eternal life through Jesus Christ our Lord'. With undreamed-of generosity God has met us at our deepest point of need. He has acted with perfect justice. The curse of the broken law need never haunt us, for he has taken it upon himself (Gal. 3:10,13) and with open arms he welcomes us to his heart of love.

Actually, I do find the cross and resurrection incredible. But incredible because I am astonished that God should bother like that for sinners. It is unbelievably good news, the best mankind has ever heard.[32]

But, God, you did bother! You bothered for the sake of the unbothered; those whose sin didn't particularly bother them, and who weren't wanting to be bothered by thoughts of God and religion and bothersome stuff like that. I thank you that you are a bothered God; to such an extent that you did something about my eternal destiny. Thank you for bothering.

21 June

Thanks be to God for his indescribable gift!
(2 Corinthians 9:15)

Here was no overlooking of guilt or trifling with forgiveness; no external treatment of sin, but a radical, a drastic, a passionate and absolutely final acceptance of the terrible situation, and an absorption by the very God himself of the fatal disease so as to neutralise it effectively.

So wrote C.F.C. Moule in *The Sacrifice of Christ*, p. 28, admirably summarising what Christ did for us on Calvary. Thank God for it. Thank God too that such is only half the story. Jesus is no dead Saviour, but alive for evermore. 'If while we were yet enemies we were reconciled to God by the death of his Son, much more, now that we are reconciled, we shall be kept safe by his life' (Rom. 5:10). We are not dependent in the Christian life on a Christ who lived and died; but on a Christ who lived, died and rose again, so as to share with us the power of his endless life. Thus even forgiveness is not an end in itself. It clears the barriers out of the way so that we may live with him.[33]

No condemnation now I dread
Jesus, and all in Him, is mine
Alive in Him, my living Head
And clothed in righteousness divine
Bold I approach the eternal throne
And claim the crown, through Christ my own.[34]

Bold I approach, all thanks to him!

22 June

The Son of Man came to seek and to save the lost.
(Luke 19:10)

The three parables of Lk. 15, the lost sheep, the lost coin, and the lost son, are placed in the illuminating context of 15:1–2, which makes their main thrust inescapable. They describe Jesus's attitude, in contrast to that of the Pharisees;[35] it is simply this, to save the lost (see the refrain in 15:7,10,32). Thus we find him holding conversation with the *respectable* sinner, Nicodemus, and showing him his need of a radical rebirth (Jn. 3); we find him speaking with a *brazen* sinner (and she a hated Samaritan) and offering her the lasting satisfaction she had sought so long but in vain (Jn. 4). We find him seeking out Zaccheus, the *financial* crook, and offering what such a social outcast would never have dared to hope, that the great teacher would 'be guest with a man that is a sinner' (Lk. 19:7). He confronted the *sexual* sinner, and instead of joining the Pharisees in hounding her to death,[36] he first quietly but forcefully indicated their own sinfulness to such effect that they shrank away ashamed, and then told the woman that she was not to think of herself as condemned, but to go and sin no more (Jn. 8:1–11). He had come to save sinners. And thus when a *sick* sinner was presented to him, he went straight to the man's deepest needs, and said, 'Your sins are forgiven' (Mk. 2:5). In doing so, of course, he incurred a charge of blasphemy from the Pharisees. Forthwith he vindicated his claim to have God's authority to forgive sins, by showing that he had God's power to heal – to the amazement of them all.[37]

A God who seeks.
A God who finds.
A God who (humbly) takes the initiative.
A God who declines to discriminate.
A God who befriends the marginalized.
A God who directs the lost.
A God who forgives.
A God who heals.
A God who challenges prejudice.
A God who amazes.

23 June

Of this gospel I was appointed a herald and an apostle and a teacher.
(2 Timothy 1:11)

Preaching is a very humbling thing. You feel such a fool. Paul catches the feeling precisely in 2 Corinthians 4:1–6. The preacher is involved in a titanic confrontation, in which he is a tiny Lilliputian. He becomes aware that 'the god of this age (i.e. the devil) has blinded the minds of those who do not believe, lest the light of the glorious gospel of Christ, who is the image of God, should shine on them'. Every effective preacher knows that proclamation involves not mere communication, but confrontation. 'For we are not contending against flesh and blood, but against principalities and powers, against the world rulers of this present darkness' (Eph. 6:12). We don't get anywhere by what Paul calls 'preaching ourselves: gimmicks do not help. It is by being prepared to be people's servants for Jesus' sake so that the light may shine through to them.[38]

> **Lord, it's probably the case that I haven't prayed for the preacher(s) in my church as often or as diligently or as kindly as I might have done. I beg your pardon. It's also probably true that I have criticized or found fault more often than is fair or reasonable, especially if I have neglected to pray for the one making the mistakes. Please forgive me. In the light of today's reading, perhaps I can pray for those who faithfully minister to me by preaching, a bit more often. Maybe every Sunday? Please remind me to do so.**

24 June

They show that the requirements of the law are written on their hearts, their consciences also bearing witness.
(Romans 2:15)

Conscience [is] a pointer to God if ever there was one. Your conscience doesn't argue. It acts like a lawgiver inside you, acquitting you or condemning you. It doesn't say, 'Do this because you will gain by it' or 'Do it because you will escape trouble that way.' It just says, 'Do it.' It is a most remarkable pointer to the God who put it there. Oh, of course it is not the voice of God straight and simple. It has been warped by all sorts of things, your environment, your rationalisations, your disobedience. But equally certainly conscience can't just be explained away as the pressure of society. It was not from any pressure by society that Newton and Wilberforce conscientiously fought for the liberation of slaves, or Martin Luther King championed the cause of the blacks. Their action was carried out in the teeth of opposition by society, and so it has always been with every moral advance.

Despite the diversity of human cultures the world over, there is actually remarkable agreement on the essential values to which conscience points: the general condemnation of murder and theft, of adultery and lust, or hijacking and hate. There is universal agreement that peace is right and war is wrong; that love is right and hate is wrong – however little men manage to carry it out in practice. And it is conscience that points us to this difference between right and wrong, and the claim that right has upon us.[39]

Most merciful Redeemer,
Friend and Brother,
May we know you more clearly,
Love you more dearly,
And follow you more nearly,
Day by day.[40]

Lord, answer this prayer through means of my conscience.

25 June

I am the vine; you are the branches. If you remain in me and I in you, you will bear much fruit; apart from me you can do nothing. (John 15:5)

Light is not lacking: 'the God who commanded light to shine out of the (primeval) darkness has shone in our hearts to give the light of the knowledge of the glory of God in the face of Jesus Christ (2 Cor. 4:6). But how is this glory to shine through to others? Only as the Holy Spirit takes the 'foolish' message of the gospel home to people's hearts, and convinces them of its truth; that it is indeed 'the wisdom of God to everyone who believes' (1 Cor. 1:18ff). We come back to this theme of the double witness, by the Holy Spirit and ourselves, which the New Testament continually brings before us. A preacher can talk till he is blue in the face, but he can never bring anyone to faith in Christ. Yet the Holy Spirit can take his words home to the conscience of the hearer and bring that person low in repentance and faith before the crucified and risen Christ. Anyone who has been instrumental in this transformation of another person's life through the impact of the Word of God and the Spirit of God will know that it is not his own doing. I have on occasion preached the same sermon in two different churches. In one, between twenty and thirty people professed conversion. In the other, nobody did. The Spirit and the message and the messenger all combine to carry out this strange alchemy of new birth. But only the Spirit is indispensable.[41]

'Indispensable' – help me never to forget that; in life, in ministry, at work and at home. Bring that thought to mind whenever I am about to step out of my house into a world that needs Christ. By the same token, let me relax in that dependency: the weight is off my shoulders! With your help, I'll play my part, safe in the knowledge that the 'real' work of transformation is in your hands.

26 June

This is what happened during the time of Xerxes, the Xerxes who ruled over 127 provinces stretching from India to Cush.
(Esther 1:1)

I heard a remarkable story recently from a leading Indian Christian, the Revd. Samuel Kemelesan. A friend of his, who was engaged in Christian colportage work, decided to go to the heart of Brahmin country in Kumbbakoman in Southern India . . .

This brave man entered the courtyards of the main temple, and began to preach Jesus. He expected to be killed. Instead, he had hardly begun before he was embraced by a Brahmin woman and was asked, 'Why did you not come sooner?' Her story was a fascinating one. This rich, high-caste woman had had terminal cancer. She was given a very short expectation of life by the doctors. So she went to Madras, in whose pleasant climate she could live out the few remaining weeks of her life. Then, apparently, she died. She was laid out in the mortuary. But she was not dead, only deeply unconscious. In this state she had a vision of Jesus, about whom she knew nothing. In the vision the Lord looked on her with love. 'If you will let me live again, Lord, I will give my life for you', she promised.

While the woman was lying there in the mortuary unconscious, a crossing sweeper happened to notice a faint movement in this supposed corpse. She went immediately to the doctor who had signed the death certificate. The doctor examined her, found a faint pulse, and immediately swung into action to resuscitate the patient. A blood transfusion was necessary. It so happened that the crossing sweeper had blood of the same group as this rich Brahmin lady. And she happened to be a Christian. She gladly gave her blood for a substantial blood transfusion, and the patient was told afterwards by the doctor, 'You owe the fact that you are alive today to the crossing sweeper who first detected a movement in you when you were in the mortuary and then gave her blood for you' . . . The Brahmin lady was as good as her word. From that day onward she worshipped Jesus only, and renounced her Hinduism.[42]

God of miracles, God of last-minute grace, I pray specifically for India today. I pray for Christians there, that you would bless their witness, especially if they encounter hostility, misunderstanding or apathy. Touch India with your great love.

27 June

He made himself nothing
by taking the very nature of a servant,
being made in human likeness.
(Philippians 2:7)

Jesus of Nazareth was executed at Passover time in the year 30, 31 or 33 – the experts continue to debate the matter. It was while Pontius Pilate was prefect (his proper title, as an inscription found at Caesarea makes clear) of Judaea. Shortly after his death a new and very dynamic religious movement arose, maintaining that death had been unable to silence Jesus: he was alive, and he was Lord.

This seemed so improbable as to be laughable. But it was the sole belief which differentiated the new movement from Judaism. They were ordinary Jews in every other respect except this: they believed that God's Messiah had actually come, been unrecognised by the people, been done to death on the cross, and had been gloriously raised by God to the power of an endless life. Such was the conviction. And it spread so fast that within thirty years large numbers of the Jewish priesthood had become believers; Rome had been heavily affected, so had Alexandria, Ephesus, Antioch and the other main cities of the Empire. More, it had spread into the country parts, in North Africa, inland Turkey and to the Russian border.[43]

Lord, the spread of the gospel was (and is), patently, rooted in ordinary places, facilitated by ordinary people. This is a gospel of solid reality. Yours was a real human life, Lord Jesus. Likewise, yours was a real human death. I give thanks for these realistic elements, because they remind me of your loving concern for humanity; nothing out-of-touch or unrealistic. This is a grounded gospel.

28 June

His compassions never fail. They are new every morning.
(Lamentations 3:22–23)

We suffer today from a false distinction between the secular and the sacred, the physical and the spiritual. The Christian Church has sometimes behaved as though only the spiritual element in man was the subject of God's concern. The actions of Jesus as recorded in the Gospels give the lie to this, and show that God's salvation concerns the whole man (Mk. 3:4). Indeed, the word is used most frequently in the Gospels with reference to the healing of disease. Both Matthew and Mark summarize Jesus's healing ministry thus: 'As many as touched him were saved' (Mk. 6:56; Matt. 14:36. Indeed, Matthew uses a compound *diesōthēsan*[44] to emphasize his point). Blind Bartimaeus was 'saved' (Mk. 10:52), so was the Samaritan leper (Lk. 17:19), the man with a withered hand (Mk. 3:4–5) and a host of others. Jesus showed concern for the whole man. The Gospels speak a good deal of the compassion of Jesus (e.g. Matt. 9:36; 20:34; Lk. 7:13). In every instance we are told that the *cause* of this compassion was the sight of human need, perhaps a hungry crowd, or a diseased body; in every instance it is made clear that the *effect* of this compassion was the alleviation of that need . . . The sight of marred humanity filled Jesus with profound and passionate emotion against the forces of evil which had wrought this damage.[45]

'Jesus, thou art all compassion.'[46]

A God of great compassion: my God. 'Every morning': thank you, Lord, for this delightful and reassuring truth. Thank you, too, that your compassion encompasses every aspect of my life. This too is reassuring.

29 June

What must I do to be saved?
(Acts 16:30)

I well recall one tough Yorkshire girl who was on drugs at the time, coming to a service where I was preaching, and being pierced to the heart by a throwaway line I had never intended saying, about God hardening Pharaoh's heart. I knew nothing about this convicting work of the Spirit in her, until a week later when she rang me from Halifax and asked, 'Does God really harden people's hearts?' It was through this most improbable passage of Scripture, taken home to her by the Spirit, that she in due course became a Christian. I think of another man, to whom I had said something about Jesus Christ while marching down alongside him to an army parade! He had seemed very uninterested, and I had not pursued the conversation. In any case, the conditions were scarcely suitable. To this day I cannot recall what it was I said to him. Nevertheless, the Spirit took it home with unerring aim. A day later he came to see me, unable to sleep and distraught. He had begun to see what he looked like to God, and now he was not in the least uninterested to hear what Jesus Christ had done about it. Before the night was out he had surrendered himself to Christ.[47]

Jesus of Nazareth – Jesus of Halifax. How wonderful!

30 June

The person without the Spirit does not accept the things that come from the Spirit of God but considers them foolishness, and cannot understand them because they are discerned only through the Spirit.
(1 Corinthians 2:14)

It is the Spirit who bears witness to Jesus and glorifies him (John 15:26; 16:14). Sometimes this happens over a long period, as a person finds himself constrained to attend a Christian place of worship, or drawn to read the Christian scriptures. Time and again I have met folk who have been warmed by the Spirit to perceive the beauty of Christ in the life of a group of believers or in the story of the New Testament, and have come to faith in that way. Sometimes the attraction to Jesus happens instantaneously. The penny suddenly drops, and he is revealed as the one who makes sense of life. I remember an English don once coming to me at the end of a meeting, and saying that she had suddenly seen that evening in Jesus Christ the answer to the rather negative existentialist framework into which her life had been cast. That was the work of the Spirit, revealing Christ to her.[48]

Gracious Spirit, dwell with me. I make no apology, Lord, for praying once again for those whose lives I would dearly love to see coming under your influence. Over a period of time or spontaneously, as you see fit, but in your mercy, hear my prayers for those I love and care for. Come to them with revelation. Grant understanding.

1 July

Godliness with contentment is great gain.
(1 Timothy 6:6)

Man is a religious animal. In the sixth century BC philosophers in Greece poured scorn on religion, and invited men to grow up. Religion continued. The Russians sought to abolish religion after the Revolution in 1917. They failed. They tried again with violent persecution under Stalin. They failed. It is the same with China. Man is incurably religious. He is going to worship either God or pseudo-god, but worship something he will, even if it is something very physical like his material prosperity or something very abstract like the idea of progress.

There is one fact about man that has distinguished him from his first appearance on earth. It marks him as different from all other creatures. That is, he's a worshipping animal. Wherever he has existed there are the remains, in some form or other, of his worship. That's not a pious conclusion: it's an observed fact. And all through history and prehistory when he's deprived himself of that he's gone to pieces. Many people nowadays are going to pieces, or they find the first convenient prop to tie their instincts on to. It's behind the extraordinary adulation of royalty. It's behind the mobbing of TV stars. If you don't give an expression to an instinct you've got to sublimate it or go out of your mind.

Such is the conclusion not of a philosopher or priest, but of a novelist, Winston Graham in *The Sleeping Partner*. He's right, isn't he?[1]

Tell me the same old story
When you have cause to fear
That this world's empty glory
Is costing me too dear.[2]

Loving God, help me never to treat you as a last resort in my life; if and when all else has failed. Show me today if I am in fact using any props in my life, even unwittingly, and lead me, teach me, to depend upon you for my utmost fulfilment.

2 July

Stretch out your hand to heal and perform signs and wonders through the name of your holy servant Jesus.
(Acts 4:30)

We must beware of supposing that the mighty deeds of Jesus are simply philan-thropic works of mercy.[3] They are nothing of the sort. They are tangible evidence of the presence of the kingdom of God in the person of the Son of Man (Matt. 12:28). St John calls them 'signs' rather than 'mighty works'; the healings are not complete in themselves. They point to spiritual realities. Quite apart from the individual parabolic meaning of particular miracles (brought out in each of the seven signs John selects), supremely they *all* point to Jesus being the Servant of the Lord. Isa. 32:2–4; 35:5–6; 42:7; 61:1 speak of the lame walking, the blind seeing and so forth, in the days of salvation. This is exactly how Jesus described what was happening in his work (Matt. 11:5).[4] He was bringing in the days of salvation, and the main purpose of the miracles was to indicate this to those who had eyes to see (Jn. 10:37–8).[5]

Thank you for this, Lord: a gentle reminder to look for the meaning behind the miracles – and, indeed, the man behind the miracles. Lord Jesus, I pray for those in need of your healing touch today, whether that be in a physical sense or some other way. Impart healing by im-parting your presence into their lives.

3 July

I am the Living One;
I was dead, and now look, I am alive for ever and ever!
(Revelation 1:18)

It might be said, and has been said, that since Jesus apparently expired in such a short time, about six hours, he might not have been really dead, and could subsequently have emerged from the tomb. This is substantially the position maintained in H. Schonfield's *The Passover Plot*, but quite apart from its psychological improbabilities such a view is hard put to explain away the plain facts of the case. They were very plain, and very public. A squad of four executioners put him to death in full view of a large crowd. They were experienced at this grisly task, since crucifixions were not uncommon in Palestine. They knew a dead man when they saw one. They could see that the other two men were not yet dead: that is why they broke their legs so that they could gain no relief from the 'saddle' on the cross, and would rapidly expire. Jesus they saw was already dead. Their commanding officer had heard Jesus' death cry, and certified the death to Pilate (Mark 15:39,44). But just to make doubly sure, the soldiers pierced his heart through with a spear. So we are told on the authority of one who claims to be an eyewitness, and this testimony is included in St John's Gospel (19:34–5). It is clear that the eyewitness attached great importance to what he saw: it is no less clear that he did not understand it. Hardly surprising. Nobody did until the rise of modern medicine. The witness maintains that when the side of Jesus was pierced, out came 'blood and water'. Had Jesus been alive, strong spurts of bright arterial blood would have emerged. Instead, the observer saw semi-solid clots seeping out, distinct and separate from the accompanying watery serum. This is evidence of massive clotting of blood in the main arteries, and is exceptionally strong proof of death.[6]

A God who bled. For me. A God who died. For me. A God whose heart was broken. For me.

4 July

Without faith it is impossible to please God.
(Hebrews 11:6)

When it comes to faith, we are left in no doubt that this is a gift of God brought about by the Holy Spirit. No man can make the Christian confession 'Jesus is Lord' without the Holy Spirit enabling him to do so (1 Cor. 12:3). Seen in its context, that is a most significant verse. For the Corinthians were fascinated with the charismatic and ecstatic aspects of the work of the Spirit. St Paul tells them at the outset of his three-chapter discussion on spiritual gifts, that ecstasy is no sure mark of inspiration by the Spirit. So-called spiritual men could, and did, call Jesus accursed in ecstatic cries in the Corinthian assembly (12:3). The true mark of the Spirit's operation is when a man can say from the heart that Jesus is his Lord. Once again we see the Spirit is related securely to the person of Jesus, and it is when the Spirit enables a man to see who Jesus is and respond to him in allegiance that faith is born. It is the Spirit who takes the things of God and reveals them to us (1 Cor. 2:12), and Paul can rightly say that the very capacity to respond in faith is a gift from God and no man-made attribute of which we can boast (Eph. 2:8). The Spirit can therefore be called 'the Spirit of faith' (2 Cor. 4:13). And to possess the pledge of the Spirit is interpreted as living the life of faith (2 Cor. 5:5–7).[7]

Thank you, Holy Spirit, for the gift of faith, whereby everything else begins to slot into place. This is all to your glory. Spirit of faith, fill my heart and mind today, that I may approach this day's activities with faith in your love, your goodwill, and your power.

5 July

**To each one the manifestation of the Spirit is given for the common good.
(1 Corinthians 12:7)**

It is due to the work of the Holy Spirit that we become Christians at all. He is the Spirit who adopts us into the family of God alongside Jesus (Rom. 8:15; Gal. 4:6). Though by nature we Gentiles are 'without Christ, aliens from the commonwealth of Israel, strangers from the covenant of promise, having no hope and without God in the world', the Holy Spirit has given us access, through Christ's self-sacrifice for us (Eph. 2:12–18). 'Now you are no longer strangers and foreigners', Paul exultantly reminds his readers, 'but fellow citizens with the Old Testament believers, and in the very household of God'. The New Testament writers use a variety of terms to speak of the Holy Spirit's work in making us Christians. 'You received the Spirit', says Paul to the Galatians. 'You began in the Spirit.' You accepted the 'gracious provision of the Spirit', or 'the promise of the Spirit' (Gal. 3:2,3,5,14). Sometimes this initial encounter with the Spirit is seen as a great washing (1 Cor. 6:11). Sometimes it is a new birth (Titus 3:5; John 3:2,5) brought about by the entry of the Spirit into our lives. Whatever the imagery, one thing remains constant. It is only through the agency of the Holy Spirit, enabling us to repent and believe, convicting us of sin and making Jesus attractive to us, that we ever become Christians.[8]

Convicting, cleansing, citizen-crafting, Christian-creating Holy Spirit, thank you for this wonderful sequence of divine activity and initiative. Thank you for quietly and humbly going about your work in my life, all because of love.

6 July

Come near to God and he will come near to you.
(James 4:8)

Bartimaeus was in a sorry plight, blind and destitute. He heard of Jesus; he called to Jesus; he came to Jesus, throwing away all that impeded him. He laid his request before Jesus. Immediately he received his sight from Jesus, and followed Jesus in the way . . .[9]

The statement 'Thy faith hath saved thee' . . . spoke of the complete and instantaneous righting of that wrong relationship with God induced by sin,[10] which comes about when a man recognizes his need, hears of Jesus, and comes to him in simple trust.[11]

Lord, there is a sequence of 'faith steps' described here that reminds me of an evangelistic campaign; something the likes of Billy Graham would have deployed in years past. There is an attractive simplicity about these steps, not least the fact that you are only too willing to meet people at the point of their need. I pray, Lord, for churches and mission groups who are working hard to present such a pattern of repentance. Such templates might not be perfect, Lord, but as long as they are designed to lead people to Jesus, I ask you to bless them and use them. Thank you for the gracious promise of James 4:8.

7 July

I chose you and appointed you so that you might go and bear fruit.
(John 15:16)

It is indisputable that shortly after the execution of Jesus an entirely new religious movement of great vitality sprang into being. It was normal when charismatic leaders arose in the troubled province of Judaea for the followers to return, disillusioned, to their homes once the leader had been disposed of. Josephus records a number of such events: the Acts of the Apostles alludes to one of them, the abortive rising of Theudas (Acts 5:36 cf. Josephus *Ant.*, 20.97–9). But in this case the disciples did not melt away. They grew and spread rapidly over the known world. Tacitus records with distaste that 'a most mischievous superstition, thus checked for the moment (i.e. by the crucifixion of Jesus) again broke out' (*Annals*, 15.44). Their own account of these origins was plain. They were brought into being as the community of the resurrection. Nobody could deny that such was their claim.[12]

The 'indisputable' growth of the early church, Lord! Was this meant to be a template for churches throughout subsequent generations? If so, it appears we haven't always done so well in some quarters, and have pretty much substituted soul-saving for coffee mornings and outreach for craft clubs. Revive us again, Lord, for you are the only hope of a church that, in Europe at least, is in some countries dead on its feet. Accompany your modern church as you accompanied your early church, that we might once again be known as 'the community of the resurrection'. Have mercy and make us fruitful once more.

8 July

One Lord, Jesus Christ.
(1 Corinthians 8:6)

[Regarding] the healings of Jesus. It will have been noted that these healings are normally granted in response to faith. 'Thy faith hath saved thee' is, as we have seen, a constant refrain.[13] Surely this is significant. The early Christians will have used such sayings to show that the ultimate salvation, God's salvation which Christ came to bring, is entered by faith alone,[14] and not by 'the works of the Law' as the Pharisees held. This takes us back to the strand of vindication which we saw in the Old Testament doctrine of salvation. Salvation is of the Lord, and must be accepted in simple, trusting faith, if it is to be enjoyed at all.

Secondly, these healings are bound up with the person of Jesus. It is Jesus who heals, just as it is Jesus who forgives sins . . . All aspects of salvation are Christocentric. It is by his words (Jn. 5:34), by his person (Jn. 10:9), by his total mission (Jn. 12:47) that men can be saved. Salvation is inseparable from the person and work of Jesus, and that is why there is more about it in the Epistles than in the Gospels.[15] [16]

It is, after all, all about Jesus! Jesus, be my focus.

9 July

1 Corinthians 15 in its entirety

It is impossible to exaggerate the importance of 1 Corinthians 15. This . . . embodies the oldest document in the Christian church. It derives from the key people concerned, and within a very few years of the event. It is not surprising that it became 'tradition' very early on in the Church.

The main thrust of this remarkable passage is the sequence of appearances by the risen Jesus which convinced his followers that he was alive. The Gospels record many more such appearances: the two on the way to Emmaus, the women at the tomb, Mary Magdalene, the disciples on the Lake, Thomas, and so forth. The appearances of Jesus are as well authenticated as anything in antiquity . . . There can be no rational doubt that they occurred, and that the main reason why Christians became sure of the resurrection in the earliest days was just this. They could say with assurance, 'We have seen the Lord'. They *knew* it was he.[17]

The paschal greeting is a custom among Orthodox Christians, consisting of a greeting and response. Instead of 'hello' or its equivalent, one is to greet another person with 'Christ is risen!' The response is 'Truly, he is risen!' (or 'Indeed, he is risen!'). This greeting is used during liturgical services and informally at other times.

Risen Lord, eternally victorious and always undefeated, I worship you.

10 July

Guard the good deposit that was entrusted to you – guard it with the help of the Holy Spirit who lives in us.
(2 Timothy 1:14)

The New Testament writers sometimes speak of Christ living within Christians, sometimes of the Spirit doing so (Gal. 2:20; Col. 1:27; Rom. 8:10; 8:11; 1 Cor. 3:16). They sometimes speak of Christians being in Christ, and sometimes of being in the Spirit (Phil. 1:1; 1 Cor. 3:1; Rom. 8:1; 8:9; Col. 1:8; Eph. 2:22). It does not seem to matter very much which way we look at it. If you intertwine your fingers together, it is equally true to say that your right hand is in your left, or that your left hand is in your right. The point is that they are firmly connected. And that is what the New Testament wants to say about our relationship to Christ and his Spirit. On the whole there is a tendency to speak of us being in Christ, and of the Spirit being in us. That is the predominant emphasis, and it is a helpful one. Christ is the new man, the last Adam (1 Cor. 15:45), and Christians are members of his body (1 Cor. 12:1ff). The Spirit comes and takes up residence in our bodies, which he wants to use as his temple (1 Cor. 6:19) . . .

The first requirement, when a man passes 'out of darkness into light, from the power of Satan to God' (Acts 26:18) would seem to be that he needs assurance. He needs to know he belongs to the new family, that he is 'accepted in the beloved one' (Eph. 1:6). And that is just what the Spirit does. St John tells us that this is one of his main functions. 'This is how we know that he remains in us, by means of the Spirit whom he has given us (1 John 3:24). He repeats it in 4:13, 'This is how we know that we remain in him, and he in us, because he has given us a portion of his Spirit.'[18]

A God who wishes to dwell within! A God who adopts, and then kindly reassures us of our adopted status! A God who leads us from darkness to light! A God who gives of himself! A God who is faithful! This is my God.

11 July

Everyone born of God overcomes the world. This is the victory that has overcome the world, even our faith.
(1 John 5:4)

The exorcisms performed by Jesus must be seen as having a dual function. Jesus had no more doubts about the reality of demon possession than modern missionaries who work in primitive areas have. There can be no doubt at all that he did exorcize demons.[19] And he taught that his exorcisms showed that the kingdom of God had come (Matt. 12:28 and parallels), and from henceforth the kingdom of Satan was doomed. The religious authorities, who could deny the fact of these exorcisms, attempted to attribute them to satanic power, only to be met with the unanswerable argument that if Satan were to cast out Satan, his house would be divided against itself, and could not stand. Satan's power was real enough, as both Jesus and his opponents agreed; 'the strong man' still 'kept his house'; but Jesus's authority over demons showed that 'stronger than the strong' had come to bind the strong man, and spoil his goods (Mk. 3:27). The exorcisms presaged the crucial victory over Satan on the Cross (Jn. 12:31). Their significance was this: while the healings were related to the forgiveness of sins inherent in salvation, the exorcisms spoke of power over evil impulse which Christ can exercise in those who have tasted of salvation. They set forth Jesus in his role of conqueror.[20][21]

> See! The conq'ring Hero comes,
> Not with noise of fife and drums;
> Comes to rule each heart and love,
> As he rules the host above.[22]

Your power is divinely supreme, Lord Jesus. You need not ever fear defeat. I, therefore, if I hide myself in you, need not either. This, though, is a big thought – literally, of cosmic proportions. Help, me, therefore, to assimilate its meaning into my day-to-day life. Grant me 'power over evil impulse'.

12 July

Christ was raised from the dead through the glory of the Father.
(Romans 6:4)

It is impossible to imagine how the preaching of the resurrection could ever have got off the ground if the body of Jesus had remained in the tomb . . . As C.H. Dodd put it 'When they said "He rose from the dead", they took it for granted that his body was no longer in the tomb; if the tomb had been visited it would have been found empty. The Gospels supplement this by saying, "it was visited and it *was* empty"' (*The Founder of Christianity*, p. 166).

Matthew, Mark, Luke and John are all totally explicit on the point, and John adds some remarkable eyewitness material about the graveclothes . . . he tells how Peter and 'another disciple' (probably John himself) ran to the tomb when the first tidings of the emptiness were brought to them . . . 'Peter went into the tomb; he saw the linen cloths lying, and the napkin, which had been on his head, not lying with the linen cloths but rolled up . . . and he (i.e. the other disciple) saw and believed' (John 20:6–8) . . . The graveclothes had encircled Jesus, and were interlaced with a great weight of embalming spices. The head covering was a small distance away, retaining its original shape surrounding the head of Jesus. *But his body was simply gone!* . . . No graverobber would have been able to enact so remarkable a thing. Nor would it have entered his head. He would simply have taken the body, graveclothes and all. Had Jesus merely been resuscitated, he would presumably either have used the clothes or laid them aside . . . All the signs pointed to Jesus' having risen to a new order of life.[23]

**Lord Jesus, it seems as though you are willing to go out of your way –
and some – to convince humankind of your love and your resurrection
power. Your incarnate life here on earth was one of grace and truth,
your death on the cross was a sacrifice saturated in mercy, and your
rising from the dead was loaded with evidence. Thank you, Lord, that
you are prepared to try every which way to bring about reconciliation.
This willingness, in so many ways, is humbling and heart-warming.**

13 July

Here is a trustworthy saying:
if we died with him, we will also live with him.
(2 Timothy 2:11)

It would be ludicrous to suppose that the Jews moved the body of Jesus. They had at last got him where they had long wanted him, dead and buried. They would never have given colour to the resurrection preaching which soon began to shake Jerusalem by so crass a folly as removing the body. And if, by some egregious blunder, they had done just that, they would easily have been able to produce the mouldering corpse as soon as the Christians began to claim that he was alive. And that happened very soon. *The third day* is strongly embedded in the earliest references to the resurrection: that is embarrassingly early. It is an indication of how threadbare arguments were becoming by the end of the second century that such unlikely people as the Jewish gardener were being suggested as agents of grave robbery. 'This is he . . . whom the gardener removed,' wrote Tertullian with biting irony, 'lest his lettuces should be injured by the crowds of visitors' (*de Spectaculis* 30).[24]

Lettuces, Lord! How funny! The lengths that are gone to, sometimes, to suppress and deny the truth. Funny in one sense, and ridiculous, but not quite so amusing when the gospel is ridiculed and misrepresented by tyrants and dictators (and religious leaders) who are intimidated by its power and scared of its influence. To that end, my prayers today are with Christians who face a daily barrage of such nonsense, and whose witness is mocked and lied about. Work in the heart of those who make fun and make up stories, I pray. Help your witnesses to be strong in your grace, and not to lose heart.

14 July

It is for freedom that Christ has set us free.
(Galatians 5:1)

Since the coming of Jesus, man is no longer helpless under the domination of sin (Jn. 8:34,36), Satan (Lk. 13:16) and his powers of evil. The salvation of the Gadarene demoniac was not only a matter of healing a distraught mind and integrating a split personality. That man tasted the powers of the age to come (cf. Heb. 6:5) when he came face to face with Jesus and had his needs met. He was not only healed, but saved (Lk. 8:36).

In the same way, Jesus's saving of the disciples in the storm and of Peter on the water are parables of his ability 'to keep you from falling' (Jude 24). Why else should the stories have been treasured and recorded? Thus it would seem that even the most physical and secular uses of 'salvation' in the Gospels carry spiritual overtones which are complementary to the natural (and doubtless primary) meaning of the words.[25]

Saviour, Deliverer, Agent of salvation, Preserver, Liberator.
All of the above, for this world and the next, in Christ. What a gift.

15 July

We proclaim to you what we have seen and heard, so that you also may have fellowship with us. And our fellowship is with the Father and with his Son, Jesus Christ.
(1 John 1:3)

Even deliverance from sin's guilt and power are inadequate as a summary of salvation. They do not exhaust the ancient prophetic hope; they are no more than a foretaste here and now of what lies ahead in the goodness of God. 'Eye hath not seen', writes Paul, 'nor ear heard, neither have entered into the heart of man the things which God hath prepared for them that love him' (1 Cor. 2:9). And so we find in the teaching of Jesus, just as we did in the Old Testament, that the salvation of God is still primarily future. The difference between Jesus and the prophets is that with him the age of salvation has dawned. But its full enjoyment still lies in the future, although it may be proleptically enjoyed in the present. It is the man who endures to the end who will be saved (Mk. 13:13 and parallels, also Matt. 10:22b). It is the man who loses his life for Jesus's sake (just as Jesus lost his for our sake) who will be saved (Mk. 8:35 and parallels). What form, then, will this final salvation take?

There are many metaphors used for it in the Gospels. It is likened for safety to a heavenly barn (Matt. 13:30). It is likened for glory to the sun shining (Matt. 13:43). It is likened for spirituality to the angels of God, who neither marry nor give in marriage (Mk. 12:25). It is likened for beauty to the garden of God (Lk. 23:43), for responsibility to thrones of judgement (Lk. 22:30), for joy to a wedding feast (e.g. Matt. 22:3ff.). The simile of the wedding feast is particularly instructive, for it speaks not only of the joy of the guests, of the grace through which they are invited and of the corporate nature of their enjoyment, but concentrates the attention of all upon the central figure. For the future, salvation involves two relationships, and indeed consists in them; fellowship with the Saviour, and fellowship with the saved.[26]

Give me constantly to know, Lord, fellowship with you; moment by moment. Thank you for the fellowship of fellow pilgrims; help me never to take that for granted. We may not always get along or see eye to eye, but I wouldn't be without my Christian companions and all they bring into my life in so many ways.

16 July

The Spirit, the water and the blood . . . the three are in agreement.
(1 John 5:8)

There are three grounds for Christian assurance [John] tells us: 'the Spirit, the water and the blood'. This passage should be seen against its background. The Gnostic teacher, Cerinthus, was active in Asia Minor at the time when John wrote, and he taught that the heavenly Christ came upon the human Jesus only at his baptism, and left him before his passion: the union between them had only *seemed* to be real – actually it was merely temporary. Had this been the case, there would have been no Christian gospel to preach: no incarnation of the Son of God, no real solidarity between him and us, no expiatory death upon the cross. John therefore opposes it strongly. Jesus, the Christ, is the one who has come through the water of his baptism, through the blood of his cross, and is mediated to us through the Holy Spirit. The coming through the water, the cross, and the gift of the Spirit are all thoroughly historical events: and yet they are more than that. They are continuing factors in the life of the Church through the experience Christians have of the Spirit, and through the sacraments of water (baptism) and blood (the eucharist) which seems to be alluded to here. Baptism is a mark of belonging, a ground of assurance, which the Spirit can take home to our hearts. It was so to Martin Luther when he was tempted to despair of his spiritual state: *'Baptizatus sum'* he recalled with joy. Joy, because it did not rest upon his own faith, strongly though he valued that: but when in the morass of doubt, one has no confidence in subjective attitudes such as faith. But his baptism, administered to him by another, sealing physically upon him the objectiveness of what Christ did on the cross, that was indeed a ground of assurance. It was the sacrament of justification by grace; the physical, palpable reminder that God acted for him without his aid and prior to his response.[27]

Loving God, with these 'three grounds for Christian assurance' in mind, I pray for anyone who is, like Martin Luther, despairing of their spiritual state. Come alongside them, Lord, with reassurances that will reinstate stability and faith. Thank you, Lord, that we are not just left alone to cope, but that you are willing to help us. Furthermore, you act for us, too, without our aid and prior to our response.

17 July

The L<small>ORD</small> is our judge,
the L<small>ORD</small> is our lawgiver,
the L<small>ORD</small> is our king;
it is he who will save us.
(Isaiah 33:22)

[Perfect law-keeping] cannot be done. If you do not keep *all* the things written in the book of the law, you remain under its curse as a lawbreaker. As James put it in his Epistle, 'whoever shall keep the whole law, and yet offend in one point, is guilty of all' (2:10). If legal contract is what you are after, one slip in the contract is sufficient to invalidate it. And which of us has not broken the law of God not just once but thousands of times? So getting in the right with God is impossible for human beings to achieve by their own efforts. As guilty failures we all come beneath that 'curse' imposed on lawbreakers. 'All the world is guilty before God', Jew and Gentile, virtuous and wicked alike (Rom. 3:19). All have come short of the divine standard for human life; none can lay claim to earning the verdict of acquittal by keeping the law in its entirety: 'for there is no distinction, since all have sinned and come short of the glory of God' (Rom. 3:23). It is not only overt actions which are reprehensible, but rather the thoughts of the heart and that attitude of rebellion against God characterise us all (Rom. 3:9–20).[28]

Lord, even though, patently, none of us has a hope of reaching and keeping your standard, and even though in our own strength we fall woefully short, you have graciously made a way. You have not left us as hopeless, but have established a glorious initiative whereby spiritual success can still be accomplished. This is, literally, a lifesaver. Thank you: judge, lawgiver, King and Saviour.

18 July

Whoever does not love does not know God, because God is love.
(1 John 4:8)

The father in a family can never be satisfied if his children clean his shoes and lay the table, but never talk to him, and never hug him. How could the heavenly Father be satisfied with mechanical obedience devoid of love and trust?[29]

Heavenly Father, whatever else I may think or feel or know about you, impress this upon my heart; you are love. Love is your name. Love is who you are. Love is what you are all about. May your love be mirrored in my life.

Jesus said . . . 'I am the resurrection and the life.'
(John 11:25)

If neither the friends nor the enemies of Jesus removed his body, one possibility remains. God raised him up. Take together the empty tomb, the resurrection appearances, the launching of the church, the meaning of its sacraments, the conversions of those most opposed to the new faith, the passionate centrality of the resurrection in the church's preaching and writings, the changed day of rest, and it is very difficult to resist the conclusion to which the New Testament writers came. 'If Christ has not been raised your faith is futile . . . But in fact Christ has been raised from the dead.' Such was the conclusion of a distinguished Jewish rabbi two thousand years ago. Pinchas Lapide, a distinguished Jewish rabbi of our own day, has just published a book, *The Resurrection of Jesus*. Its conclusion? 'I accept the resurrection of Jesus not as an invention of the community of disciples, but as a historical event. No other conclusion is warranted by the evidence.[30]

Risen Lord, the evidence points to the conclusion that death could not hold you captive. This in turn leads me to believe that I too, in Christ, need not fear that last great enemy. When the time comes, Lord, grant me a resurrection experience that will carry me safely beyond the blue horizon. There's a better world, I know!

20 July

He got up and went to his father. But while he was still a long way off, his father saw him and was filled with compassion for him; he ran to his son, threw his arms round him and kissed him.
(Luke 15:20)

It is a lovely sentimental idea to suppose that all religions are basically one, and that they all represent variations on a common theme. But unfortunately it flies in the face of all the evidence. How can all religions lead to God when they are so different? The God of Hinduism is plural and impersonal. The God of Islam is singular and personal. The God of Christianity is the Creator of the world. The divine in Buddhism is not personal and is not creative. You could scarcely have a greater contrast than that. Christianity teaches that God both forgives a man and gives him supernatural aid. In Buddhism there is no forgiveness, and no supernatural aid. The goal of all existence in Buddhism is *nirvana*, extinction – attained by the Buddha after no less than 547 births. The goal of all existence in Christianity is to know God and enjoy him for ever. The use of images figures prominently in Hinduism: Judaism prohibits making any image of God. Islam allows a man four wives; Christianity one. Perhaps the greatest difference of all lies between the Bible, which asserts that nobody can save himself and make himself pleasing to God, try as he will; and almost all the other faiths which assert that by keeping their teachings a man will be saved or reborn or made whole or achieve fulfilment. Nothing spells out this contrast more powerfully than the Buddhist story which starts off so like the parable of the Prodigal Son. The boy who comes home and is met by the father, and then has to work off the penalty for his past misdeeds by years of servitude to his father. The principle of *karma* (cause and effect, paying off your guilt) is poles apart from grace (free forgiveness when you don't deserve it a bit).[31]

A Father who notices from afar. A Father who runs – runs! – towards the prodigal. A Father full of compassion. A Father who embraces. A Father who seals my pardon with a kiss. Lord, hear my prayers for people whose spiritual commitment leaves them somewhat cold, deep down, with that nagging need for love unfulfilled. Come to them as you came to the prodigal.

21 July

Choose for yourselves this day whom you will serve.
(Joshua 24:15)

What are we to make of . . . other faiths? Presumably that are all much of a muchness. Presumably they are all pathways to God, and you might as well take your pick.

Such a view has immense attractions. It avoids the black and white choice and sees everything as a shade of grey. It is essentially tolerant, and tolerance is a very fashionable virtue. It is modest, and does not make strong pretensions for your own particular religion. It seems admirable common sense. We take the views of everybody, and try to build up an Identikit picture of God. And some extremely significant people and organisations back it up. For example the saintly Indian leader Mahatma Gandhi said, 'The soul of religions is one, but it is encased in a multitude of forms . . . I cannot ascribe exclusive divinity to Jesus. He is as divine as Krishna or Rama or Mohammed or Zoroaster.' The Hindu mystic Ramakrishna used to speak of himself as the same soul that had been born before as Rama, as Krishna, as Jesus or as Buddha. The Roman Emperor Severus hedged his bets by having in his private chapel not only the statues of the deified emperors, but those of the miracle-worker Apollonius of Tyana, of Christ, of Abraham and of Orpheus![32]

The sin of indecision, Lord; of spiritual procrastination: it's quite a serious one. Likewise, the desire for a 'pick and mix' religion whereby nothing is ever decided upon and no definite commitment is made. I pray for those who find themselves, like Severus, hedging their bets and hoping for the best. Clear the mists, true and living God, in favour of Jesus, the Lord of all. Dissolve the uncertainty.

22 July

My soul faints with longing for your salvation.
(Psalm 119:81)

Perhaps the most wonderful indication of . . . future salvation given us in the Gospels is the least descriptive: 'That where I am, there ye may be also' (Jn. 14:3).[33] Heaven and its salvation is essentially right relationship with the Lord himself or, as J.A.T. Robinson prefers to reinterpret it, 'union in love with Love, the Ground of our Being'.[34] The acme of salvation is what Jesus calls 'entering into the joy of the Lord' (Matt. 25:21,23). And that includes all that a man can hope for. It represents utter and ultimate satisfaction.[35]

A free and full salvation, Lord: don't let me settle for anything less.
Grant me the fullest benefits of your saving mercies: all I can hope for.

Those who have faith are children of Abraham. Scripture foresaw that God would justify the Gentiles by faith, and announced the gospel in advance to Abraham: 'All nations will be blessed through you.' So those who rely on faith are blessed along with Abraham, the man of faith.
(Galatians 3:7–9)

The mysterious irony of salvation lay in this paradox: Jesus, the only one who kept the law in its entirety, paid the penalty of lawbreakers, by being exposed upon that accursed cross and subject to the judgment of God. He acted as the substitute and the representative for the whole human race. As a result believers under the old covenant and under the new are accepted before God as if they were sinless, for they are incorporated in the sinless Messiah who stood in their place of sin and judgment (2 Cor. 5:21). They are 'justified' by the grace of God that gives them what they do not deserve, and by the 'faith' which grasps that proffered gift and responds in obedient dedication to that proffered love. God's way of salvation is shown to be the same throughout the ages: men respond in faith to his initiative in grace. Through the crucial action of 'Abraham's seed, which is Christ' (Gal. 3:16) even the despised Gentiles can become children of that archetypal believer, Abraham, and receive the promised Spirit.[36]

A gospel of grace for the despised. A gospel for all generations. A gospel for 'the whole human race'. A gospel proffered in love as a gift. A gospel of justification. A gospel for the underserving. A gospel rooted in covenant. A gospel of adoption.

Speak afresh to me, Lord, as I ponder this multifaceted gospel.

24 July

**You will be my witnesses in Jerusalem, and in all Judea and Samaria,
and to the ends of the earth.**
(Acts 1:8)

Salvation, then, according to the teaching of Jesus, concerns the whole man. It is concerned with his past, his present and his future. It is the work of rescue achieved by God brought into history by Jesus, the Son of Man. The conditions of its acceptance are repentance and faith; the very idea of merit is excluded by grace. But it demands a radical change of life in those who accept it. And this salvation is no narrow national ideal, but intended for all men, 'that the *world*, through him, might be saved' (Jn. 3:17).

And that explains why, although Jesus came to fulfil the messianic hopes of Israel in the first instance (Jn. 4:22,25,26), he nevertheless gave hints, even within his lifetime, of his universal significance and appeal. With a great man's singleness of purpose he recognized the limitations of his earthly mission; 'I am not sent but unto the lost sheep of the children of Israel' (Matt. 15:24). This was inevitable. The corn of wheat had to fall into the ground and die before there could be a harvest (Jn. 12:24, cf. v. 32). Before the cross and resurrection there were no saving acts to proclaim to the Gentiles, no gospel to preach outside Judaism. Nevertheless, even within his earthly life Jesus made exceptions to this general principle of the limitation of his mission to Israel. He could not remain inactive in the face of crying need. Hence the Samaritan (Lk. 17:16; Jn. 4:7), the Syrophenician (Mk. 7:26) and even the Roman (Matt. 8:10) shared his blessing.[37]

International God, inclusive God, you embrace all nations and all peoples within your saving grace. I pray today for Christian mission partners whose ministry crosses borders and cultures. I pray for those who endeavour to share the news of your saving acts in lands not their own. Bless those upon whom you have bestowed that specific vocation. Bless, too, cross-cultural ministries.

25 July

Let us not become weary in doing good,
for at the proper time we will reap a harvest if we do not give up.
(Galatians 6:9)

Matthew goes out of his way to emphasize the *human* side of salvation, the necessity to persevere with Christ. Not content with reproducing the saying, 'He who endures to the end will be saved', in the apocalyptic discourse (24:13), he gives it again in the more general context of the Mission of the Twelve. In 10:22 it is made abundantly clear that hatred and opposition will be the lot of the Christian missionary, and that endurance to the uttermost is vital if salvation in its full sense is to be achieved. This was doubtless a message very necessary in the early days of the Christian endeavour for which Matthew's Gospel was written, where the discouragements afforded by the relative failure of the Jewish mission and the delay of the Second Coming must have tempted many to give up . . . The situation to which the Epistle to the Hebrews was addressed was very similar.[38]

Lord, honesty compels me to admit that there are times when I too feel like giving up. Sometimes, the mission seems not to be working very well at all, and the church appears to be making only a marginal difference in the world. Is this 'the human side of salvation'; the doubts, the discouragements and what often looks like a lack of progress? Strengthen me, Lord, in such moments. Shield my thoughts from despair, and enable me to keep going. I pray for anyone to whom this applies today.

26 July

He gives wisdom to the wise
and knowledge to the discerning.
(Daniel 2:21)

The claim that Jesus arose from the dead is so shatteringly unique that it has understandably aroused a host of objections. So it ought. Credulity is not a Christian virtue, and if the case for the resurrection is not good enough it ought to be ruthlessly and courageously scrapped . . .

The most basic objection of all is very simply expressed. Dead men don't rise, so it is inconceivable that Jesus rose. This objection is often heard in circles influenced by the natural sciences: it is scientifically impossible for the effects of death to be reversed. Put like this, the claim looks rather unscientific. Such dogmatism is not the normal way in which reputable scientists examine a problem. True, there is an impatience with miracles in many scientific circles, but it is matched by an increasing recognition of the limitations of our knowledge and of the mystery of the universe. Many things which would unhesitatingly have been declared impossible by science a century ago are a normal part of our existence: television, space, travel, antibiotics . . .

[Concerning scientific method], this is unashamedly inductive. That is to say, it begins with phenomena and then seeks to arrive at the generalisations or natural laws which account for them. It does not begin by ruling out of court facts which are inconvenient. Instead, it patiently examines them. And many of the advances in scientific knowledge have taken place when scientists have wrestled with one inconvenient fact which did not fit in with the prevailing theory of the day. In principle there is no scientific reason why Jesus could not have risen from the tomb.[39]

Sovereign God, the great thing is, the laws of science and nature are all yours in the first place! Furthermore, they are subject to your authority. As I thank you for tremendous advances in scientific knowledge which have been of immense benefit to humankind, and as I thank you, too, for pioneering scientists whose intelligence also benefits humanity, I pray for a greater (better) relationship between the worlds of science and faith. Both spheres have so much to offer. Open (all!) our eyes, Lord.

27 July

Jesus replied: 'Love the Lord your God with all your . . . mind.'
(Matthew 22:37)

We are not claiming that there is a certain class of people who are in the habit of emerging from their graves. The first-century writers were not claiming that either. What Christians do maintain is that Jesus was no ordinary man. They believe that there are good reasons for supposing he shared God's nature as well as ours. How, then, can we be so certain that he could not have overcome death, just because nobody else has been observed to rise from the dead? He lived an unsullied life, one that not even his detractors could credibly slander, one that even his judge could not fault. How can we be certain that a perfect life which had given no foothold to sin might not also master death, which scripture asserts is in some mysterious way connected with sin? We have no other example of the 'sinless' category to compare Jesus with. There are no parallels by which to measure the possibility of his unique rising from death. It ill befits the competent scientist or the open minded enquirer to say 'It could not have happened'. The proper course is to apply stringent criteria in examining whether in fact it does seem to have taken place. That is good scientific procedure. Prejudice is not appropriate in serious investigation of truth.[40]

Lord, please make mine an intelligent faith. Deliver me from laziness of thought and paucity of interest. Convert my brain.

28 July

**The rest said, 'Now leave him alone. Let's see if Elijah comes to save him.'
And when Jesus had cried out again in a loud voice, he gave up his spirit.
(Matthew 27:49)**

No one can save Jesus, for he is God's chosen Saviour for all men, and he cannot achieve this salvation short of the sacrifice of himself. As with the other synoptic accounts of the crucifixion, Matthew uses the misunderstanding of the crowd to make his point about the nature of the Saviour and his salvation. Its essence lies in his self-oblation for others. Is he not Jesus, who shall save his people from their sins? This has been the keynote struck at the outset of the Gospel, and it is continued to the end. Jesus, of course, is the Greek translation of Joshua, and its meaning was so well known in Christian circles that Matthew does not even bother to translate it. Philo had said, 'Jesus when translated means "the salvation of the Lord"' (*de Mut. Nom.* 21), and the obvious point when this title was given to Jesus was that he would be a second Joshua, delivering people from their greatest enemies (their sins)[41] and bringing them into a better Promised Land.[42] But clear from the name itself ('Yahweh saves', or 'Yahweh is salvation'), but also from the fact that the promise, 'He shall save his people from their sins' is an unmistakable allusion to Ps. 130:8, which says of God, 'He himself (*autos* in the LXX[43] is emphatically first word, as here) will redeem Israel from all his sins.' Jesus would do what the Old Testament had said God would do.[44]

A God who could, theoretically, have saved himself. A God who could, literally, have removed himself from the cross. A God who could, ultimately, have abandoned the Calvary plan. Yet, a God who chose to love and not escape. A God who rescued and didn't run away. My God.

29 July

Purify your hearts, you double-minded.
(James 4:8)

Liberty does not mean licence. If Jesus died in order to make the unjust justified, he also endowed them with his Spirit in order to make them just. God has done for us what law-keeping, weakened by the frailties of our own fallen nature, could never do. He sent his own Son in human flesh, identical with us except for sin, and he condemned man's sinfulness in Christ's person, hanging upon a cross, as a sin-offering for us. He did so in order that the just requirement set out in God's law might be fulfilled in us who live our lives not after the principle of self-effort but in the power of the Spirit. That is a rough paraphrase of Romans 8:3–4. It shows that Christ's work of sinbearing did not abrogate the moral claims of the law, but was the precondition to men being able to face up to them. In other words, we are not forgiven because we keep the law: but once we are forgiven we are called to keep it. The claim of a holy God that those who have fellowship with him should not only be acquitted and accounted righteous, but actually and progressively be made righteous in an ethical sense is strongly brought out in the Pauline letters. He will not for a moment allow that the doctrine of justification through free grace, received by faith, can lead to antinomianism (Rom. 6:1ff). Far from it. For justification, and the very baptism which is its outward symbol, means dying with Christ and rising again; dying to the old sinful ways, and being prepared to see them as characteristics of the unregenerate nature that was dealt with on the cross by Jesus and must be kept there. And it means rising with Christ too; rising to share in the new life which he makes possible, and which in the fullest detail Paul, in Romans chapter eight, ascribes to the Spirit of Jesus, resident within us.[45]

Lord Jesus, I surrender all. Put to death any double-mindedness you find within me, now and henceforth.

All to Jesus I surrender,
Make me, Saviour, wholly Thine;
Let me feel Thy Holy Spirit,
Truly know that Thou art mine.[46]

30 July

The one who is in you is greater than the one who is in the world.
(1 John 4:4)

Mercifully, the Spirit works deeply within my subconscious self. When I am so self-centred that I would not dream of asking the Spirit for his strength, preferring to go my own way, I am encouraged to recall that 'God is at work in you both to will and to work for his good pleasure' (Phil. 2:13). We shall not be mistaken in seeing that as a reference to God the Holy Spirit. He it is who not only empowers us to do right, but works in us the desire to want to do right, without which we would never dream of turning to ask him for his strength.

But that strength is available to all who are in Christ. It is none other than the superhuman power which raised Christ from the dead which is let loose within our human bodies (Eph. 1:18f). Paul is evidently referring to the Spirit when talking of his power, since he not only prays that the Spirit will reveal it to his readers, but he, in common with other New Testament writers, associates the Spirit with the resurrection of Christ from the dead (1 Tim. 3:16; cf 1 Pet. 3:18). In Ephesians 3:16 Paul makes it quite explicit. He prays that 'according to the riches of his glory, the Father may grant you to be strengthened with might through his Spirit in the inner man'.[47]

Lord, I surrender all, including my subconscious and my inner being; elements of my complex make-up that are, to a certain extent, outwith my direct control. Holy Spirit, be active in those areas of my holistic nature. Work for your good pleasure in both.

31 July

**She said to her husband,
'I know that this man who often comes our way is a holy man of God.'
(2 Kings 4:9)**

Pliny, one of the . . . main classical sources for the end of the first and the beginning of the second century AD, was governor of Bithynia in Turkey. He wrote, about AD 112, to ask the Emperor Trajan what he should do about the rapid spread of the Christians in this area. Their monotheism was threatening the sale of pagan sacrificial animals, the survival of pagan temples and the prestige of the Emperor. Pliny says the Christians lived exemplary lives, but would not worship the gods, and met on a fixed day (i.e. Sunday, the day of resurrection) and sang before dawn in alternate verses a hymn to Christ as God (*Epistles* 10.96).[48]

Lord, in the same way as 'she said to her husband' and as Pliny wrote to Emperor Trajan, may the reports of my comings and goings be good ones. Help me to witness well to those who only ever watch me from a distance, and with whom I have no direct contact as such. Keep me alert to their watching and the possibility of a silent influence for Jesus' sake.

1 August

Fixing our eyes on Jesus, the pioneer and perfecter of faith.
(Hebrews 12:2)

The healing of a Gentile soldier's servant (7:3), the forgiveness of a fallen woman (7:50),[1] the restoration to wholeness of a demented man (8:36), the provision of new life for a dead girl (8:50) – are all described in the language of salvation by Luke, and are clearly intended to be paraenetic. He wants us to understand that this is what salvation is like – new life, wholeness, forgiveness, healing. It is the response of believing hearts to the *kerygma* that brings salvation (8:12), and this *kerygma* is nothing other than the proclamation of a person, Jesus. It is Jesus who comes to save men's lives, not to judge them (9:56 in some MSS). He comes to save the lost (19:10). It is supremely by his death that he does this, as the repeated stress on salvation in the account of his crucifixion makes plain. Four times in 23:35,37,39 Luke stresses that the salvation of others was achieved at the cost of the self-sacrifice of the Saviour; he makes more of this point than even Mark does.[2]

This list of examples, Lord Jesus, constitutes a wonderful summary of your redeeming grace towards fallen humanity. It is by no means complete, but that only stresses the breadth of your saving love. I thank you for this, and I thank you, too, that this is never about theory or formulae, but always about you. You are Saviour, and these hallmarks of salvation speak of you. It's all about you, Jesus.

2 August

He saved us.
(Titus 3:5)

[Luke] leaves us in no doubt at all that this salvation, achieved by Jesus at the cost of his own life, avails even for the most degraded of outcasts; the dying robber's prayer for salvation (23:39) was answered by the promise of the dying Saviour that he would be *with him* in Paradise. Salvation is thus inextricably linked by Luke with the person of Jesus. When Jesus comes to a man's home, salvation comes there (19:9). Salvation is not a matter for speculation (13:23), but for decision (13:24). It is secured by self-commitment to Jesus, that is to say, by faith (7:50; 8:12; 8:50, etc.).[3]

Lord Jesus – Saviour – once again I am confronted with the staggering truth that salvation is you, and that you are salvation. The whole 'package' is who you are, and what you are, and what you've done. It is by no means a separate entity. Help me to understand. Help me to grasp the immensity of this.

3 August

Whoever believes in me, as Scripture has said, rivers of living water will flow from within them.
(John 7:38)

How utterly illogical it is to say that [all religions are] pointing in the same direction. It is as foolish as to say that all roads from Nottingham lead to London. They do nothing of the sort, and it is not helpful in the least to pretend that they do. They lead to radically different goals. Extinction or heaven; pardon or paying it off; a personal God or an impersonal monad; salvation by grace or by works. The contrasts are irreconcilable.

Lesslie Newbigin, Christian bishop in Madras, has been forced to examine very carefully the difference between Christianity and other faiths. How could he help it, living in the midst of a Hindu culture? He puts it like this in his remarkable book, *The Finality of Christ*. The great divide among religions, he maintains, is their attitude to history. Most religions are like a wheel. 'The cycle of birth, growth, decay and death through which plants, animals, human beings and institutions all pass suggests a rotating wheel – ever in movement yet ever returning upon itself.' The wheel offers one escape from the meaningless, repetitive movement it generates. That is to take a spoke – it cannot matter which one – and travel along it to the hub, where all is at rest, and where you can observe the ceaseless movement without being involved in it. This is the way of most religions: 'dispute among the different "ways" is pointless; all that matters is that those who follow them should find their way to that timeless, motionless centre where all is peace, and where one can understand all the endless movement which makes up human history – understand that it goes nowhere and means nothing.'[4]

Lord, preserve me from anything that 'goes nowhere and means nothing'. Keep my relationship with you alive and fluid, lest I become stagnant inside, and faith turns stale. River of life, water of life, flow through me. Keep this all fresh!

4 August

Whoever claims to live in him must live as Jesus did.
(1 John 2:6)

[Christlikeness] is the powerful application to believers of the character of Christ. Thus when Paul is talking about the spiritual battle in Galatians 5, the content of the Christian freedom he advocates is defined by the character of Jesus. This powerful, victorious Spirit which indwells believers, and can keep their sinful natures nailed upon the cross, is like a seed planted in the soil of the believer's life. If cultivated and nourished, this seed will grow into a lovely fruitful tree; and this is what the fruit is like:

> Love, joy, peace, patience, kindness, goodness, faithfulness, gentleness, self-control. (Gal. 5:22)

And what is that, but a description of the character of Jesus? A holy God requires his people to be holy. But the God who 'has called us for holiness . . . gives us his Holy Spirit' (1 Thess. 4:7–8) to enable us to fulfil his requirement. This holiness is not merely a devotion to the deity (there was plenty of such attachment in the ancient world that was far from holy – for instance the cult prostitution that was so common in the temples), nor a mere adherence to ethical rules (there were plenty of those current in antiquity, too, and they possessed all the disadvantages, while lacking the advantages, of the Jewish law). Christian holiness involves both devotion and ethics; it springs from allegiance to Jesus, who embodies in himself the ideal of human conduct.[5]

Truth to tell, Lord Jesus, none of this comes naturally; literally, it doesn't! I do, however, want to be more like you, so I am asking you to make it happen. I certainly can't do it in my own strength (not sustainably, anyway), but I believe this is all possible with your life within. Come, Lord Jesus, make me holy: pardon, peace, salvation and sanctification.

5 August

Early in the morning, Jesus stood on the shore, but the disciples did not realise that it was Jesus. He called out to them, 'Friends, haven't you any fish?' 'No,' they answered. He said, 'Throw your net on the right side of the boat and you will find some.' When they did, they were unable to haul the net in because of the large number of fish.
(John 21:4–6)

The early speeches in Acts, like the early speeches in the Gospel, are full of references to salvation. On the Day of Pentecost Peter quotes Joel to the effect that God's salvation, promised in the Old Testament, is now available for all who will accept it, 'Whosoever shall call on the name of the Lord shall be saved' (2:21). He means Jesus, of course, by 'Lord', though he is well aware that the title referred to God in the Old Testament. The whole point of the early Christian preaching was that this Jesus, although repudiated by the Jewish leaders, was the divinely appointed Saviour for men (5:31; 13:23), and that his Lordship was vindicated by the resurrection, of the reality of which they were witnesses. In his name alone is salvation for a lost world (4:12), salvation designed as much for the Gentile as the Jew. Thus when preaching in the synagogue at Antioch Paul exhorts his Jewish hearers with the words, 'To *us* is the word of this salvation sent' (13:26).[6] Yet, when they refuse to receive it, he can turn to the Gentiles confident that this is the fulfilment of the ancient Scriptures: 'Lo, we turn to the Gentiles, for so hath the Lord commended us, saying, I have set thee to be a light to the Gentiles, that thou shouldest be for salvation unto the ends of the earth' (13:47–8).[7]

God of our salvation, I pray today for Christian outreach workers whose ministry and mission is refused, despite their most sincere efforts to share the news of Christ. I pray for them as they (reluctantly) move their focus from one group of people to another and 'turn to the Gentiles', so to speak. May they never be discouraged! Guide them as they seek to do your will. I pray this, too, for churches who are faced with the challenge of switching tactics in evangelism: 'Lo, we turn'!

6 August

**The grace of our Lord was poured out on me abundantly,
along with the faith and love that are in Christ Jesus.
(1 Timothy 1:14)**

In the middle of his three chapters on spiritual gifts (1 Cor. 12 – 14), Paul sets the crowning gift of love. One has only to substitute the name of Jesus for 'love' in that chapter to see the whole thing is a pen picture of Christ's way of life. The first and foremost fruit of the Spirit is that outgoing love for others, irrespective of their deserts, which marked the Giver of the Spirit in his earthly life.[8]

What a marvellous idea, Lord – to replace 'love' with your name. This paints a beautiful word-picture of your nature. It also, though, challenges me to seek your assistance with those elements of my own nature that aren't yet up to scratch. Jesus, Lover of my soul; my God and my example, let your life be in mine.

7 August

**Christ died and returned to life
so that he might be the Lord of both the dead and the living.
(Romans 14:9)**

The disciples did not rely on an empty tomb: it formed only a very small part of their proclamation. They believed that they had met Jesus after his death. The New Testament accounts of the resurrection appearances 'are trying to justify, even to rationalise, what was for the original witnesses an immediate, intuitive certainty needing no justification. They were *dead sure* they had met with Jesus, and there was no more to be said about it'. So wrote C.H. Dodd (*The Founder of Christianity*, p. 170). If that assurance of the earliest disciples can be reduced to mere subjective visions, hallucinations, wish fulfilment or delusions (all have been suggested) then it is not one doctrine of Christianity which collapses, but the whole structure. For the Christian faith rests fairly and squarely upon the resurrection of Jesus from the dead and his appearance to his disciples for a limited period of forty days before he ceased to manifest himself in that way but continued to abide with his followers worldwide through the Spirit.[9]

Thank you, Lord Jesus, that I too can claim to have met with you, courtesy of your Spirit. I may not have encountered you in any physical, tangible sense, as the disciples did, but my testimony is as valid as theirs, nevertheless. Their witnessing to your resurrection made a great impact; grant me that same privilege, I pray.

8 August

Do this, do that, a rule for this, a rule for that; a little here, a little there.
(Isaiah 28:10)

In [Acts] ch. 4 Luke makes quite explicit what he implies in the Gospel, that he means to see the healings of Jesus and the apostles as paradigms of salvation. In 4:9 Peter explains to the Sanhedrin how the impotent man has been healed (*sesōtai*). Immediately he goes on to stress the other meaning of this ambiguous word, and tells them that there is salvation in none other than Christ (4:12). '*Sōtēria* combines here the two meanings which we usually separate. This healing of the lame is the sign of the messianic era; this healing of the body visualizes the totality of Christ's saving power.'[10]

The story of the shipwreck, whose length has been a source of amazement to scholars for generations, is probably to be seen in the same light. It is noteworthy that the language of salvation abounds (27:20,31,34,43,44; 28:1,4) . . . As reappears vividly in the description of heaven in Rev. 21:1 ('and there was no more sea'), the sea was to the ancient Hebrew the symbol of anti-God power, of chaos and danger, of the demonic. In the story of the shipwreck Luke would have us see the truth that not all the power of Antichrist can prevent the coming of salvation to the uttermost parts of the earth.[11]

And so [Acts] ends with Paul proclaiming without hindrance the salvation of God to both Jew and Gentile alike in the very centre of the ancient world. Although it is offered to Jew and Gentile alike, the response is once again most noticeable among the Gentiles, and the Gentile evangelist[12] ends his book with a quotation from Scripture warranting this sending of 'the salvation of God to the Gentiles' (28:28) and assuring him that 'they will hear it'.[13]

What a depth of riches you have provided, Lord; layer upon layer of hidden treasures, all there for the taking. Please sit alongside me as I read my Bible, and point out to me any gems I might otherwise miss. Reveal to me that which lies beyond the obvious, beneath the surface. Enrich my devotions.

9 August

The LORD looks down from heaven on all mankind.
(Psalm 14:2)

If there is a God, then he is the source of both man and his environment. He is the Lord over all human life.

> Have you not known? Have you not heard? Has it not been told you from the beginning? It is he who sits above the circle of the earth, and its inhabitants are like grasshoppers . . . Whom did he consult for his enlightenment, and who taught him the path of knowledge and showed him the way of understanding? Behold, the nations are like a drop from a bucket, and are accounted as dust on the scales; behold he takes up the isles like fine dust. (Isaiah 40:21ff)

This is the God we are talking about. How can we possibly climb up to him? How can the cup understand the potter who made it? It cannot be done. Man cannot find out God however hard he searches. Religion, all religion, is bound to fail . . .

If by 'religion' we mean man's search for the divine, it is bound to fail. What we need is not to compare the chinks of light that each of us may have grasped, but for the day to dawn. We need not a religion, but a revelation. And that is precisely what Christianity claims to be. A revelation from God. Unlike other holy books, the Bible does not bring us the story of men in search of God; it tells us about the God who comes in search of men.[14]

'The God who comes in search of men'. A God who cares enough to do so. A God who searches relentlessly. A God who is undaunted by rejection. A God who knows where to look. A God of revelation. This is my God.

This is what the Lord has commanded us:
'I have made you a light for the Gentiles,
that you may bring salvation to the ends of the earth.'
(Acts 13:47)

John once speaks of 'Saviour' (4:42, and again in 1 Jn. 4:14), once of 'salvation' (4:22) and six times he used the word 'save' (3:17; 5:34; 10:9; 11:12; 12:27,47). This is remarkably restrained usage for an evangelist who deliberately sets out to bring the uncommitted to faith in Jesus (20:31).[15]

A simple prayer today, Heavenly Father: I pray for mission agencies and churches who share St John's aim of deliberate evangelism. I pray your blessing on them as they endeavour to share the message of the cross. Guide those whose hearts are set towards bringing 'the uncommitted to faith in Jesus'. May they know your Spirit's anointing upon their planning and witnessing. I pray specifically for any such groups known to me personally, wherever they might operate.

11 August

Those who find me find life.
(Proverbs 8:35)

In his treatment of the subject [of salvation],[16] C.H. Dodd has shewn that three ideas underlie Jewish usage of this term; in all three cases there is reference to life beyond the grave. 'Life' is contrasted with death; 'life of the age', or everlasting life, is contrasted with temporary life; and 'life of the age to come' is contrasted with the 'life of this age'. Dodd recognizes that it is from such a background that John develops his doctrine of eternal life. It is something not merely quantitively but qualitatively different from the life we know before becoming Christians. It is defined primarily not by length but by relationship. 'This is life eternal, that they may know thee, the only true God, and Jesus Christ whom thou hast sent (17:3). Not only so, but it is experienced now (3:36; 5:24; 6:47,54), although its fullness lies beyond the grave (5:21–9; 11:23–6). John sees that the life which the Jews expected in the age to come is present in Jesus, and can be enjoyed here and now by relationship with him who is the resurrection and the life (11:25). This is the utterly new thing in Christian salvation, something undreamed of in rabbinic Judaism, that men can enjoy living in God's eternal today through knowing God and Jesus Christ whom he has sent to reveal him . . .

So strong is John's emphasis on realized eschatology, on present salvation, on the qualitative element in eternal life, that the judgement is seen as past for the Christian (3:18; 5:24), the resurrection life is enjoyed by relationship with Christ now (5:24; 11:25–6), and the parousia of Christ is anticipated by the coming of the Spirit of Christ (14:16,18). Salvation, the life of the age to come, is no timeless abstraction nor future hope, of God's own life, a category of existence so radically new that you have to be born again if you are to understand and enjoy it (3:3,5). That is how John sees salvation. Though the terminology is different, his standpoint is characteristic of the early Church.[17]

This is a wonderful concept, Lord Jesus – a wonderful reality; not so much this life and then the next (although it is that too!), but one life, unbroken in Christ, here and now. This is a continuum of grace, and I pray that you will help me 'to understand and enjoy it'.

12 August

LORD . . . examine my heart and my mind.
(Psalm 26:2)

Is Renan[18] right when he says, beautifully, 'It was love which resurrected Jesus'? Is Guignebert right (*The Life of Jesus*, p. 503) when he imagines Peter back home in Capernaum lovingly remembering Jesus while hope dawns in his breast which demands that the Crucified appear? As Strauss[19] cryptically assumes, did the disciples pass from the position 'He must live' to the position 'He does live! He has appeared'? (*Life of Jesus*, 2, p. 643ff).[20]

That crucial leap, Lord, from head to heart! That essential component of life-changing faith, whereby what I believe in terms of mental assent begins to resonate with my heartbeat. That journey from 'must' to 'does'. Lord, my prayers this day reach out to those whose experience of you is quite sincere and genuine, but only something intellectual, as opposed to something deeper and transformative. Bless their searching and honour their interest.

13 August

**Mary Magdalene went to the disciples with the news:
'I have seen the Lord!'
(John 20:18)**

The Jerusalem gospel, proclaimed by Jews, would not have made use of female testimony. One of the oldest commentaries on the Law of Moses rejects testimony from a woman (*Siphre* on Deuteronomy, 190). In the light of this, is it not charmingly in character for Jesus to reveal himself alive first of all to despised *women*? And is it not totally incredible that if anybody had been fabricating the resurrection appearances they would have made the first witnesses of the resurrection women, unqualified to give evidence?[21]

Lord Jesus, this statement is charming indeed, and full of grace. Thank you that your message is often counter-cultural. Thank you that your love is inclusive. I pray that my own church will always be so; that we, as a congregation, will go out of our way to make sure we have (to the best of our ability!) thought to include one and all.

14 August

**Those God foreknew he also predestined
to be conformed to the image of his Son.
(Romans 8:29)**

The divine presence, concentrated in Christ, and universalised through his death and resurrection, becomes available to transform his people. As we fix our gaze upon the Lord Jesus, worship him, and reflect on his character brought before us in the Gospels, our faces will shine, as Moses' did when he went in to seek the presence of the Lord. But the glory will not fade from the Christian as it did from Moses. It will increase. God's purpose is to change us by his Spirit within us (the word 'change' is used in the Gospels to denote Jesus' transfiguration!); and to change us from one degree of glory to another. 'Glory' indicates the person and character of God, under the imagery of light. If we want to see the glory of God (which no man can do in all its unmediated radiance, and live, Exod. 33:20) then we must seek it in the person of Jesus. In him the glory of God shines out in human form (John 1:14; 2 Cor. 4:4). Well, the work of the Spirit in the believer is supremely to transform us from one degree of glory to another: that is to say, to make us more and more like Christ.[22]

**Changed from glory into glory,
Till in heav'n we take our place.[23]**

In this quiet moment, Lord Jesus, as I wait before you now, make a better me.

15 August

**Declare his glory among the nations,
his marvellous deeds among all peoples.
(1 Chronicles 16:24)**

Jesus came, not to be saved himself but to save others; he would do so by his death on the cross. That is the context in which the famous saying about the corns of wheat occurs ([John] 12:24). The same thought is present in 3:16–17 . . . It is in the background in the Lazarus story in ch. 11. Lazarus will indeed be 'saved' (11:12) by the coming of Jesus to raise him from the tomb. But the real salvation of Lazarus and of all men will be achieved by the death on the cross in which that last visit to Jerusalem issued (the evangelist makes this plain in 11:8,16,53). The theme of life through death is even evident in the mention of salvation in 10:9, whether or not Dodd is right in detecting echoes of the Servant terminology from Isa. 49:9–10 (*op. cit.*,[24] p. 246). For the good shepherd . . . gives his life for the sheep (10:15,17).

The life of God, released for men through the death of Jesus, is made available to them through the Spirit . . . Such was one great way in which John looked at salvation. It meant life, the life of the age to come, made possible here and now by relationship with the crucified and risen Lord Jesus through the Spirit. His other great concern was to stress the universality of this salvation. It was meant for the whole world.[25]

**We thank Thee that Thy church unsleeping,
While earth rolls onward into light,
Through all the world her watch is keeping,
And rests not now by day or night.
As o'er each continent and island
The dawn leads on another day,
The voice of prayer is never silent,
Nor dies the strain of praise away.[26]**

The world for God! The whole world for God! What part can I play in this mission, Lord? I give my heart, afresh, in pursuance of this aim. Hear the prayers of your never-sleeping, ever-praying church.

16 August

Our God is in heaven;
he does whatever pleases him.
(Psalm 115:3)

The [resurrection] appearances ceased with the ascension of Jesus. It was as if Jesus spent six weeks showing [the disciples] that he was indeed risen from the dead, and training them for mission; then he made a decisive break. Thereafter he would be known by his Spirit in the hearts of believers, not by appearances to a limited number of people on spasmodic occasions. But Paul was sure that the Lord had made an exception in his case. He knew a vision when he saw one: he had considerable experience of visions, as 2 Corinthians 12:12ff makes plain. He was quite clear that the Damascus Road experience was no vision. It left him physically blinded for a few days. This appearance was extremely important to Luke: he seems to recognise that it was quite exceptional. He tells the story three times in Acts (chs, 9, 22, 26). Luke believed, and Paul believed, that this appearance of the resurrected Christ was in some sense objective and not simply a vision. He placed it in the same genre as the appearances to the original disciples over the forty days. Despite the ascension, despite the cessation of these appearances, Paul was confident that an exception had been made in his case, summoning the apostle to the Gentiles to the service of Christ. 'Last of all, he appeared to me, as to one untimely born (or 'afterbirth', v. 8).' This untidiness, attested also by St Luke, is perhaps a salutary reminder that it is impossible to tie God down.[27]

Exceptional God, help me to remember that you wrote the rules, and that I didn't.

17 August

Jesus replied, 'Blessed are you, Simon son of Jonah, for this was not revealed to you by flesh and blood, but by my Father in heaven.'
(Matthew 16:17)

Paul develops an interesting and original line of argument in 1 Corinthians 2. He is explaining that the Christian message is no earthly wisdom, such as the travelling philosophers of the day peddled, and with which some of the Corinthians were confusing it. No, it is nothing less than God's truth mediated to them by God's Spirit (2:9). And just as human wisdom is only perceived and passed on by the human spirit inside us, so it is with the truth of God. No man can comprehend the things of God: if there is to be any comprehension on our part, then the onus is on God to reveal himself. That he has done. The Spirit has been given to us to enable us to understand not the future, but the gracious gifts God has already made over to us (2:12).[28]

> **'Nothing less than God's truth'. Help me, Lord, to rely on you for interpretation of truth that 'is no earthly wisdom'. Keep me close to you to that I may discern the truths of the spiritual life. I thank you, Lord God, that you understand that the onus to reveal yourself is yours entirely; moreover, that you are only too willing to do so. Thank you for such revelatory grace and goodwill: love revealed on earth in Christ.**

18 August

**Grow in the grace and knowledge of our Lord and Saviour Jesus Christ.
(2 Peter 3:18)**

'The salvation brought in by Jesus is the theme of the entire apostolic age. Wherever we turn in the New Testament, whether it be the Acts, Hebrews, St Paul or St John, we are conscious of a note of confidence and triumph, as of men possessing a supreme good, in which they not only themselves rejoice, but which they are anxious to share with others. More significant than any change in doctrine is this consciousness of salvation as a glorious fact, dominating and transforming life.' So wrote W.A. Brown over sixty years ago,[29] and it is a fair assessment. Salvation is a theme common, and indeed central to the whole of the New Testament. Or, to be more precise, it is everywhere taught that Jesus saves men; Christians are always seen as the objects of his saving activity. For the verb 'to save', either in the active or the passive, is a good deal more frequent in the New Testament than the noun 'salvation'; and this leads to some scholars[30] to conclude that the New Testament writers are not so much interested in a doctrine as in the experience of God's saving work brought about by Jesus.[31]

I pray for your help in such matters, Lord. Doctrine without experience is of little value. However, by the same token experience without doctrine is by no means ideal. Having said that, I love the fact that 'it is everywhere taught that Jesus saves'. May that truth ever be the strong foundation of both my experience and doctrine, as I look to build from there.

19 August

**You will not abandon me to the realm of the dead,
nor will you let your faithful one see decay.
(Psalm 16:10)**

There is something to be said for Theodor Keim's[32] belief that in the resurrection appearances we have 'a telegram from heaven'. They were divinely sent objective visions. Something rather like this view has been reverently and competently revived by M.C. Perry in *The Easter Enigma*, where he argues that a telepathic hypothesis best fits the material of the Gospels. But not only does this accord ill with the empty tomb, and the conviction of Paul that although he knew visions this was not a vision: it also comes up against the strangely physical streak in the appearances. In 1 Corinthians 15 this is not apparent, because Paul is tabulating the appearances very briefly. But the repeated *ōphthē* ('he was seen' rather than 'he appeared') is emphatic. In Mark's original short ending there are no appearances, so the physical aspect does not arise. But in Matthew 28:9 we read that 'they took hold of his feet and worshipped him': subsequently he came and met them on a mountain in Galilee. All very physical. In Luke the physical side is even stronger; Jesus walks, talks and eats with the two disciples on the Emmaus road, and then we find him eating with the whole group of his followers. 'Why are you troubled, and why do questionings arise in your hearts? See my hands and my feet, that it is I myself. Handle me and see; for a spirit has not flesh and bones as you see that I have.' They gave him a piece of boiled fish, and he took it and ate before them' (Luke 24:13–35,38–43). In St John, Mary tries to hold on to his feet. Thomas is presented with his wounded hands, feet and side, and the disciples have breakfast with him by the lake (Chs. 20, 21).[33]

**See from His head, His hands, His feet,
Sorrow and love flow mingled down!
Did e'er such love and sorrow meet,
Or thorns compose so rich a crown?[34]**

Oh, it was real alright! Physical, tangible, touchable. No pretence with this God! Nothing telepathic. Only that which is authentic and solid; reliable to the last. The genuine article.

God has brought to Israel the Saviour Jesus, as he promised.
(Acts 13:23)

Peter is represented as quoting Joel 2:28–32 *in extenso*,[35] concluding with 'whosoever shall call on the name of the Lord shall be saved' (Acts 2:21). Joel, of course, was speaking of God's cataclysmic break into history of which the plague of locusts was a foretaste. He was looking to the last days, messianic days we might call them, in which the Spirit would be generally available; critical days in which God's judgement as well as his mercy would be revealed, days that would drive many to repent and call on the name of the Lord. Those days would be days of salvation, for those who fulfilled the conditions.

On the day of Pentecost, Peter tells the crowds that these days have come. The essentially apocalyptic picture of Joel has been brought about by the human deliverer of prophetic expectation, the man of David's house (2:25,30). This man bore the ancient name of 'God the Saviour', Jesus. His mission was from God. It proved to be so by the signs and wonders that God did by him in their midst, and these they could not deny.[36]

Lord Jesus, help me to see beyond the stories: when I read about 'the signs and wonders that God did by him', prompt me to realize the massive significance of such actions in their prophetic context. You came as the literal embodiment of prophecy fulfilled, and that connection is remarkable. Grant me a better understanding of just who you are, and what these things mean, that I might worship you all the more.

Of the greatness of his government and peace there will be no end.
He will reign on David's throne.
(Isaiah 9:7)

[Peter] glories in the cross. Not only does he dare to blame the religious leaders for their wickedness in putting Jesus there ([Acts] 2:23,36, and this is a constant pattern, cf. 3:13–15; 4:10–11; 5:30, etc.), but he claims that the fate of Jesus was no disaster. It had to happen. So far from putting out of court his claim to be the Messiah, it was all part of the eternal plan of God (2:23 cf. 3:18; 4:28).[37] God had proved it by raising him from the dead. Fantastic though this might seem to them, the resurrection is fact. It is attested not only by eyewitnesses (2:32, cf. 3:15; 4:20,33; 5:32, etc., cf. 1 Cor. 15:6), but by their own Old Testament Scriptures as well. This is particularly plain in Ps. 110:1 and Ps. 16:6–11,[38] where David confesses that his descendant, who will sit upon his throne (2:30, cf. 2 Sam. 7:12–13), is not only greater than himself (his 'Lord') but will, instead of 'seeing corruption', find life and joy in unclouded communion with God (2:28).[39]

Again, Lord Jesus, I see prophecy fulfilled in your life and being. You were spoken of long before your incarnation, which makes your appearance as a human being all the more remarkable. When I stop to think of all that came to pass when you were born, I am humbled in your presence. You are God eternal.

To each one the manifestation of the Spirit is given for the common good.
(1 Corinthians 12:7)

In Ephesians 1:17f Paul prays that the readers might have the spiritual illumination afforded by the Spirit. But this illumination is granted by the God of our Lord Jesus Christ and is possible only 'in knowing him'. The Spirit enables us to know the Master, to sense his will, to grasp his mind and to see things his way. In particular it is Paul's prayer that the Spirit would reveal to them three things.

First, 'the hope of his calling'. In that phrase the Spirit characteristically mediates between the 'already' and the 'not yet'. The calling is past. The hope of the calling is future. The first instalment of heaven, the Spirit himself, enables us to see the reality of our calling and its future consummation.

Second, 'the wealth of the glory of his inheritance in the saints', a deliberately ambiguous phrase which could mean inexhaustible riches lie there! But it could also mean the even more staggering truth that the saints are God's inheritance, and pose the question to what extent he is allowed the freehold of that inheritance which is our lives.

Third, Paul prays that they may perceive 'the extreme greatness of his power to aid believers, the very power that raised Christ from the dead of God's right hand'. And so we are brought by the Spirit's revelations back to Christ again. No further light has broken, nor will break, from God than Christ: the Spirit's task is to illuminate him to us. And to make this centrality of Christ even more emphatic the apostle ends his paragraph by reminding the readers that this mighty, risen, ascended Christ is the head of the body constituted by the Church, and his fullness fills their lives (or, perhaps, their lives are the complement of his fullness, Eph. 1:23).[40]

The thing is, Lord, this can be a dark old world at times. What I mean is, it's not always easy to see you at work. Sometimes, the lamp of faith glows dim! I pray, therefore, for anyone known to me whose pathway is gloomy at present. Help them, Lord, by coming as a lamplighter of old, with illumination for the moment.

23 August

To live is Christ and to die is gain.
(Philippians 1:21)

The resurrection of Jesus was never intended to be a matter for academic discussion. It has very practical implications, and they touch the most profound areas of human life and enquiry . . .

When Paul discusses the resurrection in 1 Corinthians 15, he shows a ruthless integrity in drawing the inferences. If Jesus did not rise from the grave, then Paul's preaching has been a waste of time, their preaching is futile, and they remain unforgiven. What is more, all Christians misrepresent God, dead Christians are finished, and live Christians are deluded. This is how he summarises the importance of the issue in verses 12–19 of that chapter.

On the other hand, if Christ did rise from the grave, then he is alive to be encountered (15:4ff). He has cleared our accusing past (15:3). He has broken the fear of death (15:54). His resurrection is the pledge of our own (15:22). He can change human nature (15:57). And he has a plan for our lives (15:58). In other words, it is very difficult to exaggerate the importance of the resurrection of Jesus from the dead. Its implications are immense.[41]

So many benefits of grace! I thank you, Lord, for this forensic analysis, and I turn my prayers towards friends and family who have yet to avail themselves of all that is listed here – and more. I pray that you, Holy Spirit, will penetrate their defences and objections by shining your light into their lives. Hear my prayers.

**Nor are you to be called instructors,
for you have one Instructor, the Messiah.
(Matthew 23:10)**

The only God known to the Bible is not the First Cause or the Unmoved Mover discussed in philosophical argument, but the living God who made man, who cares for him, and who comes to meet him in Jesus Christ. It is beside the point to argue for or against the traditional 'proofs' for God's existence. The Bible never uses them. It never argues about God's existence at all, but always assumes him as the basis for all else. It points, instead, to Jesus Christ, who claimed that he was revealing God to us. 'No one knows the Son but the Father, and no one knows the Father but the Son and any one to whom the Son chooses to reveal him. Come to me, all who labour and are heavy laden, and I will give you rest (Matt. 11:27ff). Claims like this make the imagination boggle. They mean – if they can be relied upon – that behind this world there is a loving, personal God who has created all there is. This God cares for us men so much, despite our waywardness and rebellion, that he chose to come and share our world, and to make known to us his nature and his will in the only terms we immediately understand, the terms of human life.

And what a life! A life that has influenced art, music, culture and literature more than any other before or since. A life which has inspired most of the ideals of modern education, hospitals, social services, freedom, the trade unions and the welfare state. A life which embodied every virtue known to man, and was free from all human vices. However you look at it, the character of Jesus was unparalleled. He set the highest standards for human conduct that any teacher has ever set, and unlike any other teacher, he kept to those standards.

Not only is the life of Jesus admired far beyond Christian circles. So is his teaching. It is widely recognised as the best and noblest that has ever been offered to mankind.[42]

Divine Instructor, impress your teachings upon my heart afresh. I sometimes run the risk of allowing such matters to grow stale, to the extent that they might lose some of their impact. Bearing in mind all of the above, re-educate me daily, I pray.

25 August

Do not conform to the pattern of this world, but be transformed by the renewing of your mind. Then you will be able to test and approve what God's will is – his good, pleasing and perfect will.

(Romans 12:2)

When in Colossians 1:9ff Paul prays for Christians he has never met, his first request is that the Spirit would give them understanding of the Lord's will for their lives; then, that they should lead their lives in accordance with that will by pleasing the Lord in everything.[43]

Lord of my life, this is only a small paragraph, but it constitutes an enormous prayer! In fact, it is, in effect, a daily prayer that could actually last me a lifetime. I pray for anyone who is seeking your will in one way or another; perhaps regarding a vocation or study options; maybe in terms of deciding where to live. Lord, for those hundreds of ways in which we seek your will for our lives, hear and answer prayer.

26 August

I have swept away your offences like a cloud,
your sins like the morning mist.
(Isaiah 44:22)

Jesus who died in shame has been raised in glory; he is even now with the Father in heaven; and his gift to his followers is the Holy Spirit who has already begun to transform them, by giving them a quickened understanding of Scripture, a tremendous courage, an infectious enthusiasm, and by turning them into men with a message.[44]

Gracious God, our shame is covered by your love. You transform us by virtue of your mercy. You are a merciful Redeemer.

My friend, worry not that I shall judge you, for I shan't.
Worry not that you may need to face my anger, for you shan't.
Though your wounds be self-inflicted, you shall not lose my friendship,
Nor, for that matter, any of my respect;
Let not any of these concerns add to your woes, for your burdens are heavy already.
Worry not that I may shun you, or be ashamed to share a pavement with you,
Or even reluctant, for I shan't. Nor shall I write you off.
Nor shall I behave imperiously, as though your deeds make me superior;
They do not; nor you, inferior. You are still my friend.
Nor shall I close doors, or cease contact, though you are guilty.
For who am I to judge? Or tolerate gossip? Or speculation?
Who am I to condemn, and not to love,
Especially now, when you will need friendship more than ever?
No. As the bricks and rocks upon which you have built your life begin to crumble,
Perhaps you would allow me the privilege of kneeling at your feet,
Collecting them, carrying them for you,
So that we can, one day, build a better tomorrow?
For this too will pass, and while it passes, we are friends.[45]

27 August

**Isaac reopened the wells that had been dug
in the time of his father Abraham.
(Genesis 26:18)**

The worship of Jesus as Lord was firmly grounded in the Aramaic-speaking Church before ever it embarked on a programme of expansion, and we have the formula *marana-tha*[46] to prove it (1 Cor. 16:23). Paul is clearly quoting a very old prayer (or credal statement) here; it had a liturgical usage . . . and liturgy is notoriously conservative. This phrase anchors the worship of Jesus as 'Lord' in the earliest Christian community.[47]

And what an anchor! One that keeps the soul steadfast and strong. Lord Jesus, I pray today for my fellow Christians around the world whose worship is beautified and expressed by way of formal liturgy. I pray for those whose faith experience is enriched by ancient formulae and liturgical usage. Bless them as they reach out to you in such ways. Teach me what beauty there may be in old traditions.

28 August

**Whether you turn to the right or to the left, your ears will hear a voice
behind you, saying, 'This is the way; walk in it.'
(Isaiah 30:21)**

[Regarding the Spirit's guidance], David Watson has some wise words to say on the matter in his *One in the Spirit* (p. 54ff). He draws together from the Bible four strands in divine guidance which, taken together, provide a confident basis for action, and avoid excessive recourse to that overworked claim, 'The Lord told me to do such and such.' First, God guides through circumstances (Acts 16:10). God closes some doors and opens others; our responsibility is to be sensitive to his leading, and to follow through the doors when they open. Second, God guides through other Christians, as he did in Acts 6 when the whole multitude chose the Seven, or in Acts 13 when the Spirit spoke to the church at Antioch about the need for Paul and Barnabas to go abroad. Personal convictions should be open to testing by the guidance of other Christians. If our conviction really comes from God, others, who are in touch with God, will confirm it . . . Third, God guides us through the Scriptures. The Spirit who inspired their writing is perfectly well capable of taking some part of them and writing it on our hearts so that becomes an inescapable pointer to a particular course of action. This method, also, taken by itself, is liable to abuse. To pick verses at random from the Bible proves nothing at all, except that we are gullible and are not using the Scriptures as we are intended to. Paul's advice is very different: 'Let the word of Christ dwell in you richly, as you teach and admonish one another in all wisdom' (Col. 3:16). An increasingly broad appreciation of the Scriptures will give us a developing ability to scent the will of God in any given situation. Fourth, God guides us in prayer. Watson points to Colossians 3:15, 'Let the peace of Christ rule (i.e. be the arbiter) in your hearts.' There is such a thing as praying a situation through until one is virtually sure of the will of God on the matter. One has a deep inner peace about it; not absolute intellectual certainty, but practical confidence, which allows one to proceed to action with joyful assurance. These are some of the ways in which we may expect the Spirit of God to illuminate not only the person of God but his will for us.[48]

**Guide us and guard us, gracious God. Grant us your peace, and let that
be our quiet strength, our guiding notion.**

29 August

There is but one Lord, Jesus Christ.
(1 Corinthians 8:6)

If Jesus is indeed, as the resurrection asserts, God himself who has come to our rescue, then to reject him, or even to neglect him, is sheer folly. That is why Jesus is not, never has been, and never can be, just one among the religious leaders of mankind. He is not even the best. He is the only. Among various examples of the relative he stands out as the absolute. In the risen Jesus God Almighty confronts us with shattering directness. He offers us total succour; but he demands of us total allegiance . . .

The early Christians lived in a world far more syncretistic in beliefs than even our own. But they were clear that Jesus was unique.[49]

This is challenging, Lord – and, in a society that revolves around political correctness and varying degrees of tolerance, by no means straightforward. Help me, I pray, to hold fast to the uniqueness of Jesus as Lord and Saviour, but to do so in a way that is persuasive and not counterproductive. Teach me this skill!

30 August

May God bless us still.
(Psalm 67:7)

The uniqueness of Jesus's salvation is nowhere more clearly emphasized than in Acts 4:12. It is, as the context shows, a salvation which concerns the whole man (*sōzein*[50] is ambivalent in 4:9,12, as it is so often in the Gospels). It is made possible through Jesus of Nazareth, crucified, risen and active in his disciples. He was 'the stone set at nought by you builders', says Peter courageously (as he uses the text from Ps. 118:22 which his Master had used before him, Mk. 12:10), and through God's action he 'is become head of the corner.' This verse [Psalm 118:22] became an important one among the early Christians. It comes from a psalm sung at all the festivals, and Jewish Christians would never be able to forget its words, and the striking light they shed on the fate of Jesus. There are, in fact, many verbal links between this psalm and the whole incident of the healing of the lame man to which this speech is the sequel. 'The gate of the Lord' which 'the righteous enter' (Ps. 118:20) corresponds with 'the gate of the temple' (Acts 3:2) which the restored cripple (now made 'righteous'?) 'enters' (3:8). 'This is the Lord's doing, and it is marvellous in our eyes' of the psalmist (118:23) is matched by Peter's insistence that the healing is God's doing (Acts 3:12,16), and by the repeated statements that the crowd 'marvelled' (3:10,11,12).[51]

Thank you, Lord, for those songs and choruses in my life that are 'sung at all the festivals'. Thank you for the Christian teachings of my childhood which I will 'never be able to forget'. They represent a treasure store of memories that have stood me in good stead. As I repeat the familiar festivals of the Christian calendar, year by year, and as I recite familiar words, bless them afresh to my heart, that they might serve as reminders of your faithfulness towards me.

31 August

As water reflects the face,
so one's life reflects the heart.
(Proverbs 27:19)

Religion will never win through to God. Not simply because of the nature of God, but because of the nature of man. The Bible gives a pretty unflattering picture of man, but one that is uncomfortably near the truth. It tells us several unpleasing truths.

For instance, it informs us that we are not the earnest lovers of God that we would like to suppose: on the contrary, we are 'enemies in our minds by wicked deeds'. We do not have that heart of gold which we like to think we have: on the contrary 'the heart of man is deceitful above all things and desperately sick'. It tells us that we are not impartial in our search for the truth: on the contrary, 'men suppress the truth in righteous living'. We do not follow every gleam of light that comes our way: on the contrary, 'men love darkness rather than light because their deeds are evil' (Colossians 1:21; Jeremiah 17:9; Romans 1:18; John 3:19).

There seems to be a basic twist in human nature which makes us incapable of welcoming the best when we see it. More often than not we want to get rid of it, because it shows us up. One of the more pathetic illusions of humanism is that men are all good folk at heart, and given decent environment, decent working conditions, plenty of money and secure employment they will all be good citizens, and the heart of gold will shine out. What rubbish! If we are all good folk at heart why does the crime rate go up every year along with our prosperity? . . . If we were all good folk at heart, how we would flock to the best person there has ever been, Jesus Christ.[52]

Hard truths, Lord. Home truths. Heart truths. Let me never shy away from heart surgery, Lord Jesus, if it is you who is wielding the scalpel. Like medicine that might well be unpleasant, but which can do me the world of good, let me yield my heart to you for repairs. Give me courage.

1 September

He was despised
(Isaiah 53:3)

To Jewish eyes Christ hung in the place of cursing. Hence the scandal of a crucified Messiah; not only did he fail to rid [the Jews] of their enemies, but his end shewed that he rested under the curse of God. Hence, perhaps, the cries of execration, 'Anathema Jesus!' of which we read in 1 Cor. 12:3.[1]

'Execration' – meaning 'utter detestation'. That is to say, a God who was utterly detested, with all the forces of hell hurled at the man on the cross. For my sake. All the spittle, all the loathing. For me; such was the value placed upon my soul.

2 September

'The days are coming,' declares the LORD,
'when I will raise up for David a righteous Branch,
a King who will reign wisely
and do what is just and right in the land.'
(Jeremiah 23:5)

The sermon of Acts 13 was, we are told, preached in Pisidian Antioch, where there were vast numbers of Diaspora Jews, who doubtless spoke Greek. Indeed, the juxtaposition of the two words 'a Saviour, Jesus' (13:23) could only be made in Greek; in Aramaic it would be tautologous, *Yashu'a Yeshu'a*. This Saviour is seen as the longed-for King of David's line. Paul's language reflects 1 Sam. 13:14; Ps. 89:20, and the actual promise is found in various places in the Old Testament (e.g. 2 Sam. 7:12; 22:51; Ps. 132:16–17). Both these last two references state that in fulfilling this prophecy God will bring in salvation, and this may account for the use of the title 'Saviour' here. Clearly one of the uppermost themes in the context is that of the kingly rule exercised by great David's greater son.[2]

How wonderfully prophecy was fulfilled in your incarnation, Lord Jesus. You came to us as one of us. News of your mission was shared in a language that could be understood and shared. Your arrival was no mistake, no coincidence, and no insignificant event. It was the unfolding of ancient decrees. All of this, to reach a fallen race. Such planning. Such detail. Such mercy.

Once in royal David's city,
Stood a lowly cattle shed,
Where a mother laid her baby,
In a manger for his bed:
Mary was that mother mild,
Jesus Christ, her little child.[3]

3 September

**A light for revelation to the Gentiles,
and the glory of your people Israel.
(Luke 2:32)**

In [Acts] 13:26 it is made clear that this salvation is meant, in the first instance, for Jews and 'God-fearers', as Gentile adherents of the synagogue were called. It is the culmination of God's saving activity displayed in the whole history of Israel. The content of the *kerygma* is much the same as in Peter's speeches.[4] Once again we find the use of Psalm 16. In addition, Paul uses Ps. 27 to prove the Messiahship of Jesus. It is just possible that this text was applied to the Messiah in pre-Christian times,[5] and if so might have been common ground between Paul and his Jewish hearers. In any case, it rapidly became an important text for the early Christians (Heb. 1:5; 5:5; 7:28) and is embedded deep in the story of the Baptism of Jesus (Mk. 1:11 and parallels; 2 Pet. 1:17).[6]

Lord God, I pray for the nation of Israel today. I pray for Jews, wherever they might live. I pray for Messianic Jews. I pray for mission groups whose focus is Jews. I pray for my local synagogue and rabbi.

4 September

The gift of God is eternal life in Christ Jesus our Lord.
(Romans 6:23)

Some time ago the British *Sunday Times* ran a series of articles in which distinguished men and women gave their ideas about what would happen after death. They included Christmas Humphreys the Buddhist, Lord Dowding the spiritualist, Basil Henriques the Jew, Bertrand Russell the atheist, and so on. The articles aroused a lot of interest, and were subsequently published as a book, *The Great Mystery of Life Hereafter*. The motley collection of views brought together in this way showed a number of things: that man is fascinated by this problem; that there is general belief (even among rationalists) in some sort of survival; and that there is a most bewildering difference of opinion on the matter. One view seems as good as another: nobody knows for sure, for none of the writers had experienced life after death. It would seem that mortal man is reduced to guesswork; we can, by definition, get no certain knowledge . . .

Christian optimism about the future is not (as Bertrand Russell complained in his article in the *Sunday Times*) 'built on the ground that fairy tales are pleasant', but founded on the solid basis of the resurrection of Jesus Christ from the dead (which Russell appears not to have investigated). And this same Jesus promised his followers that he would go to prepare a place for them, so that where he is, they might be also (John 14:2–3).[7]

This is indeed, nothing less than a fresh and everlasting chapter in cosmic history; a chapter that, by grace, includes me. Insignificant me! This fact is mind-blowing, yet at the same time exciting and wonderful. Thank you, Lord Jesus, for forcing open the door that had been locked: the force of love; the victory of mercy. (Oh, and Lord, I pray once more for friends and family who are 'reduced to guesswork' concerning their eternal destiny. Show them the empty cross, I pray.)

5 September

**Blessed is the one
who does not walk in step with the wicked
or stand in the way that sinners take
or sit in the company of mockers,
but whose delight is in the law of the LORD,
and who meditates on his law day and night.
(Psalm 1:1–2)**

Auguste Comte, the French philosopher . . . said he intended to found a new religion, which would sweep away Christianity and everything else in its wake. [Thomas] Carlyle's devastating reply ran something like this. 'Splendid! All you need to do is to speak as never man spoke, to live as never man lived, to be crucified, rise again the third day, and get the world to believe you are still alive. Then your religion will have some chance of success' . . .

If we want an answer, supported by solid evidence, to three of the most fundamental and baffling questions anyone can ask (and does ask very frequently), then it is the resurrection of Jesus Christ which provides the clue. We are constantly reminded of the importance of asking the right questions. The trouble is that in religious matters we do not know what the right questions are. So we pose these disconnected queries about the existence of God, the different religions, and life after death. However, the Bible does not encourage us to ask these questions at all. The New Testament writers urge us to make up our minds about Jesus of Nazareth and his resurrection. For the resurrection shows us clearly that there is a God, that Jesus Christ is the way to God, and that death for the Christian leads into the nearer presence of God.[8]

A faith based on 'solid evidence', Lord – in triplicate! This indicates, yet again, your willingness to reach out, to persuade, to convince, all because of love. Help me, I pray, to assimilate the counsel of Psalm 1, so that the roots of my faith may grow strong. Keep me standing in all the right places, Lord, beginning with today.

6 September

Taste and see that the LORD is good;
blessed is the one who takes refuge in him.
(Psalm 34:8)

[In Acts] Ch. 16 . . . we see here the Gentile mission in operation. Paul preached to such effect that Lydia, an Asian businesswoman, believed and was baptized. A slave girl whom Luke calls a 'pythoness', that is to say a woman inspired by the god Apollo, followed the missionaries around, and advertised them as the 'servants of the most high God' who proclaimed 'the way of salvation' (16:16f). Gone are the days when it was thought impossible for a pagan medium to speak in such terms.[9] The longing for salvation was prevalent throughout the ancient world . . . and 'the most high God'[10] was a title for the supreme deity among the Jews and pagans alike.[11] Apollo was primarily a saviour in the sense of healer;[12] he was the god of prophecy and divination;[13] and in Rome from the time of Augustus[14] he was virtually equated with Jupiter Optimus Maximum – the most high god! And it was the slave of this healer god, this inspired god, this most high god, who recognized in a superior power a greater inspiration and a better saviour. She was not disappointed, but came to taste the salvation she had recognized.[15]

Let it be, Most High God, that those caught up in dabbling with the occult, be that at a 'moderate' level or to a more serious extent, come to taste your true salvation. I pray for those who are trapped by horoscopes, ouija boards, séances, tarot readings and other dark arts, that you would bring light and freedom. Visit those who rely upon readings and the like, and those who even in these supposedly enlightened times earn a living from such artistry, just as you visited the slave girl.

7 September

I will repay you for the years the locusts have eaten.
(Joel 2:25)

There is no carefully thought out soteriology in the Acts of the Apostles. That is to be expected. These men knew from their experience that Jesus was the bringer of that ultimate salvation of which all the Old Testament prophets had spoken. 'This is that which was spoken of by the prophet', said Peter, and it was the conviction they all shared. *This is that!* The days of salvation had dawned. The Last Day, the day of the age to come, had become a present reality to them through the achievements of the Messiah and the gift of the Spirit. Experience preceded theology, and these men rejoiced in salvation as a glorious reality. Reflection on the significance of these great events would come later. It would not add anything to what they had experienced and what they preached, though it would interpret it. But they were so conscious of their risen and ascended Lord, and his ability to save men by curing their ills, forgiving their sins and giving them the Holy Spirit, the mark of the new age, that they 'went everywhere preaching the word' (Acts 8:4) and before long 'turned the world upside down' (Acts 17:6) with their gospel of a God who has saved men from their sins, can save them from themselves, and will save them eternally.[16]

Lord, I can't help but think of the great denominations you have raised up, whose early-day missionary zeal was a reflection of this account, full of Holy Spirit passion and zeal, yet whose work and witness nowadays is diluted largely into, and characterized by, social work and/ or community involvement. Nothing wrong with either of those expressions of church life, but everything wrong with them if they have replaced the lifeblood of denominations that once 'went everywhere preaching the word'. Restore, Lord, in your major denominations – as well as fresh expressions – that which appears to have been lost somewhere along the way. Send the fire!

8 September

Our Father in heaven.
(Matthew 6:9)

The Spirit not only teaches us the truth of God, he opens our eyes to the one in whom that truth became incarnate, and guides us in our lives. He also enables us to approach God in prayer . . . It is the Spirit who enables the adopted sons to call God 'Father', 'Abba', that intimate form of address first found on the lips of Jesus. Bearing in mind that 'Abba' is the opening word of the Lord's Prayer in Aramaic, we could rightly say that only through the Spirit can we pray and live out that prayer.[17]

How blessed I am, if my God my Father be!

Abba, Father, fulfil the office of Thy Name towards Thy servants; do Thou govern, protect, preserve, sanctify, guide, and console us. Let us be so enkindled with love for Thee, that we may not be despised by Thee, O most merciful Lord, most tender Father; for Jesus Christ's sake. Amen.[18]

9 September

Surely God is my salvation . . .
the Lord himself . . . he has become my salvation.
(Isaiah 12:2)

In contrast to a good deal of pietistic and evangelical usage, St Paul does not often speak of salvation as a thing of the past. He would not, I think, have been too happy to say, 'I was saved on such and such a day', because he was intensely aware that salvation, in its fullness, was something that belonged to God's future. Accordingly, most of his references speak of this future aspect of salvation. Nevertheless, for him as for all the New Testament writers, the unitary eschatological event of Jewish expectation has been shattered by the coming of Jesus. The age to come is no longer entirely future. It has invaded this age in the person of Jesus, and this bridgehead is, so to speak, kept open and indeed enlarged by the presence in the Church of the Holy Spirit. He it is who is described by Paul as the *aparchē*, the first fruits of the age to come (Rom. 8:23). He whose coming was promised in the last days (Joel 2:28) has come, since Pentecost, into the hearts and lives of believers; so much so that, 'If any man have not the Spirit of Christ, he is none of his' (Rom. 8:9).

The early Christians, in short, were confident that 'the last days' had broken in upon them (Acts 2:17; Heb. 1:2; 1 Jn. 2:18), and that they tasted even now the powers of the age to come (Heb. 6:5). Of that justification, that acquittal before the ultimate Judge, which properly belonged to the last day, the Christians were assured now (Rom. 5:1; 8:1); of that final salvation, involving deliverance, safety and victory which also belonged to the age to come, they were no less confident. The man in Christ is justified, and he is saved. Paul dares to say that in several places.[19]

Once (now) and for all (then, in eternity). This is a reliable salvation; a durable promise. Thank you, Heavenly Father, that this condition (being saved) is one that will never lose its sparkle or polish. Nor will it ever fade, for salvation belongs to you and you are imperishable; you cannot diminish. In you, Lord, I place my trust, for that which is past, that which is present, and that which is future. How blessed I am, if my God my Saviour be!

10 September

Hear the supplications of your servant.
(2 Chronicles 6:21)

The Spirit . . . is also the prime inspirer of prayer. Not only does he enable us to cry 'Abba' with the joyous obedience and trust of newly adopted members of the family; not only does he enable us to pray and articulate words of the prayer that Jesus taught us. He initiates prayer within us . . .

We read of Christians 'praying in the Spirit' (Jude 20; Eph. 6:18). This seems to indicate a deep, free, and intensive time of prayer, when the Spirit takes over and controls and leads the prayers, and one can go on praying for several hours without being aware of the passage of time. Those who have taken part in nights of prayer can, no doubt, all recall such times when the Holy Spirit has led people to pray in harmony, with intensity, with breadth, with perseverance and assurance. 'Pray at all times in the Spirit,' writes Paul, 'with all prayer and supplication. To that end keep alert with all perseverance, making supplication for all saints, and also for me . . . that I may declare the gospel boldly, as I ought to' (Eph. 6:18f). It is fascinating in this context concerning the spiritual warfare in which we are engaged to notice how he ascribes the work of the Spirit to two juxtaposed concepts: prayer, and the Word of God which addresses us primarily through the Word or message enshrined in the Scriptures; and he enables us to address God with freedom and confidence in prayer.[20]

Thank you, Holy Spirit, for your gracious willingness to help me with the mystery of prayer. I pray for anyone whose prayer-life seems difficult and heavy-going at present, and whose prayers are somewhat stilted. Visit them with 'freedom and confidence' so that matters can begin to 'flow' again and channels of communication become a lot clearer.

11 September

Every good and perfect gift is from above.
(James 1:17)

A . . . way in which the Spirit inspires prayer is by giving to the man in question the gift of tongues . . . It is sufficient to notice here that speaking in tongues is one of the gifts of the Spirit to his people (1 Cor. 12:10), and that the primary purpose is to enable the recipient to pray to God from the depths of his being and not merely from the conscious levels of his mind. Indeed, the conscious mind is not employed when the Christian prays in tongues to the Lord (1 Cor. 14:14). But perhaps we have grown over-concerned about the conscious levels of rationality and suppressed for too long the reservoirs of subconscious feeling which the Spirit seems to touch and use when a man prays in tongues, with the result that he is built up, even though he cannot understand what he is saying (1 Cor. 14:4). There is no doubt among those who have been given the gift of tongues that their prayer life and their ability to praise God in all circumstances has grown dramatically. It is one of the ways on which the Spirit evokes prayer in the people of the Messiah.[21]

Sovereign giver of gifts, it is of course entirely up to you which gifts you choose to dispense, and to whom. You know best. Allow me to be content with whichever spiritual gifts you deign to bestow upon me. On the basis that each and every gift is a token of mercy, I receive any such blessings with humble gratitude. By the same token, help me to carefully identify my gifting, and then of course to serve you to the best of my ability. Thank you, Lord, that you gladly equip your people for service.

12 September

Truly my soul finds rest in God;
my salvation comes from him.
(Psalm 62:1)

I have seen 'good' men sweating with the intensity of their struggle to keep clear of the Light of the world. Francis Thompson knew what he was talking about in that poem of his, *The Hound of Heaven*, which begins:

I fled him down the nights and down the days
I fled him down the arches of the years
I fled him down the labyrinthine ways
Of my own mind, and in the midst of tears
I hid from him, and under running laughter.

The very fact that we hide from him shows that we are self-centred creatures at heart, just as the Bible says we are. And we have another closely allied problem. There is something wrong with our will. We don't seem to be able to live up even to our own occasional efforts after high standards. How long do your New Year resolutions last, for instance? How long does your peace and goodwill of the Christmas period continue in your office?

No wonder Paul comes to the conclusion that the Old Testament had reached before him, as he draws to the end of his shattering indictment of contemporary pagan and religious society. 'There is none righteous, no, not one. There is none that understands and seeks after God' (Romans 3:10–11). The myth is exploded. We are not honest seekers after God. Most of us, most of the time, are only too thankful to keep out of his way. All men are disqualified, whether they come from the so-called Christian West, the Communist bloc or the mystic East. None have arrived at God, both because he is too great for any of his creatures to pierce his incognito; and because his creatures are too twisted, too self-centred to want to. The greatness of God and the sinfulness of man are two massive barriers to our supposing that all religions lead to God. They do nothing of the sort. No religions lead to him.[22]

All my hope is founded upon you, Heavenly Father. Help me to abide
within your heart of love.

13 September

Jesus of Nazareth . . . went around doing good.
(Acts 10:38)

A great many religions stress the character of their founder. His life, his character, his personality, are held up to the faithful as an example. While there is a sense in which the example of Jesus was unparalleled, in that he not only taught the most exacting standards but kept them, it is noteworthy how little the example of Jesus figures in the evangelistic preaching of the early church. Naturally, enquirers and new believers would be asking the original missionaries, 'What was Jesus like, and what was his teaching?' and the Gospels sprang, partly at least, out of the need to answer that legitimate enquiry. But that is not what the apostles preached. They gave only enough material about the historical Jesus, it would seem, to ground him very firmly in recent local history. That done they proceeded to speak of his death on the cross and his resurrection. There lay the heart of the matter. The longest account of the actual ministry of Jesus to be found in any of the Acts sermons comes in 10:38f. 'God anointed Jesus of Nazareth with the Holy Spirit and with power; he went about doing good and healing all that were oppressed by the devil, for God was with him. And we are witnesses to all that he did both in the country of the Jews and in Jerusalem.' That is all about Jesus' ministry. Immediately Peter proceeds to the cross and the resurrection. 'They put him to death by hanging him on a tree; but God raised him up the third day and made him manifest, not to all the people but to us who were chosen by God as witnesses, who ate and drank with him after he rose from the dead.' Peter does not leave it there. As constantly in the apostolic kerygma, he challenges his hearers to repent of their sins and receive the forgiveness God wants to offer them through Jesus.[23]

This is an interesting concept, Lord Jesus. Help me to understand it. It speaks of a distinctly humble God, whose actions in loving, dying and rising again speak volumes for themselves. Those deeds represent and portray your great example: love in action! May it be seen of my example that God is with me.

14 September

Be alert and always keep on praying.
(Ephesians 6:18)

'The Spirit helps us in our weakness. For we do not know what to pray as we ought, but the Spirit itself intercedes for us with sighs too deep for words. And he who searches the hearts of men knows what is in the mind of the Spirit, because he intercedes for the saints according to the will of God. And we know that in all respects he co-operates with those who love God.' There are some profound truths here for the Christian to ponder. For many of us, prayer in the Holy Spirit is something about which we know very little. Our prayers tend to be mechanical or at best self-centred, and prayer in the Holy Spirit allows the Spirit of Christ to pray in us, to pour into our souls the overflowing life of intercession.[24]

Gracious Holy Spirit, I warmly invite you to overhaul my prayer life. Meet with me there, in my devotions, to teach me and to overflow those moments. Fully inhabit those private, quiet times, I pray.

Christ with me,
Christ before me,
Christ behind me,
Christ in me,
Christ beneath me,
Christ above me,
Christ on my right,
Christ on my left,
Christ when I lie down,
Christ when I sit down,
Christ when I arise,
Christ in the heart of every man who thinks of me,
Christ in the mouth of everyone who speaks of me,
Christ in every eye that sees me,
Christ in every ear that hears me.[25]

15 September

The LORD confides in those who fear him;
he makes his covenant known to them.
(Psalm 25:14)

Would the [pagan] world have understood [the gospel] message? Would it have appeared double Dutch to the first hearers? Martin Hengel of Tübingen has brought a superbly documented answer to that question in his book, *The Atonement*. He has unearthed and put together a mass of classical material which shows beyond all possible doubt that the first hearers of the gospel, Jews and Greeks alike, had more than enough pointers within their own background to understand the heart of the good news about a saviour who suffers for our rescue . . .

The [Greek] ancients were well aware of death being the necessary precondition for the exaltation of a hero, like Achilles or Heracles. They knew of many instances of voluntary death 'for mankind'. The Greeks greatly valued those who died for the city, or for their friends, for the law or for the truth . . . It was a common theme in Greek tragedy. Agamemnon sacrificed his daughter Iphigenia to avert the wrath of Artemis and secure the success of the Trojan War . . .

But Euripides went further. He took up the theme of atoning sacrifice and saw it as the voluntary surrender of one's life for a higher end . . . Furthermore, the phrase *apothnēskein huper*, 'to die for', passed into common Greek usage. We meet the scapegoat in many places (significantly the scruffiest, most broken-down animal in your flock!). The averting of divine wrath was a commonly accepted idea, and it was done through the death of an innocent animal, or, sometimes, a person. This atoning sacrifice was often called *pharmakos* or 'medicine'.[26]

Lord, you very graciously provide an abundance of hints and signs as to your presence and your purpose. You have done so throughout history. In so many ways, you prepare human hearts and minds for your arrival. You distribute 'more than enough pointers' in all kinds of ways. I pray for some of those pointers to lodge in the hearts of those who don't yet acknowledge your living reality. Lord, bless your church at large as it seeks to welcome those whose lives you touch. Make known your friendship and your covenanted love.

16 September

**If we claim we have not sinned,
we make him out to be a liar and his word is not in us.
(1 John 1:10)**

Sin is *parabasis*[27] . . . It is the deliberate breaking of divine law (Rom. 2:23,25,27, etc). It is what Adam did when he deliberately disobeyed God's plain command (5:14). It is what the man with standards does every time he breaks them (2:23). Sin is also, and most frequently in Paul, described as *hamartia*, 'missing the mark' – the metaphor was originally drawn from archery. All have sinned, i.e. come short of the mark for human conduct, the glory of God (3:23). What that 'glory' or glorious standard of God is can be seen from the life of Jesus (2 Cor. 4:6). All, whatever their respective merits, fall far short of *that* quality of life. A third devastating description of sin can be seen in the word *anomia*, 'lawlessness'. 'We have turned every one to his own way' was how the prophet described this attitude we adopt of keeping God out of our lives (Isa. 53:6). Like the men in the parable, we say of God, 'We will not have this man to reign over us' (Lk. 19:14). Transgression of God's laws, falling short of God's standards, rebellion against God's loving rule; this to Paul is what is meant by sin, and it holds sway over Jew and Gentile alike (Rom. Chs. 1–3), so that 'all the world is guilty before God' (3:19).[28]

It's a wonder, Heavenly Father, that you stick with any of us, given that this is what we are like. Yet, you do, and, more than that, you provide a means of redemption. Actually, Lord, I thank you for this diagnosis, as uncomfortable as it is, firstly because I know it springs from a heart of love, and secondly because there is a cure. You do not leave us in this wretched state, but you cover us with amazing grace. What a God you are: diagnoser and doctor.

17 September

The scripture was fulfilled that says, 'Abraham believed God, and it was credited to him as righteousness,' and he was called God's friend.
(James 2:23)

[Jesus] was no hero dying for his city, no philosopher dying for his friend, but God in human form dying for the sins of the whole world. Here was no averting of personal wrath by human sacrifice: here was God himself providing the means of atonement for his enemies who could now become his friends. Here was no occasional intervention to atone for a particular crime, but the eschatological salvation, the judgment and the salvation of the whole world. The pagan in the ancient world was, therefore, provided with the categories of sin and suffering, atonement and ransom which enabled him to understand the message of the gospel: but the message utterly transcended any concept of atonement that could have crossed his mind. Such was God's *praeparatio evangelica* in the pagan world.[29]

God whose name is Love, there is something dreadfully poignant about the statement, 'here was God himself providing the means of atonement for his enemies who could now become his friends'. This speaks of a friendless God and in doing so, summarizes sin: that is, the hurt and pain it inflicts upon your heart. Thank you, Lord, for reaching out to your enemies and wanting to befriend us. Forgive us for all the ways in which we have grieved you; for every fall and deliberate act. Have mercy.

18 September

When the woman saw that the fruit of the tree was good for food and pleasing to the eye, and also desirable for gaining wisdom, she took some and ate it. She also gave some to her husband, who was with her, and he ate it. Then the eyes of both of them were opened, and they realised that they were naked.
(Genesis 3:6–7)

Sin finds a surprising ally in the Law. This is conceived of in a number of slightly different ways in Paul's letters, but God's standard, as set out in the Decalogue, the Five Books of Moses, or the whole Old Testament covers most of these. The Law thus conceived is 'holy and just and good' (Rom. 7:12). It is God-given and enshrines his principles for human life, but as a means of communication with God it is wholly defective. Whilst it is true that if any man could keep the Law he would be fit for life with God (Rom. 10:5), the fact is that nobody keeps it (Rom. 3:19,22f.). So far then from being an agent of life, the Law becomes an agent of death (Rom. 7:9–10). It is not, of course, the Law that 'kills'. If there were no such thing as sin, the Law would not be a power of destruction. It would merely delimit the path of duty in which we were in any case walking. But because sin has taken hold of us, the Law finds itself in a paradoxical situation. God-given though it is, it exposes sin (Rom. 7:7,13), it inflames sin and brings it out of seclusion into open disobedience (Rom. 7:7–8). Paul knew from bitter experience that an explicit 'Thou shalt not' produces the reaction 'I most certainly will'.[30]

What a curious paradox this is, Lord! Be with me as I explore it. I can't help but think of other expressions of your love which have somehow become misunderstood or misapplied, ever since the original fall. I think of creation, for example, which humankind has abused and neglected, but which originally spoke so magnificently of your power. It still does, of course, but is all-too-often sullied. Likewise, humanity itself, made in your image but marred and spoilt by disobedience. Forgive us, Heavenly Father, for all our misunderstandings and the way we have mismanaged so much. Restore our proper perspective, so that we might see as you see.

19 September

Did God reject his people? By no means!
(Romans 11:1)

What of the Jewish world? Would they have understood the apostolic proclamation of a personal atoning sacrifice? . . . The whole New Testament *kerygma* is rooted in the Old Testament revelation, which lay at the heart of Judaism. The sacrificial system, the Passover lamb, the expiation of sin, the sprinkling of blood, the creation of covenants, the sin offering, all this and more is taken up from the Old Testament and applied to the atonement achieved by Christ. It is seen as the shadow of the real thing, the trailer for God's main film. So from one point of view, the Jew was ideally prepared for what was to come to him in the proclamation of Jesus.[31]

It does seem strange, Lord, how so many clues and pointers don't seem to have been picked up by those who are fluent in Old Testament knowledge. Nevertheless, I return to prayer for those who deny the Lord Jesus as Messiah; particularly, today, Jews who deny the connection of so many prophetic notes and his Messianic reality. Bless those for whom I pray, that the eyes of their hearts might be opened. In your mercy, grant revelation.

Let us also pray for the Jews: That our God and Lord may illuminate their hearts, that they acknowledge Jesus Christ is the Saviour of all men . . . Almighty and eternal God, who wants that all men be saved and come to the recognition of the truth, propitiously grant that even as the fullness of the peoples enters Thy Church, all Israel be saved. Through Christ Our Lord. Amen.[32]

20 September

By building yourselves up in your most holy faith and praying in the Holy Spirit, keep yourselves in God's love.
(Jude 20–21)

I came across a striking example of [prayer in the Holy Spirit] recently in the story of John Hyde – nicknamed 'Praying Hyde', a missionary to India . . . A man once asked him to pray for him. 'He came to my room, turned the key in the door, dropped on his knees, waited five minutes without a single syllable coming from his lips. I could hear my own heart thumping and beating. I felt the hot tears running down my face. I knew I was with God. Then with upturned face, down which the tears were streaming, he said "O God". Then, for five minutes at least, he was still again, and then, when he knew he was talking with God, his arm went around my shoulder and there came up from the depth of his heart such petitions for men as I had never heard before. I rose from my knees to know what real prayer was.' Prayer in the Spirit need not, I think, always have that emotional intensity. It does need to have that direct meeting with God.

This is where the Spirit's aid is so crucial in our prayers. For the Holy Spirit understands not only the mind of the Lord . . . but the mind of struggling Christians. He knows we find it hard to pray. He knows there are times when we feel so deeply and yet so confusedly that we cannot frame petitions, but simply come in silent pleading to the Lord. He knows that we are very often unsure what is the will of God, and therefore cannot pray with clarity and confidence about it. He knows the varied and perplexing circumstances in which we are placed. And he helps . . . He grasps the situation *for* us and *with* us. He frames the petitions in our lips; and he prays within us to the Father, with sighs too deep for words. As for the variety of circumstances to which we are exposed, the Spirit works with us in them all, and his aim is to promote our good.[33]

'He knows.' 'He grasps the situation.' 'For us.' 'With us.' 'He helps.' 'He prays within us to the Father.' 'The Spirit works with us.' This is God; my divine prayer-partner.

21 September

I will strengthen you and help you.
(Isaiah 41:10)

There is a fascinating passage in Hebrews 7:25, where the Lord Jesus is said to be able to 'save to the uttermost those who come to God by him, because he is always alive to make intercession for them'. The word for 'make intercession' is the same in Hebrews 7:25 as in Romans 8:26; except that in Romans it has a prefix which indicates intensity, or, perhaps, stresses that it can be done *for* us. But the basic thought is the same in both cases. It does not say that the Spirit or the Son beg the Father to give us what he otherwise might not. The usual word for 'ask' is not used; instead, we have this strange, rare word which literally means 'to be around'. Is that, perhaps, significant? What higher confidence could a Christian have than to reflect that in heaven the risen Christ in his ascended manhood 'is around' on our behalf? His presence at the Father's side is the silent guarantee that we are accepted. There is in the Godhead in heaven one who fully understands us and is there as our representative and our head. Equally, what an encouragement it is to know that there is, in struggling Christians on earth, one of the Godhead who 'is around' on our behalf; and that when we are agonising in prayer, we do not approach the Almighty on our own, in all our poverty. We have the Spirit as the divine representative in our hearts who enables us to pray acceptably.[34]

Thank you, Lord Jesus, that you ever live to intercede. Thank you that you do not despise my weakness. On the contrary, you are content to 'be around' in order to help me. Enabling God, thank you for your understanding.

22 September

I am the LORD, who heals you.
(Exodus 15:26)

In saving us, God has replaced the old spirit of *deilia*, 'cowardice and dread in the face of the unknown' (particularly death [2 Tim.] 1:7) by the Holy Spirit, who brings love, and power, and self-control. There was much dread, *Angst*, in the ancient world of the first century . . . There was a hankering for salvation from war, famine, death and disease, yes, and from personal failure as well. This is what gave the Mystery Cults such popularity. They offered some sort of assurance, however illusory, to those who were racked by *deilia*. It is interesting that the language in 1:9–10 has a distinctly Hellenistic flavour. In reminding Timothy of the glorious gospel of the *Saviour* Jesus, whose royal *advent* has seen the end of death's tyranny, and brought *life* and *immortality* to *light*, Paul perhaps unconsciously expresses himself in terms used by the pagan world to enunciate their hopes and fears.[35]

Lord, you do not merely observe our fears and our cowardice and our dread and our angst in order to soothe and pacify, but you offer to take them from us, to gently dissolve them within us, and to import better qualities altogether. You are a God who transforms; you can change the hearts of men, women, boys and girls. You bring not only comfort, but healing too. You replace. I pray for anyone I know whose angst is great, that you would perform such works of grace and power in their lives; the highly-strung, the anxious, the frightened. Come, Great Spirit, come.

23 September

Make every effort to live in peace with everyone and to be holy.
(Hebrews 12:14)

One of the notable ways in which the Spirit expressed himself in the Christian community was through creating unity. When in Ephesians 4:3–4 Paul is sketching some of the things all Christians have in common, he has this to say: 'Endeavour to keep the unity of the Spirit in the bond of peace. There is one body, and one Spirit, as you are called in one hope of your calling; one Lord, one faith, one baptism, one God and Father of all, who is above all, and through all, and in all. But grace was given to each of us according to the measure of Christ's gift.' He then goes on to outline some of the gifts of the ascended Christ. 'His gifts were that some should be apostles, some prophets, some evangelists, some pastors and teachers.' Whilst therefore making full allowance for the diversity of gifts God has given to his Church in the varying capacities he has accorded to different members, Paul insists that the Spirit creates unity, and that it is the job of the Christians to keep that unity and not spoil it. Paradoxically, like so much in the Christian life, unity is a gift from God, and yet we have to work at it.[36]

Easier said than done at times, Lord, even in the best of churches! However, rather than regard this is as some sort of corporate manner, perhaps I should take it personally. To that end, show me, I pray, any ways in which I can put this into practice. Show me especially if I need to make amends with anyone, and then grant me the grace to do so. I want to play my part in fostering unity, so I bring my life before you afresh today. Likewise, I pray once again for my own fellowship.

How good and pleasant it is when God's people live together in unity! It is like precious oil poured on the head, running down on the beard, running down on Aaron's beard, down on the collar of his robe. It is as if the dew of Hermon were falling on Mount Zion. For there the LORD bestows his blessing, even life for evermore.
(Psalm 133)

The first Christians were aware that the Spirit of the Messiah had come to indwell them. Hardly surprising, then, that with this Spirit of their Master making them into sons of God, they should be conscious of the closest ties with other members of the family. In this family, seen as one Body indwelt by one Spirit, there was no place for distinctions of wealth or station, sex or nationality; no room for pride in education or religious privilege (Col. 3:11; Jas. 2:1ff). After all, not one of them had anything to boast about. All had been rescued by their Lord when they could never have earned their salvation. As for their differing gifts, well, they were God's gifts to them, and no reason for pride. 'Who makes you different from anybody else? And what have you that you did not receive? If, then, you received it, why do you boast, as if it were not a gift?' (1 Cor. 4:7). This concern to preserve the unity the Spirit had created, accounts for so much in the life and teaching of the early Church. It accounts for the determination of the Jerusalem leaders that there must be no independent Samaritan church growing up without the age-old split from Judaism being healed (Acts 8). It accounts for the decision of the Council of Jerusalem that the issue of circumcision must not be allowed to split the Church (Acts 15). It accounts for the constant visits of the apostle to the Gentiles back to the Jerusalem church (Acts 18:21; 20:16; 25:1 etc.), and his organisation of a great collection for their benefit, little though he could have approved of their theology (Rom. 15:26; 1 Cor. 16:1; 2 Cor. 8:1ff). It accounts for Paul's repeated call to the Christians at Philippi to pull together and stand together (Phil. 1:27; 2:1ff; 4:1–3).[37]

I pray for the church at large, Lord – your church across the world. There are several lines of denominational disagreement, cultural points of view whereby we don't see eye to eye, and so on. In every discussion, grant us grace and charity towards one another, lest our witness be hindered.

25 September

He makes nations great.
(Job 12:23)

The ancient world was hungry for salvation, exhausted by a century of civil war which had devastated the known world before the emergence of Augustus to undisputed pre-eminence in 28 BC. Grateful subjects called him . . . 'saviour of the world', and hailed his principate as the start of 'the eternal age' . . . There was a lot of truth in all this: the roads and seas were safe, the pirates and brigands quelled, the frontiers of empire secured, and much more. And yet the hunger of the human heart remained unmet. Men and women were oppressed by guilt, by powerlessness, and by total uncertainty about the world to come. The gospel of the crucified and risen Jesus met those needs.

Because Jesus made full atonement for all the sins of the world upon the cross, men were offered, if only they would be humble enough to accept it, complete forgiveness from all their sins and guilt. Another had dealt with them.[38]

In one sense, Lord, maybe it would be a good thing, were the world 'hungry for salvation' once again. Not as a consequence of war, and not in terms of devastation, but so that 'the hunger of the human heart' turns people to faith and salvation. More to the point, only you, Lord Jesus, can meet the deepest holistic needs of humanity. However you choose to do it, Lord, I pray for an international move of your Spirit 'because Jesus made full atonement for all the sins of the world'. Have mercy.

26 September

**We proclaim to you what we have seen and heard,
so that you also may have fellowship with us.
(1 John 1:3)**

The Spirit is constitutive of Christian fellowship. On two occasions we actually read of 'the fellowship of the Holy Spirit', once in the grace of 2 Corinthians 13:13 and once as the ground for Paul's plea that the Philippians should stand united (Phil. 2:1). The phrase may mean 'the fellowship which the Holy Spirit gives' or 'joint participation in the Holy Spirit' which all Christians enjoy. Actually, these two are not far apart, for the Holy Spirit gives a share of *himself* to all believers, so all alike are partakers of the Spirit. The quality of this fellowship is best gauged by the early chapters of Acts. The new converts, having responded to the offer made by Peter of forgiveness and the Spirit, were baptised, and 'devoted themselves to the apostles' teaching and fellowship, the breaking of bread and prayers' (2:42).

Their fellowship was no mere glow of warm feeling. It involved communalism of living, financial sacrifice and sharing, the care of those in need, and making time just to be together (2:44f). You would find them revelling in each other's company, sharing their possessions, praising God in the temple, regular at the meetings for prayer, vigilant to see that widows and other defenceless folk did not get overlooked in the share-out of money and food. In 4:32 we find the same picture. 'Now the company of those who believed were of one heart and soul, and no one said that any of the things which he possessed was his own, but they had everything in common . . . There was not a needy person among them, for as many as were possessors of lands or houses sold them and brought the proceeds of what was sold and laid it at the apostles' feet; and distribution was made to each as any had need.'[39]

Take us beyond tea and biscuits and chit-chat, Lord. Anyone can have that. What we need is a fellowship that edifies, challenges, and strengthens, whereby we meet with one accord. I pray for my own church, that you will take us deeper in these ways.

27 September

**I pray that out of his glorious riches he may strengthen you with
power through his Spirit in your inner being,
so that Christ may dwell in your hearts through faith.
(Ephesians 3:16–17)**

Faith is the hand, the empty hand, by which we receive the divine gift of justification, redemption and reconciliation. It is not the ground on which God accepts us; for then it would become a meritorious 'work', something of which we could boast before God. That is very far from being Paul's view of the situation. He is careful to say that we are accepted 'by faith' (*pistei*), 'arising out of faith' (*ek pisteōs*), 'through faith' as through a door (*dia pisteōs*), but never 'because of faith' (*dia pistin*). Faith is man's personal response to God's personal initiative. It is the total response of man to the total self-giving of God – 'thus by grace you have been saved, through faith' (Eph. 2:8). Faith is opposed to the principle of works, of earning the favour of God (Gal. 2:16); it is wholehearted reliance on what Christ has done. Or, if we prefer to think of it in this way, faith is counting on the promises of God, as Abraham did (Gal. 3:6–7; Rom. 4:3–5). Faith is born when men hear these gracious promises, this glorious gospel of God (Rom. 10:8–9,17). This is why the Scriptures (2 Tim. 3:15), that is why the preaching of the gospel, or of the cross, is described as a means of salvation (Rom. 1:16; 1 Cor. 1:18). For it is the proclamation of what God has done to save man which demands his response. That response is faith, and that faith is seen in Paul both as an initial act (Rom. 10:9) and as a constant attitude (Gal. 2:20). Trust is at the beginning and at the end of the Christian way; 'we walk by faith not sight' (2 Cor. 5:7) and faith will never be superseded until we meet him whom now we trust (1 Cor. 13:8–13). Such faith in the Lord means obedience to him . . . (cf. 'the obedience of faith', Rom. 1:5), and issues in love (Gal. 5:6) and good works (Eph. 2:10).[40]

**Help me to get this right, Lord, in case I've misunderstood any of these
points. Settle the sequence of matters in my heart. I pray for anyone
who is trying desperately hard to earn your goodwill and love and,
likewise, trying to strive their way into heaven with good works. Help
them, too, I pray, to understand faith.**

28 September

The kingdom of God is not a matter of talk but of power.
(1 Corinthians 4:20)

The old life was bedevilled with powerlessness, the inability to do right. That is the whole burden of Romans 7, and the poignant cry rings out in 7:24, 'Who shall deliver me from the body of this death?' He means, of course, the *massa perditionis* – the whole weight of sin, frustration and death which belongs to him as to every other son of Adam. Thank God there *is* deliverance – 'through Jesus Christ our Lord'. For 'the gospel is the *power* of God unto salvation to everyone that believeth' (Rom. 1:16).[41]

Great Deliverer, I pray for those who would be free from their burden of sin, that they might come to know the power in the blood. I think of those troubled by besetting sins, and I ask you to set them free. I think of those whose lives are troubled by enslaving substances, and I ask you to impart liberty. I pray for those who feel powerless in one way or another, and I ask you to touch their lives with powerful grace. May they find healing in Calvary's tide.

29 September

Life does not consist in an abundance of possessions.
(Luke 12:15)

It is one of the ironies of history that a movement which professes to follow a penniless carpenter-rabbi and his needy bunch of disciples; a movement which cherishes among its foundation documents an image of communal living . . . should have become so opposed to communism and so closely associated with capitalism's deification of personal possessions! Of course, Christianity can have no truck with communism's atheism and indifference to truth and the value of persons; but their communalism of possessions is very much more Christian than our glorification of wealth and our obsession with individualism. No doubt the primitive attempt at communal living at Jerusalem was a failure, but what a glorious failure! Until there is a real sharing of money and possessions, an equitable distribution of resources and living conditions in so far as the Christian Church can achieve it, unbelievers are unlikely to remark on the quality of our fellowship. Real *koinōnia*[42] in the Holy Spirit means that we cannot stand apart from those with whom we have this fellowship, no matter what it costs. I am told that some years ago President Nyerere of Tanzania sent out a copy of those verses in Acts on communal living to all the clergy, with the brief appended comment: 'That is the policy of the President.' There is a man who from Christian principle is attempting to apply communalism of possessions to a developing African state. He is an example to Western, capitalist Christendom.[43]

Speak to me, Lord, about the conversion of my wallet, my bank account and my fundamental attitude to material possessions. Tutor me in your ways regarding these issues. In the meantime, I pray your blessing on charities and churches whose ministry reaches out to the poor and less privileged. If that is a strong element of their mission, then they will need an extra measure of blessing in a world that increasingly marginalizes those whom they seek to help.

30 September

Above all, love each other deeply.
(1 Peter 4:8)

The Jerusalem experiment was a failure. The church went broke, and richly merited the name in which they gloried, the *ebionim*, God's poor. A few years passed. The Gentile mission sprang into being and produced a flourishing church at Antioch, hundreds of miles away. The church received a prophetic warning from a Jerusalem prophet Agabus, that there would be a widespread famine. So what did they do, these Gentile Christians of Antioch? They did not even wait till the famine happened; on the word of the Jerusalem prophet (whom they might well have thought was prejudiced!) they had a collection; each of the disciples contributed according to his means; and they sent it to Jerusalem by the hands of Saul and Barnabas (11:28ff).

This seems to me a most remarkable thing. They could well have said, 'Those Jerusalem folk are a long way away; what do we owe them, anyway? Let us make sure that our own churchmen are all right when famine comes, and not bother our heads about them.' They might have said, 'Those fools at Jerusalem will be taught a hard lesson in this famine. They will learn the hard way that when you realise your assets and share out your capital it does not last very long. They will learn some business sense for a change. And a good thing too.' They might have said, 'We don't see why we should do anything to help those most unsatisfactory Christians (if the name is not too good for them) at Jerusalem. Their theology is narrow; their ritualism is offensive; and they even attempt to mount a counter mission and force circumcision and food laws on our mixed church at Antioch.' They could have made these strictures, and with no small justification. But they did not allow theological differences, differences of churchmanship, differences in church organisation, and sheer distance to prevent them from making a most moving and eloquent expression of fellowship in the Spirit. It is hardly surprising that such a quality of life could find no parallel in antiquity, and drew many into the Christian fellowship.[44]

What a challenging example, Lord! This speaks of the Holy Spirit's influence. Give me such a heart, Lord; one that will give, in love, to those who might have brought about their own downfall, and even to those by whom I might feel threatened.

1 October

He gives strength to the weary and increases the power of the weak.
(Isaiah 40:29)

It was not only pardon, but power that was such an attractive feature of the early preaching of the empty cross. Here was the one who had broken the power of death. He was risen and alive, and very much to be reckoned with. The powers of the age to come were clearly being dispensed by the risen Christ to the disciples. The spiritual gifts of tongues and prophecy, of healing and exorcism were displayed in their assemblies. The grip of greed and lust, of sectarianism and materialism was broken among these people of Jesus. Their lives made their talk about the new age credible to many. If you had to put it in three words, they could be the ones thrown at Paul in Athens: he was always going on about *Iēsous kai anastasis*, 'Jesus and the Resurrection'. Although the preaching of the resurrection at Athens caused much mirth, a church was born there, and before long produced one of the great intellectuals of the second century AD, Athenagoras. He wrote two books. One of them, *Resurrection from the Dead*, is a stout defence of that resurrection faith which had brought a new power to Athens and to his life. Tatian, his contemporary, discovered the power of the risen Jesus breaking the grip of demonic forces in his life. He bursts out in praise to God who has snapped the power of 10,000 tyrants within him (*Orat.*, 29). The empty cross spelt moral power such as Jewish and Stoic ethics had never been able to inculcate.[1]

> **Help me to understand, Lord, how this applies to my daily life. I'm all for it, and it would be lovely to think my days might go some way towards making an impact upon any Tatians I encounter. I make this prayer for their sake, for mine, and for the sake of the kingdom.**

2 October

**Just as we have borne the image of the earthly man,
so shall we bear the image of the heavenly man.
(1 Corinthians 15:49)**

The empty cross meant that death was vanquished by Christ, and what was true for the master would be true for the servant too. The fear of death was as common in ancient society as in our own, and more readily admitted. At some palatial banquet a remembrancer would stand near the head of the table and say to him during the feast, *'Memento mori'*, 'remember, you must die!' Skull and cross-bones are common wall décor in Herculaneum and Pompeii, as is the phoenix, the mythical bird which was said by the poets to die and be reborn from its own ashes. That shows the prevalent hunger for life after death. One mid-first-century picture of the phoenix in Pompeii has this envious inscription, 'O phoenix, you lucky thing.' And Clement of Rome, writing in the nineties of the first century, after arguing the reasonableness of the resurrection from the fact that seeds die and come to life again in new flowers, makes the phoenix the climax of his argument. He really believed it existed! Naturally, in this he was a child of his age. Nevertheless it is not the phoenix he was interested in. It served merely as an emblem of the risen Christ. Jesus by his resurrection had brought life and immortality to life, and had solved the problem of life after death. Here was something far more tangible than could ever be offered in the Eleusinian Mysteries. Nobody but Jesus had died and risen again.[2]

So many emblems and symbols of your resurrection, Lord; pictures and images that serve as aides-mémoires of your rising from the dead. Thank you, Lord, for all such reminders; in the words of hymns, perhaps, or in church fittings I might see from time to time. Grant me a tender heart towards such visual metaphors, I pray, so that your sacrifice and victory might remain uppermost in my mind.

3 October

Our days may come to seventy years,
or eighty, if our strength endures;
yet the best of them are but trouble and sorrow,
for they quickly pass, and we fly away.
(Psalm 90:10)

Do you know that anonymous piece entitled 'One Solitary Life'? Here it is:

He was born in an obscure village, the child of a peasant woman.

He grew up in still another village, where he worked in a carpenter's shop till he was thirty. Then for three years he was an itinerant preacher.

He never wrote a book. He never held an office. He never had a family or owned a house. He didn't go to college. He never visited a big city. He never travelled two hundred miles from the place where he was born. He did none of the things one usually associates with greatness.

He had no credentials but himself.

He was only thirty-three when the tide of public opinion turned against him. His friends ran away. He was turned over to his enemies and went through the mockery of a trial. He was nailed to a cross between two thieves. While he was dying, his executioners gambled for his clothing, the only property he had on earth. When he was dead he was laid in a borrowed grave through the pity of a friend.

Nineteen centuries have come and gone, and today he is the central figure of the human race and the leader of mankind's progress. All the armies that ever marched, all the navies that ever sailed, all the parliaments that ever sat, all the kings that ever reigned, put together, have not affected the life of man on earth as much as that one solitary life.[3]

Only one life, 'twill soon be past,
Only what's done for Christ will last.
And when I am dying, how happy I'll be,
If the lamp of my life has been burned out for Thee.[4]

I have but one life to live, Lord; oh, may I live for you.

4 October

Seek the peace and prosperity of the city.
(Jeremiah 29:7)

If Jesus was just a good man, I wonder what it was that made his life so different? David Essex called him 'a kind of Che Guevara figure that wasn't political'. Che is a marvellous parallel . . . and contrast. Son of a rich family, himself a highly educated banker and doctor, he gave himself to the cause of the underprivileged in Bolivia. Like Jesus before him, 'though he was rich, yet for your sakes he became poor . . .' Like Jesus, he led a movement of radical opposition to the corrupt existing regime. Like Jesus, he was betrayed and killed. Like Jesus, he evoked the admiration and dedication of a worldwide band of followers. But there the similarity ends. Unlike Che, Jesus did not preach or practise hatred and violence against his foes: rather, love. Unlike Che, he did not take up arms. Unlike Che, he was not tricked to his death, but went to it in the dignity of a voluntary choice. Unlike Che, he does not remain dead and gone, with nothing but his memory and ideals to cheer his followers. For Jesus lives . . . and it is highly significant that in the last couple of years or so there has broken out a Christian revival in Bolivia, in which over 60,000 people have turned from the shadow to the reality, from Che Guevera to Christ.[5]

Lord, I pray for Christians who are seeking to make their mark in the political and social arena. Bless them and help them, I pray, as they try to implement Christian principles and standards for the common good. Be with them as they speak truth to power, and minister to them if and when theirs is an unpopular stance. Grant them all requisite courage and wisdom.

Now to him who is able to do immeasurably more than all we ask or imagine, according to his power that is at work within us, to him be glory in the church and in Christ Jesus throughout all generations, for ever and ever! (Ephesians 3:20–21)

I must become, what, in Christ, I already am. That means I must carry about in my body the dying of the Lord Jesus, in order that his risen life may be manifested in my mortal body (2 Cor. 4:10). I must be made conformable to his death, if I am to know the power of his resurrection (Phil. 3:10). This is the secret of victorious living which made the cross and resurrection a daily source of power to the apostle [Paul]. This enabled him to progress in Christ's triumphal procession, not, like Roman captives in an imperial triumph, a sullen prisoner of war; the paradox of Christianity was just this. Once he had allowed himself to be utterly conquered by Christ, he *shared in* Christ's triumph (2 Cor. 2:14). He found unleashed within his life the very power of God which raised Christ from the dead. This was good news indeed, and he prayed that the Holy Spirit would make known to his Asian friends 'the surpassing greatness of his power towards us believers, according to the working of the power of his might which he wrought in Christ when he raised him from the dead . . .' (Eph. 1:19). Paul piles word upon word to depict the mighty power of the resurrection which can raise the Christian, who was dead in sin, to a new quality of life altogether. This is what salvation as a present reality meant to him.[6]

Unleashing God, I pray for my Christian brothers and sisters, I pray for your church universal, and I pray for myself, that this 'paradox of Christianity' might become (present tense) an increasingly lived reality amongst us all. Grant your church this 'daily source of power' so that our witness might be edged with glory.

Do your best to present yourself to God as one approved, a worker who does not need to be ashamed and who correctly handles the word of truth. (2 Timothy 2:15)

Theologians are among God's important gifts to his church. They are charged with the responsibility of examining the Christian revelation in depth, and relating it to the contemporary need and thought forms of the society in which they serve. Theirs is the privilege of being paid to spend their time working on the content of the faith, wrestling with its problems, relating it to secular thought and other world views. Theirs is the responsibility of feeding the church with their studies in such a way that leaders on the ground, the clergy and teachers, can be helped to a more balanced, well-considered and relevant presentation of the gospel to which both theologian and preacher are committed. The theologian is not in bondage to the church, as if he might never be allowed fresh opinions and discoveries; nor is he independent of the church, as if what he has to say has no relation to its life and faith. He is part of the church, and he is called to love within its fellowship and witness. He has a position of great trust, responsibility and privilege.

But he also occupies a most difficult and dangerous position. Pressures come on him from all sides. Often the churchman regards him as a threat, and his academic colleagues as a sort of appendix, left over from some previous age of man. Gone is the day when theology was seen as the queen of the sciences, concerned as it was with God, the ultimate source of both man and matter. She has become the Cinderella instead, and is often only acceptable at the ball of university disciplines if she dresses up as a student of ancient Near Eastern literature or of the phenomenology of religion. In many a university today the theologian is a very lonely person: his colleagues think of him as a quaint oddity who retains belief in God, and the Christian often regards him as a sceptic – or a quisling.[7]

Lord of the church, I give thanks for those whose intellects are devoted to your service. I think of St Paul and his brilliant insights, and all his successors, many of whom receive little credit. Bless those who might be discouraged, Lord, or 'very lonely'. May they know that their labours are not in vain. May we never take their work for granted.

Come, let us bow down in worship,
let us kneel before the LORD, our Maker.
(Psalm 95:6)

The earliest disciples were led by the Spirit not only to a sharing of possessions but to a tremendous depth of worship. They 'broke bread from house to house' or 'at home': this seems to indicate house communion services. They ate their meals with generosity of disposition and exultation (a word which Luke uses to characterise the joy of the messianic community as it delights in what Christ has done for them, and what they are now experiencing of his goodness, and what will await them at his return). They were notable for their praise of God even when threatened or in prison ([Acts] 4:24ff; 16:25). Indeed, praise is one of the special results of the Spirit coming on them (Acts 2:47; 3:8–9). They were to be found in the formal worship of the temple as well as the warm informality of the home meetings. They were regular in synagogue worship; sometimes in a great Jewish centre like Antioch in Pisidia (13:14ff): sometimes in a place like Philippi, which had too few Jews to form a synagogue. The tiny congregation went down to a prayer place by the river, and Paul and his company joined them to such good effect that they led Lydia to faith (16:14).[8]

This is a beautiful word-picture, Lord: your people gathering for worship, whether that be in large groups or congregations or as a handful of worshippers meeting at 'a prayer place by the river'. I pray for churches far and wide, Lord; those who number hundreds or thousands within their membership and those who, as it were, have 'too few Jews to form a synagogue'. In your mercy, meet with those whose sincere intention is to exalt your name. Graciously receive our worship, whether we meet as six hundred, sixteen, or six. Come, inhabit our praises. Be especially close to those whose circumstances mean that they are unable to worship freely, in public spaces, and whose gatherings need to be in secret.

8 October

**A bruised reed he will not break,
and a smouldering wick he will not snuff out.
(Isaiah 42:3)**

In [Christ], the Christian is invulnerable. The demonic powers cannot touch him (Rom. 8:38f.) – they were disarmed by Christ's victory on the cross, when he 'stripped off the cosmic powers like a garment; he made a public spectacle of them, and led them as captives in his triumphal procession' (Col. 2:15).[9] Danger and opposition cannot thwart him; even a rigorous imprisonment can turn out to be the furthering of his salvation (Phil. 1:19). For God will not scrap what is precious to him; he will not discard what he has saved. He who has begun a good work in the Christian will continue it until the day of the Lord Jesus (Phil. 1:6).[10]

God of love, I pray for this truth to settle in the hearts of those who are feeling vulnerable today. I pray, too, for those who are imprisoned on account of their faith; may they be reminded of this, in a way that will strengthen them. Draw alongside the bruised, and rekindle the spiritual energy of those whose confidence is smouldering.

He saved us through the washing of rebirth and renewal by the Holy Spirit.
(Titus 3:5)

When we heard the gospel of our salvation and believed, we were sealed with that Holy Spirit who had been promised long ago (Eph. 1:13). 'Seal' is a property word. It speaks of ownership. He is given to us in order to possess us, and mark us out as God's people by transformed lives. He is given, moreover, here and now as an 'earnest' or 'first instalment' of our future inheritance, until the day when God comes to collect his purchased possessions (Eph. 1:14). Paul changes here to a commercial metaphor, one that should be very readily intelligible in these days of 'down payments'. The Holy Spirit is that part of the age to come which is already present, the foretaste and the guarantee of heaven. The transforming, sanctifying work of the Spirit in the Christian is the consequence of his calling by God, and the prerequisite of his final salvation. We must, as those who have been saved and will be saved, evidence the fact by working out in our lives that salvation which God by his Spirit is working in us (Phil. 2:12–13). The Bible nowhere encourages us to think that any man can have tasted the past deliverance of God who does not manifest in his life any of the signs of the Spirit's work and power. If he cannot show a blameless, shining life as a son of God in a dark world, if he is never holding forth the word of life to those who perish for lack of it, then Paul fears his labour has been bestowed in vain upon such a man (Phil. 2:13–16).[11]

Lord, you do not just call us to holy living and then leave us floundering. You are not unreasonable. As you call, so you equip. Day-by-day, I need your 'washing of rebirth and renewal', sufficient for each day's demands. Teach me the truth of that lesson: the more you own of me, the more I possess of you.

Teach me thus thy steps to trace,
Strong to follow in thy grace;
Learning how to love from thee,
Loving him who first loved me.[12]

10 October

These are the words of the Amen, the faithful and true witness,
the ruler of God's creation. I know your deeds, that you are neither
cold nor hot. I wish you were either one or the other!
(Revelation 3:14–15)

The modern theologian is not exempt from the pressures of ordinary modern society. There is a great tendency towards universalism in a world that makes God in its own tolerant image. There is a tendency towards syncretism in a world that has shrunk to a global multi-faith village. There is a tendency towards secularism: with both the historic faith and the future hope soft-pedalled in so much modern theology, Christianity is frequently presented in terms of love alone. And finally, there is an ever growing tendency towards indifferentism. Alongside a shrinking world, a shrinking hold on biblical revelation, a growing ecumenism, goes a declining interest in doctrine. It derives . . . from the philosophical question of the absolute and contradiction. Truth is relative. The black I see and the white you see are no longer contradictory: they are complementary. Heaven and hell are all one, for truth is no longer objective. Doctrine is arrived at, both in politics and religion, largely by head counts: norms have degenerated into what most people of good sense and good will approve.[13]

This makes for sad reading, Lord. It speaks of a worrying decline that won't help a hurting world one bit. When truth is on the scaffold, assist your church to take a bold(er) stand for truth, and not to shy away from controversy and unpopularity. Save us, your people, from the tyranny of popularity. Bless church leaders as they grapple with issues like these. Grant clarity of thought, strength of conviction and durability of purpose.

11 October

One generation commends your works to another.
(Psalm 145:4)

[The theologian] must seek simplicity. This is rarely to be found among theologians. They are as difficult to understand as any other technical expert who has not taken the trouble to translate his jargon for the benefit of those who are laymen in his discipline. When one considers that the greatest theologian of all, Jesus himself, clothed his unfathomable truth in the simplest and most memorable of language, often stories, and when one considers that Paul and Peter and John wrote to a constituency which had no biblical encyclopaedias or dictionaries and consisted largely of ill-schooled members of the ancient world, it is tragic that so much theological writing these days is practically incomprehensible to the lay ear. If the theologian is to serve the church he must learn to put profound thought into language which is not only easily understood but is graphic and memorable in this television age when competition runs high.[14]

This is no small challenge, Lord, so I hold in prayer those theologians who need and deserve my support and goodwill. I pray for them, Heavenly Father, asking that you would continually inspire their efforts. Help them as they endeavour to present ancient truths in a modern context. The church relies upon good theologians to get things right. It therefore behoves me to pray for them. I do so, here and now.

12 October

Be strong and courageous. Do not be afraid or terrified because of them, for the LORD your God goes with you.
(Deuteronomy 31:6)

Nobody ever taught [as Jesus did]. This was the conclusion of the soldiers sent to arrest him. St John tells us that when the Pharisees asked them why they had not obeyed orders, they replied 'No man ever spoke like this man' (John 7:46). He taught them, says the earliest evangelist, as one who had authority, and not like the teachers of the day. These men would prop up their opinions by endless references to teachers before them who had held the same view – rather like the acres of footnotes in modern scholarly books about God. Jesus prefaced his teaching with the remarkable formula, unknown in all literature, 'Truly, truly I say to you.' Who was this 'I' who spoke so much about the Kingdom of God, and calmly announced that he was bringing it in? 'Until John, it was the law and the prophets', he once said. 'Since then, it is the good news of the Kingdom of God.' In other words, his forerunner, John the Baptist, marked the end of the old era: he inaugurated the new.[15]

Lord Jesus, it must have taken great courage for you to come out with statements like that. You must have known how incendiary they would seem, yet you nailed your colours to the mast in no uncertain terms. Thank you, Lord, for this specific aspect of your coming to earth. It took bravery to confront all the forces marshalled against you, but you were undeterred. I worship you because of this. Grant me similar mettle in the fray, when it is my turn to speak up.

13 October

The God of all grace, who called you to his eternal glory in Christ, after you have suffered a little while, will himself restore you and make you strong, firm and steadfast.
(1 Peter 5:10)

At some time or other in life, everybody has to suffer. It is universal. Physical suffering, mental suffering, spiritual suffering affect every household, and embrace every nation and colour and creed. The problem of suffering is the greatest stumbling block for many to believing in a good and loving God. What has Christianity to say to this most pressing cry of the human heart in anguish, 'Why should this happen to me?'

God has given us the cross of Christ *non ut dicamus sed ne sileamus*.[16] It is not the final and complete explication of the problem of pain, but it does shed a blazing patch of light upon it. A chapter like Matthew 27, depicting Jesus on his cross, enables us to see . . . positive factors even in the midst of outrageous suffering and injustice. This chapter displays Jesus supremely as the sufferer . . . The St Matthew Passion indeed! . . .

Never does the obscenity of innocent suffering affront us so sharply as in the crucifixion of Jesus of Nazareth. We see suffering these days as an unmitigated evil without redeeming quality. We go to great lengths to avoid it for ourselves and others. But Jesus dared to call the sufferers blessed (Matt. 5:11).[17]

Lord God, suffering is a deeply problematic mystery. I understand that the suffering of Christ was for the good of my soul. I wholeheartedly thank you for such a Saviour. Yet, I continue to grapple with suffering that appears to bear no such fruit; wars and conflicts saturated in bloodshed, people enduring years of pain or torment, children who suffer abuse. I know the cross speaks volumes about your identification with anguish; yet, I remain somewhat at a loss to comprehend suffering's riddle. God of all grace, bear with me, I pray, as I continue to wrestle with this.

14 October

I long to see you so that I may impart to you some spiritual gift to make you strong – that is, that you and I may be mutually encouraged.
(Romans 1:11–12)

The cross of Christ is a many-splendoured thing. Like a diamond, it has many shining facets. And the preacher is charged with the responsibility of holding those facets up to the gaze of the congregation he serves. He is failing in his responsibility if he always speaks about the same aspect of the cross. It is the wisdom of God and the power of God, and he needs to dig deep into its mystery. This is all the more necessary because of the great spread of moods and needs in mankind. In any one church there will be represented a whole host of needs, of prejudices, of approaches, and of personality types. No preacher can reach them all at any one time with any one presentation of the empty cross. But he ought, in the course of a balanced ministry, to expose them to a variety of interpretations of the empty cross of Christ, for it is indeed the broad-spectrum antidote to the maladies of the human spirit.[18]

> God's love is sufficient for me! Lord, preserve me from any statements like that one if they are ever trite or ill-advised. I do believe, though – I am encouraged to believe – that 'the maladies of the human spirit' find their remedy at Calvary. To that end, I pray for preachers everywhere who are doing their best to present at least some of the 'many shining facets' of the cross. Theirs is an unenviable task, and I owe them my prayers. I pray for those who preach within my own church fellowship. May your blessing and guidance rest upon them as a source of encouragement.

Since we are receiving a kingdom that cannot be shaken, let us be thankful, and so worship God acceptably with reverence and awe.
(Hebrews 12:28)

True worship is in the Spirit, as Jesus made clear to the Samaritan woman ([John] 4:24). This passage is often misunderstood; as if it means that locality does not matter in worship, and that our human spirits have an affinity with God's Spirit. But this, as G.S. Hendy has pointed out in *The Holy Spirit in Christian Theology* (p. 32), is the precise opposite of the truth. 'Spirit' for John, as for Paul, is the opposite of 'flesh', and 'flesh' stands for all our fallen humanness. To say that God is Spirit, and that the only way to worship him is in Spirit and in truth, is first and foremost to slam the door in the face of our approach to God in our own strength or goodness. How can 'flesh' approach God who is 'Spirit', how can sinners approach the Holy One? They cannot. But the good news is that God has opened up a way. God has made himself accessible in the Word made flesh, and he is now to be worshipped in the place where he has revealed himself, i.e. Jesus Christ, who proclaimed to the woman, 'I who speak to you am he.' Hendry concludes, 'God actively seeks men to worship him in spirit and in truth, by making himself accessible to them in his Son, who is truth incarnate, and by the mission of the Spirit, who is the Spirit of truth. The worship of God in spirit and truth is, therefore, Trinitarian worship; it is to worship God through Jesus Christ, in the Holy Spirit.'[19]

I marvel, Lord Jesus, at the fact that a conversation you had with a Samaritan woman some 2,000 years ago, beside a relatively obscure watering hole, is relevant for me today, and for your church. Yet, such are your words, and they span generations without losing any of their impact or relevance. Help me to be like that woman, who listened to you with reverence, that I too may learn more about worship.

16 October

The student is not above the teacher, but everyone who is fully trained will be like their teacher.
(Luke 6:40)

God intends those who are already the objects of his saving power to be helped along the way of salvation by the life and words of Christian brethren. Thus Timothy, by taking heed to himself (in meditation, dedication and stirring up the gift within him) and to the doctrine (teaching, exhortation and public reading of the Scriptures) will further his own salvation and that of his presumably Christian hearers (1 Tim. 4:14–16). When God saves a man like Paul, it is in order to make him a pattern to those who should hereafter believe (1 Tim. 1:15–16). By this it is clear that he means an example not only to the outsider but to the fellow Christian (Phil. 4:9; 1 Thess. 2:10). All Christians have this responsibility to their fellows, a responsibility which the Thessalonians discharged so well (1 Thess. 1:7).[20]

This is a dual responsibility, Lord – and one for which I often feel ill-equipped. I accept the challenge, but I immediately call upon your grace so that I may attempt to fulfil it in your strength. I do at least place myself at your disposal, time and talents presenting, and hope that you will take it from there. Teach me, I pray.

17 October

The Spirit of the LORD spoke through me;
his word was on my tongue.
(2 Samuel 23:2)

Closely associated with the Spirit's presence in worship is his inspiration of the Scriptures . . . The prophets of old claimed to have been sent and inspired by the Spirit of the Lord. Jesus himself set his seal on the Spirit's inspiration of Psalm 110, for instance, 'For David himself said by the Holy Spirit' (Mark 12:36). We find the same attribution of the Old Testament to the inspiration of the Holy Spirit in Acts 1:16; 4:25 etc., and it is entirely in keeping not only with Christian but with Jewish orthodoxy when we find the blanket claim in 2 Timothy 3:16 that 'All Scripture is inspired by God'.

We never get any nearer to an explanation of the divine inspiration of the human writers than in 2 Peter 1:20f where the author tells us that prophecy came from God, not from the prophet's own ideas. It came as the human writers were moved or carried along by the Holy Spirit. This is a fascinating maritime metaphor in the original Greek, suggesting the way a ship is carried along by the wind. The prophets raised their sails, so to speak (they were obedient and receptive) and the Holy Spirit filled them and carried their craft along in the direction he wished. The writers were not robots but men; men of their time, men of varied backgrounds and intellects, prejudices and outlooks. But those men were yielded to the leading of the Holy Spirit in such a way that he could speak through them.[21]

This is a lovely illustration, Lord, and it says so much. It speaks of surrender, yielding and infilling. It speaks of co-operation and partnership. What a privilege that is! Help me today to raise my sails and to catch your breeze, according to your will.

18 October

**We know that suffering produces perseverance;
perseverance, character; and character, hope.
(Romans 5:3–4)**

Not only a Christian's example, but his prayers (2 Thess. 3:1–2; Phil. 1:19) can further the salvation of his brethren in Christ. So, too, can his suffering, if patiently borne. Paul sees his 'afflictions' in this light as contributing to the salvation of his friends to whom he writes (2 Cor. 1:6). Presumably the encouragement of his example would deepen their dependence on their Saviour. Similarly, in 2 Tim. 2:10, Paul sees his sufferings as contributing to the salvation of others. It is possible that by 'the elect' in this verse, Paul means those whom God has chosen but have not yet responded to his call; it is more probable, however, that he sees his sufferings as encouraging other Christians to follow suit, and as demonstrating the sustaining power of the Lord to keep him.[22]

Thank you for these insights, Lord. They shed a helpful little light on suffering and a Christian perspective. Lord, if I am called to suffer, then I pray for courage so that my example, even then, might speak of your 'sustaining power'. Teach me to mine those deep treasures. For all I know, that could make all the difference to someone who notices faith at work. I pray, too, for those known to me personally who are suffering today, in one way or another. Be alongside them by your Spirit, to meet their needs. Thank you, Lord. Help me not to turn back when crosses come.

19 October

Guide me in your truth and teach me.
(Psalm 25:5)

The same Holy Spirit who was active in the prophets was active in the apostles. There was, therefore, no anachronism when 2 Peter 3:16 sets Paul's letters alongside the other Scriptures. They had to wait another three hundred years for the formal promulgation of the books of the New Testament in precisely the form we have them today, but from the days of the apostles themselves it was quite clear to the Christians that the Holy Spirit who inspired the prophetic writings was also standing behind the words of Jesus and his apostles. Paul could claim to have the very mind of Christ, to proclaim not the word of men but of God, and to teach not merely in broad outline but in detailed words imparted by the Spirit of the Lord (1 Cor. 2:16; 1 Thess. 2:13; 1 Cor. 2:13). Hence his abrupt challenge to any who thought themselves 'inspired' to recognise and abide by what he said (1 Cor. 14:38). Hence his expectation that the letters would be read in the Christian assembly at worship, alongside the inspired writings of the Old Testament (Col. 4:16).

It is, therefore, in the Scriptures of the Old and New Testaments, with Jesus as the centrepiece, that the Spirit is most readily to be encountered. That is why Bible reading both in church and for the individual, occupies so prominent a place in Christianity. There is no sniff of bibliolatry about it. It is simply the fact that the Spirit who inspired the Scriptures is to be met there. We read them in order to gain illumination from him and be transformed by him into greater likeness to our Lord. 2 Corinthians 3 is the classic chapter for the role of the Spirit as illuminator of the Scriptures. It is when men turn to the Lord the Spirit that the veil is taken away from the eyes of their understanding. One sees once again the aptness of Bishop John Taylor's name for the Spirit as the go-between God. He is the one who inspired the Scriptures in the first place. He is the one who interprets them to the humble, seeking reader.[23]

Thank you, Heavenly Father, for this lovely cohesion between Old and New Testaments: cohesion of thought and of intent, with a crimson thread linking everything together as a plan of salvation. Thank you, too, for the idea of Jesus as the 'centrepiece'.

20 October

My soul yearns for you in the night.
(Isaiah 26:9)

The crucifixion of Jesus shows that there can be a fellowship in suffering. God does not torment us and leave us on our own. He may not have given full explanation of pain, but he has come to share it. God is a suffering God. He does not stay immune from the anguish of his creatures. It breaks his heart. The cross of Christ means we can never say to God 'You don't care' or 'You don't understand'. He is in there with us. There is no suffering we can bear which he does not know from the inside. There is no injustice we can suffer which he does not comprehend from personal experience. And in times of greatest suffering it is not explanation we need so much as companionship. That God has provided for us in the sufferings of Jesus, and in his risen presence . . .

We see from Calvary that there is a value in suffering. It is not fruitless and in vain. For much of our suffering Hebrews 12:11 holds true: 'For the moment all suffering seems painful rather than pleasant; later it yields the peaceful fruit of righteousness to those who have been trained by it.' Certainly the cross of Jesus has been incalculably fruitful. He has seen the fruit of the travail of his soul, and been satisfied (Isa. 53:11). There is always value to be found somewhere in suffering, though it is usually only afterwards that this becomes apparent.[24]

Thank you, Lord. This too is helpful. As I continue to look to you for insights on this complex subject, I pray specifically for anyone I know who is struggling with physical pain; those whose nights are long, with painful hour after painful hour. May they find you as their night-time companion. I seek your blessing upon them. Likewise, medical professionals who do their best to alleviate discomfort and devise suitable courses of treatment. Help them, Lord.

Search me, God, and know my heart.
(Psalm 139:23)

To save others became Paul's master passion. It sent him all over the Middle East, wearing himself out in the service of the gospel. It was his deepest concern and most earnest prayer that all Israel should be saved (Rom. 10:1). A remnant had indeed been saved, as Isaiah had foretold (Rom. 9:27), but the majority of Israel had rejected their Saviour. Why? He concludes that God has allowed it, in order that the Gentiles might be grafted into the olive, and find salvation (11:11). Surely God will, in due time, provoke his old people by the sight of the Gentiles streaming into salvation (11:14). This is one result which Paul hopes his Gentile mission will have; when the 'fullness of the Gentiles has come in, then all Israel shall be saved' (11:25f.).[25] [26]

He is no fool who gives what he cannot keep to gain that which he cannot lose.[27]

How will I wear myself out, Lord? What is it that I can honestly call my 'master passion'? What is my 'deepest concern and most earnest prayer'?

22 October

As the rain and the snow come down from heaven, and do not return to it without watering the earth and making it bud and flourish, so that it yields seed for the sower and bread for the eater, so is my word that goes out from my mouth: It will not return to me empty, but will accomplish what I desire and achieve the purpose for which I sent it.
(Isaiah 55:10–11)

Throughout all his missionary work, Paul has this great concern to save the lost, just as his Master had. That is why he accommodates himself, so far as conscience allowed,[28] to the scruples of Jews when he was with Jews, and of Gentiles when he was with them – 'so that by all means I might save some' (1 Cor. 9:22; 10:33). The Christian partner in a mixed marriage has the same responsibility to seek to save his partner (1 Cor. 7:16). Not, of course, that the Christian can save anyone by himself. But by bearing testimony to the gospel of God's saving work, he can (Rom. 1:16). In the New Testament the work of saving is predicated of human agents just as readily as it was in the Old. It is the task of every Christian to pass on what he himself enjoys. For this is the will of God (1 Tim. 2:3), who is in design the Saviour of all men, but in practice the Saviour of those who believe.[29] 'And how shall they believe in him of whom they have not heard? And how shall they hear without a preacher?' (Rom. 10:14). God's answer to this problem is the principle of incarnation; he entrusts his message to redeemed men and women whom he trusts to pass it on. 'He manifests his word through the *kerygma*, which is committed to me,' says Paul (Tit. 1:3). That responsibility and privilege drives him on to preach even when men 'receive not the love of the truth that they may be saved' (2 Thess. 2:10), or when others 'forbid us to preach to the Gentiles that they may be saved' (1 Thess. 2:16). For in the *kerygma* lies the power of God to save men (Rom. 1:16). [30]

> **'Responsibility and privilege', indeed! Thankfully, Lord, this missionary work does not depend on me, except in terms of my availability and obedience. The Bible has still its ancient power, so I pray for your Holy Spirit's backing to my modest efforts. Yours is the saving power. I'll play my part if you show me how.**

23 October

Let us consider how we may spur one another on toward love and good deeds, not giving up meeting together, as some are in the habit of doing, but encouraging one another.
(Hebrews 10:24–25)

[Preaching] is by no means a one-man effort. The congregation can 'meet' the preacher by the way they respond, the way they support him in prayer, the way they assess what is said, and the way they worship. They create the atmosphere in which the Spirit of God has ease of communication, if I may put it that way. I well recall an evangelistic service in the North of England at which I preached. I *knew* that God was going to lead many people to Christ in that service by the time we had got halfway through, long before we reached the sermon: the sense of worship was so real, the love and dedication to Christ so obvious. It was moving to stand in the aisle for half an hour afterwards and meet a steady flow of individuals who had been brought to the service by friends, and those same friends had stayed with them to help them on in the early days of their Christian life after many of them that night committed their lives to Christ and asked his Spirit into their hearts.[31]

Points taken, Lord! Received with thanks.

24 October

He took bread, gave thanks and broke it, and gave it to them, saying, 'This is my body given for you; do this in remembrance of me.'
(Luke 22:19)

There is a lovely passage in 1 John 5:7–8 which seems to indicate that the Spirit uses the sacraments to assure his people that they belong and to act as physical vehicles of spiritual blessing. 'The Spirit is the witness, because the Spirit is the truth. There are three witnesses, the Spirit, the water and the blood, and these three agree.' This letter of John is written, among other reasons, to combat Docetism, an early heresy which maintained that the heavenly Christ was too holy and spiritual to be soiled by permanent contact with human flesh. The heresy had a number of variations, but they would all have repudiated the idea that the Christ of faith could have been identified with the Jesus of Palestine. But John's point in these verses is that identification is essential to the gospel. God really became man, and Jesus came not with water only (his heavenly nature? His baptism?) but with blood (his human nature? His crucifixion?). Whatever the precise meaning of this difficult phrase, John is saying that in Jesus the divine did become accessible to human touch and sight. And the same continues to be true! The sacraments of the water and the blood (and there must surely be at least an *allusion* to baptism and the Lord's Supper in those words) are used by the Spirit to bear witness to us of the reality of our salvation, and of the fact that we are indeed sons in the heavenly Father's family. More, they are the physical bearers of spiritual blessing, for the Spirit can and does work through the sacraments in the Church, just as he worked through the life of Jesus of Nazareth.[32]

A God who made himself 'accessible to human touch and sight': we could stop there, Heavenly Father, for that would be miracle and grace enough. Yet, the narrative continues, with plentiful reminders, via the sacraments, of the tremendous sacrifice that Jesus made. Bless those who will partake of the sacraments on the Sunday following my reading of this word, I pray, wherever they might be in the world. May your blessing be present in their midst. Bless, too, those who administer those sacraments, with equal blessings.

**The peace of God, which transcends all understanding,
will guard your hearts and your minds in Christ Jesus.
(Philippians 4:7)**

Peace is possible in suffering. Even in the paroxysm of death Jesus maintained a peace which enabled him to hand over his spirit to his Father (Matt. 27:50). His example was not lost on Peter. 'Therefore let those who suffer according to God's will do right and entrust their souls to a faithful Creator' (1 Pet. 4:19). In the midst of anguish and desolation, there is a rock beneath. God knows what we can bear, and will temper our trials to enable us to endure them in peace, the peace to which Christ showed the way.[33]

A shorter reading today, Lord, which might enable me to lengthen my moments in prayer on behalf of those whose peace is hard-won today; those enduring mental anguish and/or what seems to be unanswered (delayed) prayer. I pray for them. I pray too for your people who are persecuted for their faith, that – somehow, in a way that really does pass understanding – you will enable them to find peace in the midst of their ordeal. I pray for those individuals whose lives just seem to be permanently chaotic. Bless those for whom I pray, Prince of Peace.

Give harmony and peace to us and to all who dwell on the earth, just as you did to our fathers when they reverently 'called upon you in faith and trust', that we may be saved, while we render obedience to your almighty and most excellent name, and give harmony and peace to our rulers and governors on earth.[34]

26 October

'Where, O death, is your victory?
Where, O death, is your sting?'
The sting of death is sin, and the power of sin is the law. But thanks be to God!
He gives us the victory through our Lord Jesus Christ.
(1 Corinthians 15:55–7)

One of Paul's most characteristic convictions about heaven [is] we shall be *with the Lord*. In the early lessons like 1 Thessalonians, his assurance about the present state of the dead Christian is this; they are with the Lord. Furthermore, this is the supreme description of the bliss of the saved after the Parousia – 'the dead in Christ shall be raised first, then we which are alive and remain shall be caught up together with them in the clouds, to meet the Lord in the air; and so we shall ever be with the Lord' (4:16–17). When he wrote the Corinthian letters, in the middle part of his ministry, Paul is still clear on this basic theme. 'He which raised up the Lord Jesus shall raise us up also by Jesus, and shall present us with you' (2 Cor. 4:14) – and even before that final resurrection, when the soul after death is disembodied and lacks its full bliss, the overriding compensation is this, that we are present with the Lord (2 Cor. 5:8). As Rom. 6:8 expresses it, 'Now if we be dead with Christ, we believe that we shall also live with him.' And in his later letters the picture has not changed. When, in a context where he is considering his salvation, Paul weighs up the pros and cons of life and death, he acknowledges that his continued life would be more useful for his Philippians friends than his death, he confesses to them his 'desire to depart and to be with Christ, which is far better' (Phil. 1:23). Christ was already his 'life'; how could it be other than 'gain' to depart into his closer presence (Phil. 1:21) where faith would be exchanged for sight (2 Cor. 5:7)? Nothing could break the union between the Christian and his risen lord; this, 'when Christ, who is our life, shall appear, then shall ye also appear with him in glory' (Col. 3:4).[35]

The key word here, Lord, is 'with'. With you in this life, day by day, in the ordinary stuff of human existence, and then, when life's little day is done, still with you. And that word is everything, because being with you guarantees eternal safety and a bond that not even death can sever. With, and never apart.

**I did not speak on my own, but the Father who sent me commanded me to
say all that I have spoken.
(John 12:49)**

The farmer who has been sowing and tending his seed now has to harvest the
crop: if he lets the moment pass, the crop is lost. The pearl fancier who finds
the best pearl he has ever seen, or the ploughman who turns up a bag of buried
treasure in a field – for both zero hour has arrived: they must go for it even if it
means gambling their whole capital. The generous householder has spread his
banquet and invited all and sundry; to make excuses at this juncture, to refuse
the invitation would be disastrous – it would mean final exclusion from the party.
No wonder that the whole countryside was agog at teaching like this. There was
nothing comparable in the religious history of the world.

You only had to compare Jesus' teaching with the Old Testament to get the message.
Now, don't get me wrong. Jesus took the Old Testament as his Bible. He believed that
it was inspired by God, and was therefore decisive both for himself and his hearers. But
still he can contrast his teaching with it, not as black against white, but as fulfilment
over against promise. 'I have not come to abolish the law and the prophets, but to
fulfil', he claimed (Matthew 5:17). And he proceeded to show what he meant. 'Your
goodness has to be better than that of the religious leaders', he maintained – and explained that many religious men make a show of their piety in order to impress men;
they give to be praised by men; and they pray to be seen by men. Secret prayer, unseen
generosity, unostentatious religion is the order of the day for the follower of Jesus.[36]

**With love at the heart of everything, Lord Jesus, your teachings set
the compass for the whole of human behaviour; in thought, word and
deed. Whatever else I might know about life pales into insignificance
compared to getting this right.**

Saviour, teach me, day by day,
Love's sweet lesson to obey;
Sweeter lesson cannot be,
Loving him who first loved me.[37]

28 October

LORD, you alone are my portion and my cup.
(Psalm 16:5)

Just as one could look at Jesus, listen to him, and touch him in the days of his flesh without gaining any benefit from him or even realising who he was, so it is with the sacraments. They may be bare signs, or they may be vibrant with the life of the Spirit; it depends, not a little, on the receptivity and faith of the recipient. Certainly churchmen are not to sit back confident that they must be all right with God because of their sacraments. 1 Corinthians 10 is written to that situation. The Corinthians seem to have been regarding their sacramental life as a sort of talisman which would allow them to engage in idolatry and fornication with impunity. Paul reminds them that the Israelites of old had their counterpart to the Christian sacraments and relied on them for security – but in vain. They went in for fornication and idolatry like the Corinthians, and 'God was not pleased; for they were overthrown in the wilderness'. The sacraments in the Church are a means of grace and an objective, palpable ground of assurance. But they are not magic.[38]

No magic required, Lord – not even 'religious magic'. Guard my heart, I pray, from superstition of any kind, and especially that which might masquerade as Christian-ese. Prompt me often to check my ways, lest I inadvertently lapse into relying on anything except you personally, and you alone. Govern my spiritual priorities, however subtly some options make themselves apparent. Ritual and liturgy definitely have their place, but not as anything except useful (valuable) forms and blessings that help to facilitate my primary relationship with you.

29 October

Each of you should use whatever gift you have received to serve others, as faithful stewards of God's grace in its various forms.
(1 Peter 4:10)

Corinth was a richly gifted church. And they rated very highly among these gifts the ability to speak in tongues. The value they set upon it was very understandable from either a Hebrew or a Greek background. One has only to think of the *ruach adonai*[39] coming with a supernatural violence upon Saul so that he danced like a dervish, or upon Ezekiel so that he was carried away to another place, to sympathise with the Corinthians in supposing that extraordinary manifestations like this were the sure mark of the Spirit's activity. In the Greek world it was the same. Even that great intellectual Plato could write in the *Phaedrus*, 'It is through *mania* (ecstasy due to divine possession) that the greatest blessings come to us' and in the *Timaeus*, 'No one in possession of his *nous* (rational mind) has reached divine and true exaltation'. The non-rational was the mark of divine inspiration; the more *pneuma*, the less *nous*. The Corinthians would have rated in ascending order of value the teacher (in reliance on his rationality), the prophet (who spoke under divine inspiration but intelligibly), and the man who spoke in tongues (whose inspiration was marked by unintelligibility).[40]

Thank you, Lord, for the range of gifts you bestow upon your church, equipping your people for service. You have not left us short, nor unable to fulfil mission. Grant us wisdom, though, when it comes to handling gifts of all kinds. Show us what to do with them, so that their usage may glorify you, the giver, and may only ever be edifying. By the same token, make us each hungry for gifting, but wise and humble too.

30 October

Do not take revenge, my dear friends, but leave room for God's wrath, for it is written: 'It is mine to avenge; I will repay,' says the Lord.
(Romans 12:19)

'You have heard that it was said to the men of old, "You shall not kill; and whoever kills shall be liable to judgment." But I say to you that everyone who is angry with his brother without cause shall be liable to judgment' (Matthew 5:21). Jesus is not abolishing the Old Testament law of manslaughter. He is fulfilling the principle behind it, for he is showing how God hates the evil thought of uncontrolled fury no less than the bitter outcome of murder. Again, he takes the famous maxim from the Old Testament, 'An eye for an eye and a tooth for a tooth' and adds, 'But I say to you, "Do not resist one who is evil"' (Matthew 5:38). Is he repudiating the Old Testament principle? Not at all. He perceives the principle that lay behind it (that of limiting revenge to the equivalent of the wrong done) and fulfils that principle by allowing love to banish revenge altogether.

The matter of love was hard enough to fulfil, even to the folk you liked. So the Old Testament had said, 'You shall love your neighbour', and to it the scribes had enthusiastically added what the Old Testament did not add, 'and hate your enemy'! To this Jesus brings an undreamed-of fulfilment, a new thing in the history of thought, an ethic which is the most difficult and the most powerful in today's world as it was then: 'But I say to you, Love your enemies, and pray for those who persecute you, just as your heavenly Father does' (Matthew 5:43).[41]

This is, Lord, perhaps the biggest challenge of them all. It's easy for me to love when the sun is shining and I am spending my time with people whose company I enjoy, and when nothing is rubbing me up the wrong way. It's a different kettle of fish, though, when I am amongst 'enemies' or even those I don't, honestly, like very much. All the more reason, then, for me to pray that your love would be poured afresh into my heart; daily, but especially when I need it most. Uproot anger.

How much more, having been reconciled, shall we be saved through his life!
(Romans 5:10)

Eternal life to Paul is only secondarily life that will go on for ever; it is primarily a new quality, a new dimension of living . . . It is this quality of life which is the Christian's present enjoyment and his future hope together. If he does not know it now, he will not know it then. If we are strangers to the life of God here, we shall be strangers to it there. Indeed, life with God hereafter would not be heaven but hell if we have not learnt to 'crucify the flesh' and 'live in the Spirit' (Gal. 5:24f.). It would be what Althaus[42] calls 'inescapable godlessness in inescapable relationship to God' (cf. 2 Thess. 1:9). 'Life with God for ever' means salvation from death and the associated 'wrath' which we saw to be one of man's greatest enemies under the old aeon. Paul is at pains to stress this ultimate eschatological deliverance from death and wrath (1 Thess. 5:9–10 – contrast 1 Thess. 2:16; 2 Tim. 1:10; Rom. 5:9). For the Christian is, in his present life, only delivered 'in hope'. Thus Paul can say we have been delivered from the wrath to come (1 Thess. 1:10), or that our deliverance is past and at the same time future (see the contrasted uses of 'redemption' in Eph. 1:7,14). These foes of man have received their death blow, but are not yet dead; their sentence is signed but not yet executed.[43]

That which is, but is yet to come! Time-bound as I am at present, Lord, maybe my best plan is to get used to living alongside you now, in this life, so that my transition to the life to come includes that same element of relational fellowship, but in a way that is incomparably better and, this side of the matter, unimaginable. Allow me to walk with you, my God, and to talk with you, often, bearing in mind that the best is yet to be. I want to develop the habit of daily communion.

And He walks with me, and He talks with me,
And He tells me I am His own,
And the joy we share as we tarry there,
None other, has ever, known![44]

1 November

Comfort, comfort my people, says your God.
(Isaiah 40:1)

There is an outcome to suffering. For the Christian the cross can never be separated from the resurrection. And the resurrection speaks of God's triumph over suffering. Jesus drained the cup of suffering to the dregs, and it failed to poison him, or embitter him, or make him distrust his Father. Accordingly, Good Friday was followed by Easter day. Suffering, if this world were all, would be inexplicable and unjustifiable. But this world is not all there is. What is sown in tears will be reaped in joy. It was so for Jesus. It will be so for his suffering followers.

The cross empty of Jesus, therefore, has much to say to the sufferer. We should not be surprised when suffering strikes, nor expect to be exempt from it. We should allow it to draw us closer to the crucified Jesus. If we suffer with him we shall also reign with him. No tears fall unnoticed on the ground of Calvary.[1]

A compact word of comfort, Lord. Thank you.

2 November

And this is what he promised us – eternal life.
(1 John 2:25)

John Baillie, in his book *And the Life Everlasting* (p. 199), has a charming story which, as he says, is an artless tale, but embodies the authentic Christian temper. An old man lay dying, and asked his Christian doctor 'if he had any conviction as to what awaited him in the life beyond. The doctor fumbled for an answer. But ere he could speak, there was heard a scratching at the door; and his answer was given him. "Do you hear that?" he asked his patient. "That is my dog. I left him downstairs, but he grew impatient and has come up and hears my voice. He has no notion what is inside that door, but he knows that I am here. Now is it not the same with you? You do not know what lies beyond the Door, but you know your Master is there."'

The Christian does already share Christ's life (Rom. 6:10–11; Gal. 2:20), and after death he will continue to share it. We live 'in hope of eternal life' promised by God our Saviour – and he cannot lie (Tit. 1:1–3). It is interesting that Paul seems to reserve the phrase 'everlasting life' for the sequel to physical death; such is the certain meaning of Rom. 2:7; Gal. 6:8; Tit. 1:2; 3:7, and probably holds good of Rom. 5:21; 1 Tim. 6:12 (in the light of 6:19) and Rom. 6:22–3, though the last mentioned may well be thought of as a present state reaching out into the future, as 'death' in the parallel clause does. In any case, Paul freely applies 'life' both to the now and to the hereafter. Already we share 'life in God' (Col. 3:3; cf. Eph. 4:18), 'life in Christ' (2 Tim. 1:1; 2:11) and 'life in the Spirit' (Rom. 8:6,10). This life is no bare attribute; it is qualitatively defined by the Holy Trinity. So it will be in the life to come.[2]

Ratified and 'qualitatively defined by the Holy Trinity'; made legally valid by none other than the eternal Godhead. I could have no surer promise, Lord, and I give thanks today that Scripture is loaded with multiple confirmations of this contract, this agreement. I take you at your word, Lord: to do anything else would be insulting and offensive. And all of this, not of my own, not because of any merit I may possess, but all, all of grace.

3 November

He will be called Wonderful Counsellor.
(Isaiah 9:6)

'Bread and circuses' was the prescription in the days of the impending collapse of the Roman Empire. The people were kept happy by the provision of material needs for their bodies and entertainment for their minds. One does not need particularly acute insight to perceive that something very similar may be happening in Western society at the start of the twenty-first century. The threat of terrorism, the unashamed selfishness, the collapse of values, the prevalence of abortion, the spread of permissiveness, the dependence on drugs by an enormous part of the population: all these factors, together with the sheer pace of life, tend towards a strain in our world which has never been paralleled. It is hardly surprising that an increasing number of people are cracking under the strain. There can be little doubt that this will continue, and that counselling will become a major industry if the fabric of society falls apart.

A great deal of modern counselling is non-directive. It encourages the client to make his or her own decision in a mature way. The counsellor is anxious to avoid dependence, anxious, too, to avoid putting his or her own ideas into the mind of the client. All this is healthy. But there is, I fancy, another factor at work on the side of non-directive counselling, and from the Christian viewpoint this is less good. Modern counsellors abjure directional counselling because they no longer believe in norms and absolutes. This is the age of relativism run riot. Not only is it too crude, too legalistic to say 'I suggest that you do this: it seems the right course'. But the very word 'right' has ceased to have any absolute meaning. They depend on individual choice, the choice of individual or society, like whether you drive on the left or the right.[3]

Whatever the rights, wrongs and maybes of modern counselling techniques, Lord, I hope to always come to you first, regarding you as my main port of call whenever I need counsel. You may well use counsellors whom you have gifted, and I pray especially for Christians to whom you have entrusted such an important ministry. Remind me, though, to speak to you about my concerns and problems, and then to take matters from there. Remind me, too, to wait quietly for your counsel.

4 November

**Do not conform to the pattern of this world,
but be transformed by the renewing of your mind.
(Romans 12:2)**

Where can you find anything in the teaching of Jesus that does not strike you as truth? Where can you find anything that strikes you as error? How do you account for the fact that no ethical advances, no teaching of how men should behave towards their fellows has emerged in the centuries since then which represent any advance on the Man of Nazareth? Where did the man get his fantastic teaching from? He had an answer: 'My teaching is not mine, but His that sent me' (John 7:16). Could he be right? Did he come from God? Could this account at one fell swoop for his authority, his simplicity, his depth, his world-wide appeal? If you reply, 'Of course not: he was just a very impressive teacher', I want to ask you a question or two.

Why did he strike contemporaries and subsequent generations as so utterly different from other teachers? How is it that he got all this learning without having been to college? How is it that, unlike other great teachers such as Socrates and Mohammed, his teaching fits all men everywhere? How is it that nobody has dreamed up any moral advances since his teaching? What was there in his heredity and environment to account for this unique teacher, and the remarkable fact that no greater has ever looked like emerging? Yes, there was something different about this teacher. Perhaps it was not so strange when he took over the old Jewish saying 'When two or three busy themselves over the Law of God, the glory of God shines on them' and replaced it with 'Where two or three are gathered together in my name, there I am in their midst' (Matthew 18:20). Perhaps he *was* different.[4]

Lord Jesus, my divine example, if you were (are) 'different', then it follows, if I am to be like you, that I must be different too; different in my conduct, my speech, my behaviour, my standards. Not holier-than-thou (God forbid), but markedly different in a secular world. I pray that you would show me how. Show me what that difference means, so that I may make a difference. May the marks of Jesus be seen in me.

5 November

Be shepherds of the church of God, which he bought with his own blood.
(Acts 20:28)

It need not be supposed that life [in Christ] after the removal of all foes will be a dull and static affair. Life is never static, nor is love dull. If there is to be life, there must be growth; if the life to come is one of perfect understanding, it will be one of perfect love both to the Saviour and to the saved (1 Cor. 13:8,12). Instead of development *towards* goodness, there will be development *in* goodness. Professor A.E. Taylor has expressed this well. 'The moral life would not disappear even from a world in which there were no wrongs to be righted. Even a society in which no member had anything more to correct in himself, and where "Thou shalt love thy neighbour as thyself" were the universally accepted rule of social duty, would still have something to do; it would have the whole work of embodying the love of each for all in the detail of life.'[5] This emphasis is important, for the ultimate salvation is essentially corporate. Indeed, almost all the metaphors used in Scripture to describe it are corporate ones – the kingdom of God, the Messianic Banquet, the elect, the Body of Christ, the New Man (or Humanity), the Israel of God, the fellowship of the Spirit, and so on. That is why love will be the all-important quality of the saved, the very life of heaven; it is 'we with them' who will ever be with the Lord (1 Thess. 4:17). Professor Taylor again, 'If we are to think morally of heaven, we should, I suggest, think of it as a land where charity *grows*, where each citizen learns to glow more and more with an understanding love, not only of the common King, but of his fellow-citizens.' He continues, after remarking that we can begin to learn this lesson now, 'But even where there is no ill-will or indifference to interfere with love, it is still possible for love to grow as understanding grows.'[67]

Lord, if this is what life with you will be like in all eternity – an experience of the fullness of love – then is that what church life this side of eternity should represent, at least in part? I suspect so, but sometimes it can also be something of 'a dull and static affair'. Show us, how to clear the cobwebs away from church life; if, that is, they have been allowed to hang around for any length of time. May your church resemble some kind of foretaste of the community of heaven still to come.

6 November

**I have given them the glory that you gave me,
that they may be one as we are one.
(John 17:22)**

The life to come is represented as continuous with this life. Death has been robbed of its significance, and the two poles in the Christian's existence are his conversion and the coming of Christ. He does even now share Christ's likeness – increasingly as the Spirit is allowed mastery in his life. We are transformed into Christ's likeness, 'from one degree of glory to another, even by the Lord the Spirit' (2 Cor. 3:18). But that likeness is still blurred in every Christian, however sanctified. It is, as John put it, not until Christ appears that 'we shall be like him; for we shall see him as he is' (1 Jn. 3:2). St Paul's perspective is precisely the same. He knows that it has been God's purpose from all eternity that mankind should be 'conformed to the image of his Son, that he might be the firstborn among many brethren'. And this is the result of what he calls predestination, calling, justification and glorification (Rom. 8:29–30). Not until the process is complete shall we effectively and fully share his glory.[8]

What a glorious prospect! What a glorious privilege! What a panorama of grace! It is enough – more than enough – that you should want to make me more like Jesus, but to think there is so much more to come as well, culminating in glorification. I am unworthy, Heavenly Father, I know that full well, but I claim these outpourings and receive them with gratitude. More of the same, please, Lord!

7 November

**If you declare with your mouth, 'Jesus is Lord', and believe in your heart
that God raised him from the dead, you will be saved.**
(Romans 10:9)

There is good reason to suppose that 'Jesus is Lord' was the earliest baptismal confession. It was certainly something every believer could say; it was the irreducible minimum of Christian faith. Paul is concerned to show the Corinthians that genuine Spirit-possession is not marked out by tongues but by the unambiguous confession that Jesus of Nazareth is lord; Lord of the universe, and Lord of your life. That is the first and foremost criterion of the Spirit's authentic presence. And it was something that was not restricted to certain Corinthian Christians with particular gifts who despised others as not being *pneumatikoi*, 'Spirit-filled'; but was rather the basic condition of being a Christian at all, embodied in the baptismal confession!⁹

A simple, sincere prayer today, Lord. I pray for baptismal candidates, wherever they might be and whatever the circumstances of their confession. For some, such a baptismal confession will be hard-won, and might even land them in all sorts of trouble. For others, it will be expressed with equal sincerity, but might not mean quite so much in terms of opposition or societal challenge. Bless them all, I pray; each and every one, as they prepare for baptism and take this significant step. May they know your encouraging presence alongside them; now, then, and afterwards.

8 November

**He who testifies to these things says, 'Yes, I am coming soon.'
Amen. Come, Lord Jesus.
(Revelation 22:20)**

Progressively as we are transformed into Christ's image (which is 'the image of the invisible God' – Col. 3:10) we come to share his visible manifestation of character, his glory. This will be perfected at his return.[10] Even now 'Christ in you' is 'the hope of glory' (Col. 1:27). *Then* those saved by Christ will obtain glory (2 Tim. 1:10), and will perfectly reflect in a redeemed human nature the character God intended them to have; they will be like Christ. Perhaps the most famous passage which links salvation with the return of Christ and the obtaining of his glory is Phil. 3:20f. Paul is writing to a city proud of being a Roman colony. He reminds his readers that we Christians constitute a colony of heaven, and from this relationship we can expect vindication at the hand of our Saviour when he comes, just as the Roman colonists could from their Saviour, the Emperor.[11] But Christ's salvation is incomparably superior to Caesar's; for he will change the body of our low estate, our corporate existence in all its frailty and sin, and make it like the body of his glory.[12]

'They will be like Christ.' At last! When this is all over, and my redemption is nigh, when this worn-out body has breathed its last, then 'They will be like Christ'! How marvellous, how wonderful! Hallelujah!

9 November

Humble yourselves, therefore, under God's mighty hand,
that he may lift you up in due time.
(1 Peter 5:6)

'When Jesus calls a man, he bids him come and die.' So wrote Dietrich Bonhoeffer. In his own pilgrimage he had to die to family, to fame, to success, to patriotism. In the end he was led out to suffer physical execution. And as he left his colleagues in the cells he said, 'This is the end – but for me the beginning of life.' He knew that the way of the cross and the way of the resurrection were interlaced for the believer as they were for his Lord.

Jesus had made it very plain from the moment he was acclaimed as 'Messiah' by Peter, that such triumphalist notions needed translating into a different language, the language of suffering and vindication. He had not come to be a political or religious Messiah. He had come to give his life for others, and to take it again. He taught the amazed disciples that 'the Son of man must suffer many things, and be rejected by the elders and the chief priests and the scribes, and be killed, and after three days rise again. And he said this plainly. And Peter took him and began to rebuke him. But turning and seeing his disciples he rebuked Peter and said, "Get behind me Satan! For you are not on the side of God but of men"' (Mark 8:31f). Peter had a great shock when he learnt that his beloved Master was not going to bring in the kingdom by storm but was going to die. He was given another shock when Jesus continued, and showed that the cross was not going to be unique to the Master but was the way of life and death for the disciple too. 'If any man would come after me, let him deny himself and take up his cross and follow me. For whoever would save his life will lose it; and whoever loses his life for my sake and the gospel's will save it.'[13]

Lord Jesus, you have clearly shown me the way: if I wish to wear the crown, then I must, first, carry the cross. If I wish to be promoted to glory, then I must first demote myself with humility. Yours is a kingdom of paradoxes, Lord, yet that is the system you have ordained. If I wish to gain, then I must first of all lose. Enable me, I pray, to be 'on the side of God' in all my approaches to these crucial considerations.

Joseph, a Levite from Cyprus, whom the apostles called Barnabas (which means 'son of encouragement').
(Acts 4:36)

[Within the Body of Christ] some members have less outstanding gifts, and they are tempted to feel that they are inferior members in the Body. Paul encourages them in [1 Corinthians 12] verses 14–20. How awful it would be if the Body consisted of just one great eye! If all had the same gift, the harmony of 'unity-in-diversity' would give way to dreary uniformity (12:19–20); moreover they would be tacitly blaspheming God who arranged each of the organs in the Body as he saw fit (12:18). Let them take heart. An inferiority complex is out of place in the household of God. He knows what he is doing with the diverse gifts he imparts. All members of the Body are necessary and interdependent.

In the verses which follow, Paul addresses himself to those who suffer from a superiority complex. They are reminded that all members have a part to play, but that God delights to give special honour to the less showy parts; 'the parts of the body which seem to be weaker are indispensable, and those parts of the body which we think less honourable we invest with greater honour' (12:22f). If those with the less spectacular gifts are slighted, the whole Church is impoverished.[14]

Firstly, Lord, I thank you for all those within my own church fellowship whose work and ministry goes largely unnoticed and unsung, week after week. It's probably true to say that the church would very quickly cease to function, were they to down tools. Thank you for all they do. Secondly, Lord, I pray for anyone within my church who is labouring under an inferiority complex – such a horrible, crippling weapon of evil. Somehow, Lord, speak to them about this, and gently raise them up. Show them how valuable they are in your sight, and how their role in the life of your church is just as important as any other. And, thirdly, make me a sensitive encourager to those in need of a kindly word or a confidence booster.

11 November

**The eye cannot say to the hand, 'I don't need you!'
And the head cannot say to the feet, 'I don't need you!'
(1 Corinthians 12:21)**

When [Paul] says 'if one member suffers, all suffer together' he is not saying anything at all about Christian sympathy. His point is altogether more penetrating to Corinthian pride. He wants the more arrogant members of the Body there to realise that if any one member, however mean and ordinary his service, is inhibited from making that service, *then the whole Body suffers!* If, on the other hand, one member is honoured by being able to render its proper service acceptably, then the whole Body is honoured. The truth that the whole Church is the loser if it is not so constituted that all members get the chance to make their God-given contribution to its life and worship was as surprising and unacceptable to the Corinthians as it is to us. But that is what Paul is asserting throughout [1 Corinthians 12]. Always for him, the Body of Christ is primary, and the individual member secondary. This is the precise opposite of the Corinthian – and our own – atomised way of thinking. The Corinthians had to learn that they were not individually 'little Christs' with all the gifts, but rather, members of Christ with some gifts. Nobody was unnecessary, and nobody self-sufficient: they needed each other in the Body of Christ.[15]

Lord of the church, how I need my fellow Christians – even those who irritate me and with whom I don't always agree! I need to learn from others, to compensate for those qualities I lack. I need others because of the opportunities of service they create for me, enabling me to take my place in the Body. I need others to rub against my hard edges as we jog along as pilgrims together, like the grain of sand helping to produce a pearl! What a privilege it is to be a part of your body, Lord, your church on earth. I thank you for those whom you have placed me amongst; for what they teach me, for the ways in which they encourage me, for including me, and for showing me, each in their own different ways, facets of Christ.

12 November

The bolts of your gates will be iron and bronze,
and your strength will equal your days.
(Deuteronomy 33:25)

The self-sacrifice of the Christians under persecution has long been a powerful witness to the reality of their faith. In AD 203 a 22-year-old African girl, Perpetua, with a baby at her breast, was martyred for her faith at Carthage. Before her death she managed to write down her impressions. Her father had tried everything to make her recant. First he was rough with her, but found that distressed her to no effect. Then he turned to appeals: his grey hairs, her mother, and her own tiny son who would not be able to survive her. All of these were thrown into the scale to induce her to change her mind and deny Christ. But she knew the pattern of denying herself, taking up the cross, and following Christ. She went to her death with dignity and courage. Twenty-five years earlier a Gallic slave girl, Blandina, showed the same spirit of unimaginable courage under persecution. She was a recent convert and totally dedicated to Christ. Quietly, she maintained, 'I am a Christian woman, and nothing wicked happens among us'. She was forced to watch the murder of her Christian companions, then was heated on a gridiron, thrown to wild beasts in the arena, and finally impaled on a stake. Totally in Christian character, she died praying for her persecutors with love and fervency: her death nerved a 15-year-old lad, Ponticus, to follow her example.[16]

O Cross that liftest up my head,
I dare not ask to fly from thee.
I lay in dust, life's glory dead,
And from the ground there blossoms red,
Life that shall endless be.[17]

I pray for those who are persecuted, tortured, marginalized, harassed and beaten to the point of death. I ask you to be close to your people in countries where even the mention of your name is forbidden. May the 'bolts and gates' of their faith be strengthened. I pray, too, for those who carry out the acts of brutality.

13 November

Love is as strong as death,
its jealousy unyielding as the grave.
It burns like blazing fire,
like a mighty flame.
(Song of Songs 8:6)

There is a sober recognition that to follow Christ can be exceedingly costly, even to death; but death itself cannot separate the believer from Christ, and therefore the cause grows. 'The oftener we are mowed down by you', wrote Tertullian, 'the more we grow in number. The blood of Christians is seed' (*Apologeticus*, 50). He spoke from much personal experience.

This pattern of willingly undertaking the cross as the path to union with Christ and resurrection with him has continued down the centuries. The annals of the faith are red with the blood of martyrs who have not counted their lives dear to themselves. In the twentieth century probably more Christians have been martyred for their Lord than in all the other nineteen centuries put together, and still the blood of the martyrs is seed. Still the way of self-sacrifice rather than self-assertion is seen to be the Jesus way, and remains the only hope for the world . . .

Without this self-giving spirit of Jesus and his people, the lust for power becomes all-consuming, the exercise of power becomes selfish, and when arrogance induces revolution, yesterday's oppressed become tomorrow's oppressors. Heroes like Martin Luther King and Alexander Solzhenitsyn, Festo Kivengere, Richard Wurmbrand and Janani Luwum abundantly validate the Jesus way of life through death, and victory for love through the endurance of evil.[18]

Almighty God, I have to believe that love wins. Otherwise, evil has triumphed, and that would make a sorry mockery of everything the Bible tells me. This might well be a hard-fought victory, Lord – one made up of blood and nails and thorns and bloodshed and self-denial – but the outcome is secure, and that is what confirms and strengthens belief. I repeat my prayer from the previous page, for the suffering church across the world. Love wins! Keep that flame of hope alive in my heart.

14 November

Showing love to a thousand generations of those who love me.
(Exodus 20:6)

Well might Paul . . . implore the Corinthians . . . 'Make love your aim' [1 Corinthians 14:1]. His plea is taken up by John Wesley in *A Plain Account of Christian Perfection* . . .

Another ground of these, and a thousand mistakes, is the not considering deeply that love is the highest gift of God – humble, gentle, patient love; that all visions, revelations, manifestations, whatever, are little things compared to love; and that all the gifts mentioned above are either the same with it or infinitely inferior to it.

It were well you should be thoroughly sensible of this – the heaven of heavens is love. There is nothing higher in religion – there is, in effect, nothing else; if you look for anything but more love, you are looking wide of the mark, you are getting out of the royal way. And when you are asking others, 'Have you received this or that blessing?' if you mean anything but more love, you mean wrong; you are leading them out of the way, and putting them upon a false scent. Settle it in your heart, that . . . you are to aim at nothing more, but more of that love as described in the thirteenth chapter of Corinthians. You can go no higher than this till you are carried into Abraham's bosom.[19]

God my Father, your name is Love. That is entirely who, and what, you are.

Come, let us all unite to sing,
God is love.
Let heav'n and earth their praises bring,
God is love.
Let ev'ry soul from sin awake,
Let ev'ry heart sweet music make,
And sing with us for Jesus' sake,
God is love![20]

15 November

The body that is sown is perishable, it is raised imperishable;
it is sown in dishonour, it is raised in glory.
(1 Corinthians 15:42–3)

It seems probable that in his doctrine of the 'spiritual body' in 1 Cor. 15 Paul is fighting on two fronts; against those with a Greek background who believed in a disembodied immortality, on the one hand, and against the Jewish materialists on the other, who believed that the very same bodily particles which had been buried would rise again in the last day. We shall indeed rise, Paul counters, but with a spiritual body. By 'spiritual' Paul appears to mean one perfectly adapted for heavenly conditions, a body that will no longer hinder, but rather express the new life in Christ, a body that has become the perfect and transparent instrument of the Holy Spirit. By 'body' he means the whole man, his entire personality, set within the *material* context of the created world and the *social* context of his fellows. The Christian doctrine of the resurrection of the body means that our ultimate destiny is thus neither reabsorption into the Infinite, nor the resuscitation of our present existence, nor a solitary and selfish enjoyment of God *solus cum solo*,[21] but a social matter. Final bliss, the ultimate consummation, is not meant for us individually but corporately; it will not be enjoyed by *any* until it can be enjoyed by *all*, 'that they without us should not be made perfect' (Heb. 11:40).[22]

Lord Jesus, I may not know how, or when, or even where this will all take place. I don't pretend to. It is enough for me to believe that it will. I lay before you, afresh, my ignorance and my faith. I thank you for both; my ignorance helps me to retain a sense of mystery and awe, not to mention a sense of dependence, and my faith fills me with optimism and confidence. I 'will be raised to live forever'! Amen.

16 November

Do not merely listen to the word, and so deceive yourselves. Do what it says.
(James 1:22)

Time and again [Jesus] told doubters not to believe him unless his behaviour bore him out. His works, as he sometimes called them, had to match his words. And they did. Exactly. How sublime to be able to tell the story of the shepherd who goes out at night and braves danger to seek one lost sheep – and carries on until he finds it. But more sublime still to go and live it out by loving Simon Peter even when he denied knowing him, and deserted him in his moment of greatest need. It is marvellous to find Jesus talking of the love his Father has for all men irrespective of their merits; love which, like the rain and sunshine, falls on all alike. It is even more marvellous to give the favourite's portion at a supper party to the man you know is just about to betray you, and then to kiss him on the cheek as he does so! It is one thing to say 'Blessed are the poor', and quite another to be happy in poverty, as Jesus was. One thing to say 'Bless your enemies', and quite another matter to cry 'Father, forgive them' as cruel soldiers nail your bleeding body to a cross. But that is the way Jesus behaved. His actions matched his teaching.[23]

A God of authenticity, who, in Christ, talked the talk and, crucially, walked the walk. This encourages me to believe in you more fully, Lord, as I analyse just how exactly what you said, here on earth, matched up to what you did. Furthermore, Lord Jesus, you kept to your word even when it was bitterly painful for you to do so. As my faith deepens, let me learn from this, in terms of what it means for my own life.

17 November

When Judas, who had betrayed him, saw that Jesus was condemned, he was seized with remorse and returned the thirty pieces of silver to the chief priests and the elders. 'I have sinned', he said, 'for I have betrayed innocent blood.' (Matthew 27:3–4)

Socrates, Plato, Moses, Confucius, and in our own day Martin Luther King, Pope John, or Billy Graham taught wonderful things and men have hung on their words. But never did any of these great men actually manage to carry out all they taught. In all of them there has been consciousness of failure. Indeed, this is one of the surest marks of greatness – to recognise that one's object exceeds one's reach, the goal lies far beyond the achievement. And growth in greatness always carries with it growth in humility. Talk to any great individual, and he will tell you how ashamed he is of his failures and of his mistakes. The most famous saints are always most conscious of wrong within.

But Jesus was different. He taught the highest standards that any teacher has formulated, and he kept them. He really did. There is remarkable unanimity on this matter. It is interesting to note how united the opposition to Jesus is about his innocence. Three times in the account of the trial before Pilate, the governor pronounces his innocence. Pilate's wife sends a message to the courtroom to the same effect. The Jewish leaders cannot find an accusation which will stick, and so they have to get him to incriminate himself by admitting to be the Messiah. Even the traitor Judas confesses that he has betrayed innocent blood. Even the brigands crucified with him recognised that he had done nothing wrong. Even the man in charge of the crucifixion was driven to exclaim, 'This man was innocent'. Quite an impressive bunch of testimony from the Opposition benches. Jesus was different.[24]

The innocent slain for the guilty. Never was anyone more innocent, yet you were slain, Lord Jesus, for a guilty world. You were slain for me.

**There was no other good enough
To pay the price of sin;
He only could unlock the gate
Of heav'n, and let us in.[25]**

18 November

Peter replied, 'Repent and be baptised, every one of you, in the name of Jesus Christ for the forgiveness of your sins. And you will receive the gift of the Holy Spirit.'
(Acts 2:38)

It has been characteristic of holiness movements throughout Church history to claim that the fullness of the Holy Spirit depends on conformity with their particular shibboleth. The terminology changes: 'perfection', 'brokenness', 'full surrender', 'sanctification' have all been used, but 'the fullness of the Holy Spirit' is perhaps the most contemporary and explicit in its claim. It is commonplace in Pentecostal and neo-Pentecostal literature that while all Christians share to some extent in the Holy Spirit, only those who have been 'baptised in' the Holy Spirit can know his fullness. The fullness of the Holy Spirit which comes from his personal, permanent and full indwelling, is intended to equip us for service, and is obtained only by this crisis experience of 'baptism in the Holy Spirit'. Indeed, 'Spirit-filled' is often used by charismatic people to describe someone who shares their experience, in contra-distinction to run-of-the-mill Christians.[26]

Lord, I pray for my Pentecostal brothers and sisters around the world. I pray your blessing on their endeavours. Help us all, Lord, from all kinds of denominations, to continue in healthy dialogue regarding our differences. Most of all, Lord, remind us all that no one denomination has any kind of monopoly on your Spirit! That, for one thing, is an impossibility and, for another, is an unhealthy point of view. You, Holy Spirit, are Sovereign God. Teach us to live beneath, and within, that truth.

19 November

Very truly I tell you, unless a grain of wheat falls to the ground and dies, it remains only a single seed. But if it dies, it produces many seeds.
(John 12:24)

If . . . we ask, 'How are the dead raised up, and with what body do they come?' (1 Cor. 15:35), St Paul can no more draw the curtain than we can. But he does give two most illuminating insights into the nature of the resurrection body. He gives us the famous parable of the seed, an illustration which had parallels in Judaism.[27] When we sow grain in the ground, it dies and decomposes. Only the germ lives on, and from it the new body is formed. It is the old principle which Paul knew to be central to the Christian religion, of life through death. So it will be with the resurrection body; a continuity of life through death, while the physical frame returns to the dust as surely as the husk of the grain of corn. But the analogy does not stop there. We do not expect an identical grain to emerge from the cornfield, but something far more wonderful, a plant, a blade, an ear of corn. Had we never seen the latter, we could never have guessed what it would be like, simply from looking at that bare grain in our hands the autumn before. But once we have seen it, we can recognize that there is not only a continuity of life with that grain, but a real likeness, albeit greatly enhanced and beautified. 'God has given it a body as it pleased him . . . So also is the resurrection of the dead . . . it is sown in corruption, it is raised in glory (1 Cor. 15,38,42f). We cannot conceive what a 'spiritual body' will be like, but we may be sure that, once we possess it, we shall recognise that there has been both continuity of life and a real thorough transfigured likeness to the body we knew.[28]

Thank you, Lord, for all that nature shows us, season upon season, that can so easily be applied to the spiritual life. Thank you for lessons all around me, such as this one, that serve as illustrative parables. Speak to me this day, so that I may receive spiritual instruction as I go about my business – and spiritual blessing too!

Remain in me, as I also remain in you. No branch can bear fruit by itself; it must remain in the vine. Neither can you bear fruit unless you remain in me.
(John 15:4)

There is no need for sin to go on reigning in my life, though it will never be totally expelled this side of the grave. There is no reason why I should be forced, Paul says [in Romans 6], against my will, to obey sin's passions. Do not, he urges, go on yielding your members as instruments for sin to use: but make an act of unconditional surrender to God as those he has rescued from death. And put your members at his disposal. Of course, that attitude of surrender will need daily and hourly to be renewed. But without the radical act of abnegation, without the unconditional surrender, the hourly and daily surrender will never happen. If, however, that total surrender to Christ is my aim and direction, then sin will not hold tyranny in my life. I shall never be quite free of it in this life. But it will no longer dominate; and progressively its forces will be driven back as I abide in Christ, and in this dying and risen life.[29]

Lord Jesus, if and when there are those times when my will seems to be in conflict with what I believe to be yours for my life, help me to change my will accordingly; to bend in obedience and trust. And, Lord, on those occasions when I am not particularly inclined to trust and obey, and when that seems beyond me, then perhaps I can present my struggle to you, with the honest prayer that I would at least like you to do something about that dilemma. Will that do, Lord? I want to keep it real, given that you know and understand anyway. Can we work together?

21 November

I consider everything a loss because of the surpassing worth of knowing Christ Jesus my Lord, for whose sake I have lost all things.
(Philippians 3:8)

Archbishop Janani Luwum was . . . aware of the supremacy of his Christian allegiance over his personal safety. Clerics do not generally take on the leaders of their country. They are often mute in the face of injustice. They act as if they were part of the establishment. But Luwum told General [Idi] Amin that his reign of terror was evil in the sight of God; and he paid the penalty for his integrity with his life. He . . . knew this would happen. He quite deliberately chose death rather than his natural desire for safety, and to allow the Lord to rise through his death. That happened very speedily and very wonderfully. The authorities would not release his body for the funeral. It took place round an empty grave in the grounds of Namirembe cathedral. And the retired Archbishop, Erica Sabiti, preached to scores of thousands, who defied the government's ban in order to be present, on the text, 'He is not here: he is risen.'

That principle can be applied across the board. We are to die to all claims of the self-indulgent life. Ambition, love of ease and comfort, wealth, employment, marriage, family, self-will must all be offered to Jesus. We must ask him to nail to the cross all that is unworthy of him, so that his life can be seen in our mortal bodies. For the disciple, as for the Lord, the crown is unattainable without the cross.[30]

I am no longer my own, but yours. Put me to what you will, place me with whom you will. Put me to doing, put me to suffering. Let me be put to work for you or set aside for you. Praised for you or criticized for you. Let me be full, let me be empty. Let me have all things, let me have nothing. I freely and fully surrender all things to your glory and service. And now, O wonderful and holy God, Creator, Redeemer, and Sustainer, you are mine, and I am yours. So be it. And the covenant which I have made on earth, let it also be made in heaven. Amen.[31]

22 November

**I know that when I come to you,
I will come in the full measure of the blessing of Christ.
(Romans 15:29)**

What does the New Testament say about the fulness of the Holy Spirit?

Surprisingly, it says nothing at all. The Greek word for fulness, *plērōma*, is applied to many things in the New Testament, notably to both Christ and the Church; but never to the Holy Spirit. This is not an important point, because the idea may be present without the word; but it does show how ill-based in Scripture is any attempt to make the 'fulness of the Holy Spirit' into a doctrinal war cry, as if it were a most important and neglected biblical emphasis.

The second noteworthy point is that the verb 'to be filled with', *pimplēsthai*, is almost exclusively Lucan. Apart from two occasions in Matthew, all its other twenty-two occurrences are in Luke's Gospel or Acts. The adjective 'full' has a wider spread, but of its sixteen appearances eleven are in Luke or Acts. It is clear that this is a favourite word of Luke's. In addition we ought perhaps to mention the normal word for 'to fill', *plēroun*, but this is only twice used of the Holy Spirit (Acts 13:52; Eph. 5:18) and twice loosely associated with him (Rom. 15:13f; Col. 1:8–9).[32]

**Love perfecteth what it begins;
Thy power doth save me from my sins;
Thy grace upholdeth me.
This life of trust, how glad, how sweet;
My need and Thy great fulness meet,
And I have all in Thee.[33]**

'My need and thy great fulness' – one must meet the other and, thanks to your grace towards me, that meeting can, at any given time, take place. Thank you, Lord.

23 November

Be strong, and let us fight bravely for our people and the cities of our God.
(2 Samuel 10:12)

The dying and rising life which is at the heart of discipleship is very difficult. It is hardly surprising therefore that there have been constant efforts throughout human history to find some other way for the church to live.

The most common over the centuries has been simply deliberate forgetfulness. The church has chosen to take no notice of what Jesus said about taking up the cross and following him. It has taken up an establishment role and lived in the shadow of that. The church, like Rome in the Middle Ages, has so often either become a political power, wielding all the weapons of the world in establishing its own position, or else a prop of the existing establishment as was the Orthodox Church in Russia before the Revolution. Moreover, there has been a singularly complete amnesia about Jesus' teaching that Christian leadership is to be marked by the pattern of the Servant. Instead, it has almost universally adopted the mode and manners of autocratic secular leadership. The dying and rising life has not been seen. The beauty of Jesus has, accordingly, not been portrayed.[34]

Lord, I pray for the church to be brave, to be outspoken in the face of injustice. If dying and rising is what it's all about, then that has to apply to Christian witness in the political and social arena too. Improve or remove the cowards, Lord, if their leadership is timorous, and if it is costing the church too dear. 'Let us fight bravely'.

If anyone is in Christ, the new creation has come:
the old has gone, the new is here!
(2 Corinthians 5:17)

Jesus has achieved a new Exodus. All men, not just Israelites, have been ransomed from a bondage and a death far worse than Egypt's, by the costly ransom-price of the death of the Messiah; they are brought, furthermore, into an inheritance far better than that of Canaan, for it is 'incorruptible, undefiled, and that fadeth not away, reserved in heaven' for them ([1 Peter]1:4).

The *nature* of this deliverance is interesting. Peter says nothing about sin. What he does mention is the emptiness of [his readers'] own previous way of life, and that of their fathers before them. To the Jew this would speak of the burdensome traditions imposed upon the faithful by the religious leaders (Lk. 11:46 and Matt. 23 *in toto*); indeed, Peter himself refers to these traditions as the yoke of bondage 'which neither our fathers nor we were able to bear' (Acts 15:10). To the Gentile, this would speak of the old heathen life, characterised by ignorance of God, absence of objective moral standards, lack of purpose, and what Hort calls 'the yoke not merely of personal inclination and indulgence but that which was built up and sanctioned by the accumulated instincts and habits of past centuries of ancestors'.[35] It was from all this slavery to futility and custom that the suffering Messiah offered redemption.[36]

Thank you, Lord, for this interesting insight into deliverance. It adds to my awareness of what you have done for me. It also makes me pause to consider how this might apply to my ongoing walk with you. That is to say, is there anything I might be holding on to that needs to be jettisoned in my pursuance of the new life you have on offer? If there is, shine your light upon it, I pray.

25 November

**My dear brothers and sisters, take note of this: Everyone should be quick to
listen, slow to speak and slow to become angry.**
(James 1:19)

We never find [Jesus] having to apologise. We never find him having to admit he
was wrong. And this from the man who was so shrewd in spotting hypocrisy in
others! There are several occasions when we are given the substance of his prayers;
but never once do they betray any shadow of consciousness of guilt. He tells us
to pray 'Forgive us our trespasses', but significantly he does not seem to need to
do so himself. Fascinating. Unique. Here is a person of the most refined spiritual
insight who can say of his heavenly Father, 'I do always those things that please
him' (John 8:29). Here is a man who can turn to an angry crowd furious because
he was claiming that he was one with God, and with childlike innocence can ask
then, 'Which of you can convict me of sin?' (John 8:46). I do not know which is
the more remarkable: that he could ask such a question – or that he could not be
faulted by the crowd![37]

Lord, help me, today, to be:
Quick to apologize if I am in the wrong
Quick to ask your forgiveness of my trespasses
Eager to 'do always the things that please him'
And willing to respond to anger with 'childlike innocence'.

26 November

Jesus Christ is the same yesterday and today and for ever.
(Hebrews 13:8)

You cannot disentangle Jesus from miracle. Scholars in the last century spent endless ingenuity on the quest of a non-miraculous Jesus. In the end it was an acknowledged failure. Because every strand in the evidence about Jesus shows him as different from other men: through him God acted in a way impossible to understand on the assumption that he was just a good man. The miracles begin at his birth: he was God's Son, according to Mark; God's Word and agent in creation, according to John; the full repository of the Godhead according to Paul (whilst none the less being 'born of a woman'); the one who came into the world without the agency of a human father, according to Matthew and Luke. The miracles continue in his ministry: miracles of healing, or exorcism, nature miracles (such as the feeding of the multitude from a handful of loaves, and his walking on the sea in a storm), and supremely his raising from the dead Lazarus, the widow of Nain's son, and Jairus' daughter. Last of all came the greatest of all miracles, his own resurrection from the grave – not just to a further span of life but to a new quality of life over which death has no power.[38]

Lord Jesus, I pray for miracles today; miracles of healing for those who are at their wits' end, miracles of provision for those who can't imagine where their next penny will come from, miracles of salvation in the lives of those who would appear to be the most unlikely candidates for conversion, and miracles of grace in terms of forgiveness and restoration for those whose sins are as scarlet. Miracles, please, Lord, for those who stand in great need.

27 November

Dear friends, do not believe every spirit,
but test the spirits to see whether they are from God.
(1 John 4:1)

From time to time another denial of the dying and rising life emerges. This is one of the many forms of triumphalism. The crown is separated from the cross. Success is lionised, and the path of suffering despised or repudiated. This seems to have been the situation in first-century Corinth. The Corinthians were already full, had already entered on their reign, while the poor apostles remained the offscourings of the pot, suffering contumely and persecution throughout the Roman world (1 Cor. 4:8–13). Perhaps that is why in [his] letters Paul gives such emphasis to the cross, and wears his sufferings and hardships like medals (1 Cor. 2:2; 2 Cor. 11:21f). Triumphalism is a perennial danger to the church. When it overcomes the morbid, lacklustre image of the kill-joy, it tends to swing to the other extreme and claim for now what belongs to heaven. Healing, prosperity, victorious living, church growth are all suffused in the glow of the resurrection, while the shadow of the cross is carefully expunged . . .

It is a type of prosperity doctrine. If you have faith, and join their membership, you can be assured of God's prosperity, his healing, his victory and his success in your life. 'Anything you ask' is the slogan of these soldiers of the resurrection who have forgotten that they follow a crucified Jesus, and that they are bidden to 'share in suffering as a good soldier of Jesus Christ' (2 Tim. 2:3).[39]

Lord, I pray for the minister(s) and teachers in my own church. Theirs is an onerous responsibility, so the least I can do is hold them before you in prayer. Give them wisdom, so that as they minister, they may preach and teach well. Place your hand upon them, so that what they share may edify the congregation. Preserve and protect them from error and from teaching falsehood.

Do not quench the Spirit. Do not treat prophecies with contempt but test them all; hold on to what is good.
(1 Thessalonians 5:19–21)

Christians in the main line of both Catholic and Protestant traditions have for a long time been very scared of allowing that [the] gifts of the Spirit of which we read in the New Testament might be expected to occur today. They are supposed to have died out in the apostolic era.

It is much more comfortable to suppose that this is the case, and to look for the contemporary manifestations of the Holy Spirit in the peace and order of the Church of today rather than in the violent irruptions of earlier days. Both Catholic and protestant camps have been heavily infected by the rationalism of the Enlightenment, and our Christianity has been unduly cerebral (hence its appeal to the educated only). If the Corinthians were inclined to identify the work of the Spirit with the abnormal, we tend to make the opposite mistake, and suppose that he can only manifest himself in moral renewal, spiritual illumination, and through either Bible or sacraments according to our theological reference! This attitude, however, is sheer escapism from exposing ourselves to the Spirit's powerful life. He remains the Spirit of wind and fire; he remains sovereign in the Church, and is not to be boxed up in any ecclesiastical department.[40]

> **Lord God, I do sometimes wonder why you stay with your church, when so often we have relegated you in the ways mentioned above. Forgive us, Holy Spirit, if we have attempted to clip your wings or confine you to an 'ecclesiastical department'. Come, renew us. Come afresh, as of old, with your glorious winds of change. Come, Great Spirit, come. Make our hearts your home.**

29 November

**Because of the LORD's great love we are not consumed,
for his compassions never fail.
They are new every morning.
(Lamentations 3:22–3)**

Between the past and future in salvation history, the Christian has to live in the present. He is intended to have a constant experience of the keeping power of God ([1 Peter] 1:5). This is his birthright since he was initiated into the realm of salvation at his baptism (3:21). Just as certainly as Noah found the way to safety through the waters of the flood, so the Christian finds salvation through the waters of baptism. Not, of course, that baptism in itself has any quasi-magical powers, as Peter is quick to point out. The baptism of which he speaks is 'not putting away the filth of the flesh, but the answer of a good conscience towards God'. That is to say, when the condition of trusting obedience to God's way of salvation is present as it was in Noah, then there is the soldier's pledge of sincere loyalty to God – granted *that*, then baptism saves. This is not only because it is the initiatory rite of Christianity, but because it sums up all that Christ has achieved for man in his death, resurrection and ascension; all this God 'makes over' to us, as it were, in baptism.[41]

I plunge beneath the waters, Lord – not in my own merit, but by faith, in obedience to your prompting and conviction – and in doing so, a boundless salvation comes rolling over me. I pray for daily grace as I have 'to live in the present'. May those waters wash me daily, 'new every morning', as I experience your 'keeping power'.

The word of God is alive and active. Sharper than any double-edged sword, it penetrates even to dividing soul and spirit, joints and marrow; it judges the thoughts and attitudes of the heart.
(Hebrews 4:12)

It is simply not the case that healing, prophecy, exorcism and speaking in tongues died out with the last apostle. Still less can a passage like 1 Corinthians 13:8 ('as for prophecies, they will pass away; as for tongues, they will cease . . .') be adduced to attest the supposed demise of these gifts. They will pass away only when 'the perfect comes', i.e. at the Parousia – not at the end of the apostolic age or the formation of the New Testament canon! There is in fact plenty of evidence in the sub-apostolic days, and periodically throughout church history, to show that these gifts did not die out, though they were often viewed with great suspicion by the Church authorities . . . And it is perfectly evident from the widespread growth of the Pentecostal church and the neo-Pentecostal movement in the last eighty years that God has poured out these gifts in rich measure upon his people, rationalistic and sceptical though we have been about them.[42]

This passage reminds me, Lord, of the importance of analysing Scripture carefully, and of the folly of reaching assumptions that are not supported by that careful analysis. Heavenly Father, keep me close to my Bible, and as I read it prayerfully, let it also read me.

1 December

People will come from east and west and north and south, and will take their places at the feast in the kingdom of God.
(Luke 13:29)

The man on the inside is both 'in Adam' and 'in Christ'. The old nature has, alas, not gone out: nor will it before we see him [Jesus Christ] as he is. Then, and not till then, shall we be like him (1 John 3:2). In the meantime, there is a constant battle, as passages like Galatians 5 and Romans 7 (not to mention our own experience!) make plain. We are far from perfect in our present state. But we are on the winning side. And dying and rising with Christ daily is the only way to grow in holiness . . .

The 'Jesus Prayer' of the Orthodox Church . . . is meant to be repeated many times, in relaxation, faith and humility. 'Lord Jesus Christ, have mercy on me a sinner.' Such a prayer combines the humility of a sinner with the sacrifice of 'Jesus' (Yahweh saves) and deep trust in the One who is 'Lord'.[1]

I take this prayer as my own, Lord Jesus Christ, but I also take this opportunity to pray for my brothers and sisters in the Orthodox Church. I acknowledge and respect their deep, rich heritage of faith and custom, and I ask that you minister your loving presence to them as they too pray. Bless their leaders and their congregants as they look to you. Their prayer. My prayer. Their God. My God. Our God.

2 December

You, my brothers and sisters, were called to be free. But do not use your freedom to indulge the flesh; rather, serve one another humbly in love. (Galatians 5:13)

There is no stage in this life when I shall be able to say 'I have arrived'. Always there is the tension between the two backgrounds I inherit, between the two natures I share, between the life of the 'old man' and the 'new man'. Both remain active. My baptism signifies to me both my election (proceeding from God's grace, grounded in Christ's atonement, incorporating me in his body) and my calling (to become empirically in my behaviour what I already am in Christ). Paul [says] that far from being free to sin as we please after becoming Christians, we are free from the obligation to sin, because we belong to the crucified and risen Saviour, Jesus Christ . . .

In driving Christ to the cross sin overreached itself, overplayed its hand, and lost the war (cf. 1 Cor. 2:8). And so the Christian's relation to sin has been decisively broken by the death of Jesus. We are no longer under its tyranny.

Indeed, one can look at chapters 5–8 of Romans as four aspects of what it means to be put in the right with God. We find four tyrannical giants whose prisons have suffered earthquake through the death of Christ. To be justified means to be freed from the clutches of the Giant Wrath (ch. 5), the Ogre Sin (ch. 6), the Tyrant Law (ch. 7) and the Despot Death (ch. 8). In each case we are taken from the grasp of these enemies *and released so that we can fight them*! Nevertheless the tension remains. Freed from Wrath, we still have to face the consequences of our actions. Freed from Sin, we can (and still do) fail every day. Freed from Law we remain under the law to Christ (1 Cor. 9:21). Freed from Death, we still have to die. Christian deliverance is inaugurated in Christ *now*; it will be consummated in Christ *then*.[2]

Jesus, take me as I am. Continue to work in me. Let this ongoing process find its outworking in my daily circumstances – pushing on and bearing up in grace. Stay with me, work with me, until the day comes when I have 'arrived'.

3 December

When Jesus got out of the boat, a man with an impure spirit came from the tombs to meet him. This man lived in the tombs, and no one could bind him anymore, not even with a chain. For he had often been chained hand and foot, but he tore the chains apart and broke the irons on his feet. No one was strong enough to subdue him. Night and day among the tombs and in the hills he would cry out and cut himself with stones. When he saw Jesus from a distance, he ran and fell on his knees in front of him. (Mark 5:2–6)

St John's Gospel shows the true significance of [Jesus'] miracles when he calls them 'signs'. Signs of who Jesus is. Signs of what he can do for men. The one who fed the multitude can feed a hungry soul. The one who opened blind eyes can do the same for men blinded by pride and prejudice. The one who raised the dead can bring new life to someone who is dead spiritually and morally. The miracles were never done for selfish purposes; never to show off. They were evoked by Jesus' compassion for human need, and they were intended both to show that the long awaited Messianic kingdom had begun, and also that Jesus was the liberator who could unlock the various chains of man.[3]

Come with release, miracle-working Christ, to those in chains today; chains of their own making, albeit, chains of despair and confusion, chains of past traumas, chains of guilt. Come to the impure. Come to the bound. Come to those who cry out. Come in mercy. Come in power. Come to those who have seen you 'from a distance' and who desperately seek your loving touch of great authority.

4 December

**'I am the Alpha and the Omega,' says the Lord God,
'who is and who was and who is to come, the Almighty.'
(Revelation 1:8)**

The Christian . . . is deeply concerned about the future of man and his world. And from the earliest days, when believers dated martyrdoms *regnante Jesu Christo,* 'in the reign of Jesus Christ' and Augustine wrote his *City of God* whilst the civilised world was crumbling round his ears, Christians have been optimistic about the ultimate future. Why? Because of the empty cross of Jesus.

It is rather like a game of chess. At some time in the game there comes a move which is absolutely critical and determinative of the outcome. The game goes on, but struggle as he may, one player is doomed since that critical move was played by his opponent. The cross and resurrection of Jesus are that move. Since then the game goes on: the problems remain, the suffering continues and the outlook seems black. But the outcome is assured. Because of that cross and resurrection we can be confident of the final destiny of mankind and the world. It is not bound for destruction and chaos, but for the omega point of God's purpose . . .

Christians *must* strive for better conditions on earth, if the spirit of their Master really indwells them; to heal, to teach, to care, to love – this is his way. And Christians must never succumb to the liberal myth of building 'Jerusalem in England's green and pleasant land'. The 'Jerusalem that is above, which is the mother of us all', is not ours to build. God will bring it about in his time and in his way. The consummation of the kingdom will be as much God's sovereign work as was its inauguration through the coming and dying and rising of the Messiah.[4]

Alpha and Omega God, there is so much to do with 'the end times' that remains mysterious. There doesn't appear to be any one straightforward script or 'road map'. The sequence of events concerning 'the consummation of the kingdom' remains largely shrouded in prophetic mystery. Yet! I believe that the 'game of chess' has been won, and won resoundingly, and that is where I rest my hope; standing on the promises of God. Keep my feet squarely there, come what may.

5 December

If anyone speaks in a tongue, two – or at the most three – should speak, one at a time, and someone must interpret.
(1 Corinthians 14:27)

We should . . . expect the Spirit of God to show himself as God. We should neither reject speaking in tongues, nor regard it as the be-all and end-all of spirituality. A Catholic charismatic evaluation is valuable at this point: 'It is clear that the issue of renewal is not tongues, nor an insistence that praying in tongues is in any necessary way tied to the spiritual realities received in initiation. Many outside the renewal attribute a centrality to tongues which is not reflected in most sectors of the renewal. On the other hand, those involved in the renewal rightly point out that this *charisma* was quite common in the New Testament communities. It should neither be given undue attention nor despised. Since it is the lowest of the *charismata*, it should not be a matter of surprise that it is so common!'

That is a wise and balanced statement of the truth as the New Testament confronts us with it. We should, therefore, rejoice when a member of the congregation discovers that he has the gift of tongues. Of course, we should be wary. The gift of tongues does not edify anyone else unless it can be interpreted, otherwise it is for private use in a man's own devotions. But if it is interpreted it can be a valuable form of edification for the congregation.[5]

Sound teaching, Lord, based well in Scripture, and I thank you for it. This reminds me to try to make sure that I act in ways that edify the congregation at my church. Whether that be speaking in tongues or interpreting a message spoken in tongues, or in some other way of service altogether, may my presence within my church be one that edifies, builds up, encourages and helps. Help me to keep that in mind whenever we meet together.

6 December

Those who humble themselves will be exalted.
(Luke 14:11)

One has only to mention tongues speaking in church, particularly one of the mainline churches, for hackles to rise. But why should they, if this is an authentic gift from God? Fear is, of course, one reason, and a very unworthy one at that. Why should we fear what our heavenly Father allows for our edification? Order is another. But that need be no problem either, if the apostle's injunction is obeyed that there should only be two or at most three such messages in a meeting of the congregation, that they must not take place without interpretation, and that there should be sensitivity and mutual submission (1 Cor. 14:27,29,40). Of course there is difficulty in knowing if there will be anyone to give an interpretation, but that is far from insuperable. If the tongues speaker feels impelled to give an utterance in tongues, we can be confident that God will provide someone to interpret. If nobody is forthcoming, then the worship leader will, after due pause, go on with the service. Either someone was smothering the impulse to interpret, or the original speaker simply got it wrong, and should never have spoken in that tongue in the first place. In a congregation where spiritual gifts are allowed to operate there will inevitably be mistakes; and the ability to apologise and admit we got it wrong is one of the surest ways to grow in maturity and sensitivity to what God is really saying.[6]

A place where sanctified common sense holds fast, and where mistakes are allowed. I like the sound of that sort of church fellowship, Lord! Give me the grace to admit my mistakes, Lord, whatever the issue in question – and not only at church!

7 December

I am the living bread that came down from heaven.
Whoever eats this bread will live for ever.
(John 6:51)

The Christian hope for the future has nothing whatever to do with such concepts as the perfectibility of man, the evolution of morals, or the eradication of ills in society. It depends simply and solely on God. And God has pledged his future by means of his decisive action in the past: the dying and rising of Jesus. As Jack Clemo puts it in his book *The Invading Gospel*, 'Truth did not remain for ever on the scaffold. Truth came down from the scaffold, walked out of the tomb and ate boiled fish.' The assurance about God's final outcome has been given already. There is the ground for true Christian optimism. There is nothing either shallow or anthropocentric about it. It does not fail to take seriously the appalling problems in our world . . . It simply stakes all on the God who raises the dead. He has done it at the mid-point of time in one very special person, Jesus. He is the last Adam, the head of the new race, and his people's future is wrapped up in his own. Flesh and blood cannot inherit the kingdom of God. There is no way in which mortal man can win immortality. But 'just as we have borne the image of the man of dust, so we shall also bear the image of the man of heaven'. Just as we all share by our common humanity in the lot of the first Adam who became a living being; so we shall all share, by our common faith and baptism, in the lot of the last Adam who became a life-giving spirit (1 Cor. 15:45–50).[7]

'His people's future is wrapped up in his own'. What could be a more secure wrapping? There is nothing faulty or unreliable about that. In Christ, all will be well. I stake my all on the God of resurrection. Keep me eating of the bread of life, and keep me well wrapped, I pray!

8 December

**We are God's handiwork, created in Christ Jesus to do good works,
which God prepared in advance for us to do.
(Ephesians 2:10)**

The New Testament teaches that the release of the Holy Spirit in the life of believers is dependent on the death and resurrection of Jesus (John 7:39). The Paraclete could not come to the disciples unless Jesus 'went away' (John 16:7). But once Jesus had died and risen the Spirit was poured out into the lives of the waiting disciples, as the Acts records and as the whole history of earliest Christianity makes abundantly plain. 'This Jesus God raised up' Peter is recorded as saying on the Day of Pentecost, 'and of that we are all witnesses. Being therefore exalted at the right hand of God, and having received from the Father the promised Holy Spirit, he has poured out this which you see and hear' (Acts 2:32ff). The Holy Spirit is made available through the death and resurrection of Jesus, and he is the pledge . . . of God's new creation (Rom. 8:22f; 1 Cor. 15:20). He is that part of the future which we have now in the present. And the function of the Spirit in the lives of believers before the final curtain of God's drama is clearly defined in the New Testament.[8]

Almighty God, yours is indeed a gripping 'drama'. What is immensely reassuring, though, is that it is expertly scripted and planned. There is a wonderfully sequential note to every 'act'. Nothing is left to chance. Nothing is haphazard or random. Beginning and End are clearly stated. On this basis, I place my trust in you, Lord, because I can afford to do so confidently as your story (his-story) unfolds.

9 December

**Two or three prophets should speak,
and the others should weigh carefully what is said.
(1 Corinthians 14:29)**

It is fashionable to laugh at the miracles. Such things could not happen. But why not? The laws of nature do not forbid them. A 'law of nature' is simply the name we give to a series of observed uniformities; this is the way things happen. But if a contrary instance is well attested, the scientist will widen his so-called 'law' to embrace both the uniformities and the exception to the rule. In the case of Jesus there is lots of strong contemporary evidence that he was the exception to the rule. If he was just a good man, that would be astonishing, perhaps meaningless. If he was different, if he was in some way God himself coming to disclose himself to us within the limitations of human form – then perhaps it is neither so incredible nor so meaningless that he should perform miracles.

At all events the evidence is overwhelming, and it is not all contained within the pages of the New Testament. You will find the earliest Christian apologist, a man called Quadratas, writing early in the second century:

But the works of our Saviour were always present (for they were genuine): namely those who were healed, those who rose from the dead. They were not only seen in the act of being healed or raised, but they remained always present. And not merely when the Saviour was on earth, but after his departure as well. They lived on for a considerable time, so much so that some of them have survived even to our own day.[9]

Saviour Christ, as I come to the latter stages of this book, I turn once again in prayer to those whose salvation is uppermost on my heart and mind. I pray, Holy Spirit, that you will influence their thinking, and that you will remove the scales from their eyes so that they may see Calvary. I pray that you will somehow impress upon them the multiple evidences of your saving love, in order that they may believe. Have mercy. Cause them to 'weigh what is said'.

10 December

I am the LORD, the God of all mankind. Is anything too hard for me?
(Jeremiah 32:27)

I find it intriguing that this, the only passage of Quadratas to have survived, should be devoted to drawing out the implications and establishing the early truth of the miracles. It shows how confidently the early Christians could look to the miracles of Jesus as a pointer to his being more than a man, to his being different.

But there are traces of miracles in Roman and Jewish sources as well. Justin Martyr, writing his *Apology* about AD 150, can say with casual confidence, 'That he performed these miracles you may easily satisfy yourself from the *Acts* of Pontius Pilate.' It was the same with the Jews. We find them in the Gospels unable to deny the miracles of Jesus, but taking the only way out – attributing them to the devil. In the Acts of the Apostles we find Jews attempting to use the name of Jesus as a potent spell in exorcism: later on this continued, so much so that the writers in the *Mishnah* (Jewish law code) have to forbid Jews to heal in the name of Jesus! And the Tractate *Sanhedrin* tell us that 'Jesus was hanged on the eve of the Passover because he practised sorcery and led Israel astray' – a plain reference to his miracles.[10]

Miracle Man, forgive us our doubting.

11 December

Dear friends, although I was very eager to write to you about the salvation we share, I felt compelled to write and urge you to contend for the faith that was once for all entrusted to God's holy people. For certain individuals whose condemnation was written about long ago have secretly slipped in among you. They are ungodly people, who pervert the grace of our God into a license for immorality and deny Jesus Christ our only Sovereign and Lord. (Jude 3–4)

God saves men from their plight and he will preserve them to the very end, provided they continue to trust and obey their Saviour. No man will be in heaven against his will. That is why the antinomians[11] with whom Jude is dealing must not presume on the grace of God. They appear to have regarded salvation as an assured religious possession of their own, rather than a constant manifestation of God's grace – and that attitude is the foe of true Christianity, indeed it is a manifestation of the anti-God spirit.[12] The historic element in salvation cannot be used as a sanction over God, any more than the Jewish Torah could (see Rom. 10:1–3). The Christian life begins and ends with faith making response to grace. God will keep men. But men must trust him to do so, and want him to do so.[13]

Lord God, just as your people in the wilderness looked to you for daily provision, so may I look to you always for 'a constant manifestation' of your grace in my life. None of this is my doing, and my reliance upon your keeping power is total. Never let me stray from that awareness. A God who saves and keeps! Keep me near the cross.

12 December

If you think you are standing firm, be careful that you don't fall!
(1 Corinthians 10:12)

The man who thinks he is standing secure should take care lest he fall. Why, even Paul himself dare not presume. If he were to live an undisciplined and undedicated life, in repudiation of the Saviour's proffered grace, he too might face rejection at the day of testing (1 Cor. 9:16–27). For salvation is not a historic possession but an eschatological experience. To be saved or to gain salvation is neither a possession which can be obtained nor a proposition which can be proved (or even assented to), but an existential relationship with the Saviour. And one of the marks of the man who has truly entered this relationship is that he has a desire to save others from the awful loss, the separation, the state of rebellion against God which they are in. This is emphasised both by Paul and by Jude (1 Cor. 9:22; 10:33; Jude 23). The 'saved' man manifests the love of the 'Saviour' God for sinners. That is how he can be distinguished. Instead of slipping back to the ways of the world, he is always at work for God attempting to bring others to the Saviour. But lest this human sense of saving be misunderstood, Jude ends his letter with one of the noblest paeans of praise to be found anywhere in the New Testament. It is God who is able to keep you from falling. It is God who is able to bring you to final salvation. To God the only Saviour, *our* Saviour, be glory and majesty, dominion and power both now and for ever (24,25).[14]

Thank you, loving God, for this gentle warning. I realize that, outside of your grace, I am prone to pitfalls and stumbles. Keep me from slipping and falling, I pray, as I acknowledge my need of your tight grip. And, Lord, I pray specifically today for mission organizations who are geared up for evangelism on a national or international scale. Bless those whose focus is the salvation of souls; those whose formal ministry is utterly dedicated to that aim; para-church mission groups and the like who spearhead campaigns and programmes. Use them well.

13 December

When pride comes, then comes disgrace,
but with humility comes wisdom.
(Proverbs 11:2)

It may be that God has given you a gift of healing. Perhaps you will be used to heal regularly in this way . . . Perhaps God will use you only occasionally. If healing is your gift, rejoice, and use it for the good of those to whom God leads you. But remember the dangers which beset the use of such a gift: the danger of showing off; the danger of supposing that to heal without means is more spiritual than to heal with means – as if God were not the author of all healing, whether through orthodox medicine, acupuncture, hypnosis, psychotherapy, or spiritual healing. You will be tempted to think there is some special property in oil or hands imposed upon the patient. You will be in danger of playing God, and assuring men that they will recover when they will in fact die. You will be in danger of supposing that suffering may not even form part of the permissive will of God, and thereby perhaps underestimate the role which suffering has in keeping us dependent upon the Lord's strength which comes to fruition in weakness (2 Cor. 12:9). You will be tempted to think that God is using you because of some special virtue of your own. The Israelites of old had to learn that God had not chosen them because they were great or holy, but in order to show something of his love in them (Deut. 7:7) and the same is true of the election and the gifts of God today. So remember the dangers, while you rejoice in the gift for the good of others. And wise is the church that does not restrict its role in healing to spiritual solace, but allows scope for those of its members who are gifted in this way to exercise their gift with love and humility alongside the more usual medical methods.[15]

Wise and important teaching, Lord: thank you. Maybe those are the key words attached to any gifting or ministry, Lord: 'love and humility'. May such hallmarks characterize all that your church does in your name, healing or otherwise. Keep us humble – for we have much to be humble about! To God be the glory.

14 December

Come, let us sing for joy to the LORD;
let us shout aloud to the Rock of our salvation.
(Psalm 95:1)

The whole life of worship in the church is the concern of the Holy Spirit. He longs to forge Christians into a corporate temple which he can inhabit, and which we can all too easily ruin by our divisions (1 Cor. 3:16ff). He longs to control the worship (14:26f), as he did at Antioch (Acts 11:27f; 13:2), not to be organised out of the possibility of all intervention. He has gifts for his people: words of wisdom and knowledge, tongues and interpretations, gifts of healing and faith, gifts of prophecy and deliverance (1 Cor. 12:8ff). Some he wants to make teachers, some leaders, some administrators in Christ's body (12:27ff). He inspires the love and zeal, the hospitality and service, the hope and patience of different members of the Body (Rom. 12:3–13). In all this he is seeking to equip the Christian community to be, here and now in the present brutal world, a 'colony of heaven' (Phil. 3:20). The life and behaviour, the love and mutual service of Christians is all the work of the Spirit. Jesus is the chief cornerstone in the building, and 'in him the whole structure is joined together and grows into a holy temple in the Lord: in whom you also are built into it for a dwelling place of God in the spirit' (Eph. 2:21f).[16]

God to whom all worship and homage is due, I pray specifically for those whose ministry is to lead congregations in worship offered through music and song. I pray for worship leaders, musicians and singers. (I expect they face a fair bit of criticism from time to time, regarding their choices of hymns, choruses and tunes!) For those who serve you in this way, be that via an organ in a grand cathedral or a guitar in a house-group, and everything in between, I pray your blessing and guidance. Thank you for every such input into our corporate life. Bend your ear as we sing praise.

15 December

He will guard the feet of his faithful servants.
(1 Samuel 2:9)

The first followers of Jesus, being Jews, had the highest reverence for the Scriptures of the Old Testament. Yet there were manifestly incomplete sides to them. Those Scriptures spoke of a day when God would judge the earth. They spoke of a king of David's stock whose dominion would be endless. They spoke of all the families of man being blessed in Abraham, the man of faith who started the nation of Israel. They spoke of one like a Son of man coming to the Ancient of Days, and receiving a kingdom that would never be destroyed, together with power, glory and judgment. They spoke of a prophet like Moses arising among the people whose teaching would be unparalleled. They spoke of a servant of the Lord whose suffering would be intense and whose death would carry away the sins of the people. They spoke of a Son of God whose character would measure up to that of his Father. This coming one would fulfil the role of prophet, of priest and of king for ever. He would be born of David's lineage, but of a humble, despised family. His birthplace would be Bethlehem. He would both restore the fallen in Israel and be a light to the Gentiles. He would be despised and rejected by the very people he came to rescue from their self-centredness. He would die among malefactors, and his tomb would be supplied by a rich man. But that would not be the end of him. He would live again, and the Lord's programme would prosper in his hands. When he saw all that would be accomplished by the anguish of his soul, he would be satisfied. For he would have forged a new agreement between God and man by his death; indeed, his death would open up the possibility of ordinary men and women having the Spirit of God come and take up residence within their lives.

All of this came true with Jesus. Not some of it: all of it.[17]

'All of this' – and we aren't even into the New Testament yet! What a plan! What prophecy! What signposts! What a God! There is so much evidence here, Lord, of your deep desire that people should spot the clues and find their way to salvation. Thank you that you do not leave us lost, simply to wander aimlessly, but you offer us directions at every step of the way. Thank you for going to so much trouble.

16 December

Philip ran up to the chariot and heard the man reading Isaiah the prophet.
'Do you understand what you are reading?' Philip asked.
'How can I,' he said, 'unless someone explains it to me?'
So he invited Philip to come up and sit with him.
(Acts 8:30–31)

In the centuries that followed, this argument from prophecy had an enormous impact. Many distinguished pagans were won to faith in Jesus by the way he fulfilled the prophecies made in those writings of an Old Testament which seemed so much older and so much nobler than their own writings of Homer and Plato. And many still are. As Professor Moule, one of the leading New Testament scholars in England, puts it:

The notion of the 'fulfilment' of Scripture in a single individual, a figure of recent history, and he a condemned and disgraced criminal, who claimed to be the coping stone of the whole structure, and the goal of God's whole design, was new. And it was the Christian community which first related together, round a single focus, the scattered and largely disconnected images of Israel's hope. It was utterly new for images like 'Messiah', 'Christ', 'Son of God', 'Son of Man', 'Suffering Servant' and 'Lord' to be seen as inter-changeable terms all relating to one figure (*The Phenomenon of the New Testament*, p.16).[18]

Living Word, my prayers today are for those who might only ever read the Old Testament. I pray for you to shine a spotlight on the pages they read. I pray for you to prompt curiosity within them as they read. I pray for you to drop questions into their minds as they read, causing them to ponder the ways in which Old Testament prophecies might be fulfilled, and have been fulfilled. Do a great work in this way, Lord. May many be 'won to faith in Jesus by the way he fulfilled prophecies'.

17 December

Even the archangel Michael, when he was disputing with the devil about the body of Moses, did not himself dare to condemn him for slander but said, 'The Lord rebuke you!'
(Jude 9)

Increasing numbers of Christians are finding that they are called upon to perform exorcism these days. This is perhaps because when, as is so common in our society, God is driven out of the front door, demonic forces crowd into the house by the back door. Did Jesus not warn us of precisely this danger (Luke 11:24f)? At all events, there is a most notable increase in black and white magic and in demon possession. Sometimes this comes about by deliberate surrender to the power of evil, as long ago Faust is reputed to have sold his soul to the devil. Sometimes it comes by mere physical contact with, for instance, a charm brought back from an animistic country where it was offered in worship to demons. Sometimes it may be that a house is troubled by an evil spirit, or a group of youngsters start toying with Spiritism. We in the West have too long pooh-poohed the idea of demon possession, and we are paying for our arrogance by a marked increase in demonic activity . . .

[Exorcism] is a real gift of the Spirit of God, and it certainly did not die out in the apostolic era – fortunately for us. This is often how the Spirit worked in the early Church when the gospel was spreading so fast. Tertullian, for instance, could say to pagans who mocked at Christ:

Mock as you will, but get the demons to mock with you! Let them deny that Christ is coming to judge every human soul . . . Let them deny that, condemned for their wickedness, they are kept for that judgment day . . . Why, all the power and authority we have over them is from our naming the name of Christ, the Judge. Fearing God in Christ and Christ in God, they become subject to the servants of God and Christ. At our command they leave, distressed and unwillingly, the bodies they have entered. (*Apology* 23)[19]

Get thee behind me, Satan. The Lord rebuke you.

18 December

**Precious in the sight of the Lord
is the death of his faithful servants.
(Psalm 116:15)**

Confidence about the future, born from the atoning death and resurrection of Jesus, has beautiful results. It grows the fruit of peace instead of gnawing worry about the future: 'have no anxiety about anything', writes the apostle Paul from prison. 'Let your requests be made known to God, and the peace of God which passes all understanding will guard your hearts and minds in Christ Jesus' (Phil. 4:6–7). That attitude was superbly exemplified by Peter in prison, the night before he was due for execution: he was, we are told, 'sleeping between two soldiers' (Acts 12:6). Peacefully dreaming!

If you have that serene confidence about the future, you can face any hardship with confidence. The worst that can happen is that you get killed. But even that will usher you into the closer presence of your Lord, so it is to be welcomed when the time comes. Romans 8:37–9 is the classic expression of that confidence, but 2 Corinthians 1:9 runs it close. Paul had been through some terrible hardship which brought him to the edge of death. He was 'unbearably crushed, so that he despaired of life itself'. But that, he observed, was intended to make him rely not on himself but on God who raises the dead. 'He delivered us from so deadly a peril, and he will deliver us; on him we have set our hope that he will deliver us again' (2 Cor. 1:10).[20]

What a startling contrast, Lord: the secular world views death as something to be avoided at all costs. It is a dread experience filled with unknowing and terror. The aging process is denied, and resisted for as long as possible, in hopes of fending off death's dread day. Yet, for the believer, death is but the tranquil gateway to a new life, one that far exceeds anything imaginable. Lord, I pray for those who are on the brink of death even as I read these words. Carry the believers safely home, I pray, in peace and safety. And for those dying without you, speak to their hearts, even now, that they too might be saved.

19 December

To us a child is born, to us a son is given, and the government will be on his shoulders. And he will be called . . . Mighty God.
(Isaiah 9:6)

If you have read the Gospels, you may well have been struck by a remarkable contrast. On the one hand Jesus is a humble, self-forgetful figure, healing the sick, teaching the people, befriending the outcast. He is no academic theologian, but a horny-handed carpenter whose words are full of hard-headed wisdom and earthy illustrations. He has no money, no settled home, no vote, no rights. On the other hand he makes the most fantastic claims, and many of them are almost casual, throwaway remarks. For example, he takes it for granted that he is entitled to man's worship, the worship due to God alone. When Peter falls at his feet in adoration after a fishing expedition and says, 'Depart from me, for I am a sinful man, master' (Luke 5:8), Jesus does nothing to stop him. When Thomas falls at his feet after the resurrections and exclaims, 'My Lord and my God' (John 20:28), Jesus does not rebuke him – except for needing the evidence of his eyes to come to that conclusion. No good man would do that. Indeed, we have examples in the New Testament of two good men, Peter and Paul, who found themselves being worshipped by ignorant pagans, and they reacted violently against it, telling them to worship God alone. Jesus seems to have taken such worship as his due.[21]

Hints of your divinity here, Lord Jesus; 'hidden in plain sight', so to speak. Thank you for them. When I read my Bible, help me to see more of the same – little clues as to your true identity, that I might all the more worship you as God. Litter my life with such reminders, that I too may declare of you 'My Lord and my God'.

20 December

Sell your possessions and give to the poor. Provide purses for yourselves that will not wear out, a treasure in heaven that will never fail, where no thief comes near and no moth destroys. For where your treasure is, there your heart will be also.
(Luke 12:33–4)

Many Jews clearly expected resurrection at the last day (John 11:24) to be an exact replica of the present body, warts and all. In the time of the Maccabees men looked for the reassembling and restoration of the tortured limbs of the martyrs (2 Macc. 7:14–38; 14:46). Baruch asks God 'In what shape will those live who live in the day?' and the answer is 'The earth will then assuredly restore the dead, which it now receives, in order to preserve them, making no change in their form, but as it has received them, so it will restore them, as I delivered them unto it, so also will it raise them' (2 Baruch 49:2–4). Thus many dying rabbis gave detailed instructions as to how they were to be buried and how their corpse was to be clothed, for the *Tractate Sanhedrin* held that a man would be raised in the same clothes in which he was laid in the tomb (*Sanhedrin*, 90b). Naturally Jewish speculation was not entirely crass. Esdras 7:97 strikes the note of transformation, 'how their face is destined to shine like the sun, and how they are destined to be made like the light of the stars, henceforth incorruptible'.[22]

Lord, I don't particularly care what I end up wearing in the life to come, be it my best suit or a boiler suit. The point is, I will be with you. I will be safe. I will be home, amongst the ransomed. My clothes are neither here nor there compared to that reality. To that end, Lord, help me to concentrate on what matters in terms of salvation, and to leave all secondary issues aside. In the context of eternal life in your presence, they are somewhat irrelevant. Let me adopt that point of view to so many things in my life here on earth, too. Point me to perspective. I'll leave the finer details of my heavenly wardrobe to you.

21 December

We know that this man really is the Saviour of the world.
(John 4:42)

Never once do the words 'save' or 'salvation' occur in the Johannine Epistles, but the title 'Saviour' is applied to Jesus in a single, important verse, 1 John 4:14. The burden of the writer's experience and testimony is that 'the Father sent the Son to be the Saviour of the world'. It is part of the content of the Christian confession (4:15). Just once in the Gospel John represents the Samaritans as making the same confession. They believe on the ground of personal experience 'that this is indeed the Messiah, the Saviour of the world' (Jn. 4:42). The term is singularly appropriate on the lips of the cosmopolitan Samaritans. Against the Hebrew element in their heritage the term would mean that God, the author of salvation, had sent his promised deliverance by the hand of Jesus. The words of Isa. 62:11 had come true, 'Behold the Lord hath proclaimed unto the end of the world, Say ye to the daughter of Zion, Behold thy salvation cometh'. On the other hand, the Hellenistic element in their background would enable them to understand this claim that Jesus is Saviour of the world in another way; it would come as a sharp challenge to the imperial myth that proclaimed the Roman emperor to be the *sōtēr tēs oikoumenēs*.[22] [23]

This message – this 'experience and testimony' – really is quite something, Lord; beautiful in its simplicity, like strands coming together to form a ribbon. Firstly, the straightforward offer of salvation insofar as it has all been taken care of and simply has to be received; believed in. Secondly, the clear statement that this offer is for all, and reaches people of every background and heritage. Thirdly, the declaration that Messiah Jesus is the authentic Deliverer, unlike any number of counterfeits and pretenders to the throne. Thank you for each of these strands. They speak of a unique Saviour who has made himself available to the whole of humanity.

22 December

**You also, like living stones,
are being built into a spiritual house to be a holy priesthood.
(1 Peter 2:5)**

There is in many churches still a terrible famine of hearing the Word of the Lord; and that does not merely mean that the preaching is of an indifferent standard, and the Bible largely misunderstood or little used. The really shocking thing is that congregations are expected (by themselves as much by the clergy) to keep quiet and be passive apart from the singing of the hymns. In the Church of the New Testament, and in many churches today where charismatic gifts are made welcome, there is an orderly but real opportunity for those who have a message from the Lord to share it simply and directly with the rest of the congregation.

It may come through direct speech. It may come through a 'picture' which burns itself into the mind of some member of the congregation. It need not be predictive: much prophecy in the New Testament was not. It may simply be a much needed word of encouragement (1 Cor. 14:3). We have found in our church that it is perfectly simple to give a period of quiet reflection after a time of worship, or before the end of the service, when contributions are welcomed from the congregation if they are sure that in so doing they will have something appropriate to add to what has transpired already. Sometimes this will be a verse or more from Scripture; sometimes a picture or a direct word to the congregation. St Paul bids those who offer this gift to be willing to have their words tested, and in our congregation we generally expect those who are presenting some such ministry to let the leadership see it first. This keeps the whole congregation together and provides a check on what is said and when it is said on the one hand, but on the other is a healthy corrective against clericalism.[25]

What a lovely image this presents, Lord; freedom and encouragement tempered with balance and wisdom. I can think of all kinds of ways in which that 'formula' would bless and enhance church life. Thank you, Lord, for church ministers who aren't precious about such areas of ministry being solely their domain. Give us more ministers like that, Lord, so that your church may flourish as we build each other up.

23 December

I rejoiced with those who said to me,
'Let us go to the house of the LORD.'
(Psalm 122:1)

The traditional churchman is highly suspicious of any pretensions by members of the congregation to direct leading by the Holy Spirit. Such a claim seems a very horrid thing to him, just as it did to the Bishop of London when Wesley made it in the eighteenth century. Order cannot risk allowing the responsibility of freedom to the Spirit. On the other hand, the man who is drunk with the liberating experience of the Spirit of God is tempted to lose patience with the institutional Church and pull out into 'free' worship among like-minded friends. The charismatic distrusts order, and the traditionalist fears freedom.[26]

What a dilemma, Lord! These two extremes, and pretty much every hue and shade in between! Bear with your church, Lord, as we muddle our way through the spiritual life; some preferring this and others preferring that. None of us has it completely and absolutely right, Lord, but please accept our worship, despite that, if it is offered sincerely. And as we all pull along together, stay amongst us. Stay with us, not only to receive our worship, but to teach us your ways. We are by no means perfect, but we do love you, deep down.

24 December

See, I will create
new heavens and a new earth.
The former things will not be remembered,
nor will they come to mind.
(Isaiah 65:17)

The created order is subject to frustration and decay, just like its human inhabitants. But one day

> the creation itself will be set free from its bondage to decay and obtain the glorious liberty of the children of God. We know that the whole creation has been groaning in travail until now; and not only the creation, but we ourselves, who have the firstfruits of the Spirit, groan inwardly as we wait for adoption as sons, the redemption of our bodies. For in this hope we were saved. (Rom. 8:21ff)

Majestic, breathtaking hope. Hope that soars beyond what man could conceive. 'Eye has not seen nor ear heard nor the heart of man conceived the things that God has prepared for those who love him. But God has revealed them to us by his Spirit' (1 Cor. 2:9) . . .

[The empty cross of Jesus Christ] . . . is the story of God's comprehensive salvation for his rebel world. And the pledge of the validity of that future hope is the bitter cross and empty tomb. Karl Barth was strong in insisting on the physical resurrection and empty tomb of Jesus: not because the empty tomb is the Easter faith. It is not. But it is the necessary precondition of it. It is the *sign* that, in the midst of our suffering and death, God has acted decisively. He has shown us what he is going to do for the world. He will not scrap it. He will take the constituent elements and make something new.[27]

You are no scrap merchant, Lord. You do not throw out or throw away. You refashion, remould and renew. You are a God of immense creativity; reshaping and re-giving. I rejoice in this, on all kinds of levels. It's exciting, it's intriguing, and it speaks of a Creator's heart. You are my God, and because of who you are, we have grounds for optimism.

25 December

Produce fruit in keeping with repentance.
(Matthew 3:8)

[We look at] James' . . . contention, namely that faith (coupled with works) saved (2:14). Few passages in the New Testament have been so misunderstood as this one. It is James's apparent denial of the Pauline doctrine of justification by faith that made Luther dub this 'a right strawy epistle', and consign it to an appendix in his New Testament. Whether or not James is implicitly attacking Paul in these verses is dependent upon the relative dates of their writings, and that of James is quite uncertain. There were certainly those who twisted Paul's doctrine of free grace into an excuse for antinomianism (Rom. 3:8), and James may have such people in mind when he denies that faith alone can save . . . Bede has caught the meaning of the [original] Greek when he paraphrases it '*fides illa quam vos habere dictis*',[28] and so has the N.E.B. translation, 'Can faith save him?' James is not denying that faith in the sense of *fiducia*, or 'loving trust', is the proper response on the part of man to the saving activity of God on his behalf; what he is attacking is faith in the sense of *assensus*, cold intellectual assent to credal formulations which make no difference to the behaviour of the one who professes it. He insists that authentic, saving faith must issue in works of love (2:14–18), just as Paul in Gal. 5:6 stresses 'faith which worketh by love' as the only thing that will stand the test of God's scrutiny. The total initiative and self-giving of God in salvation demands the total response of man in faith and works. The faith that saves is the faith that shews itself in works of love.[29] The absence of a transformed life, on the other hand, is proof positive of the absence of salvation. And if that were the only contribution made by the Epistle of James to the doctrine of salvation, we would have ample cause to be grateful for so searching a warning.[30]

My good works, Lord, must only ever be an expression of gratitude for my salvation. My service must be rooted in an appreciation of my redemption, for I cannot earn your favour. Your love remains the same, whether I work well or not at all. Your love is not conditional in that sense. My response to your love is what this is all about. Horse before cart, not cart before horse!

**I pray also for those who will believe in me through their message, that all of them may be one, Father, just as you are in me and I am in you. May they also be in us so that the world may believe that you have sent me.
(John 17:20–21)**

Pope John XXIII prayed, 'Renew thy wonders in our day, as by a new Pentecost'. Pope Paul VI affirmed, 'The Church needs an eternal Pentecost', and it is significant that it is in the Roman Catholic Church, in some ways the most structured and traditional of all churches, that this renewal movement has broken out most strongly and been most influential. Protestants who had treated Catholics with great circumspection all their lives suddenly found themselves praying and praising God together with them in the release of the Holy Spirit. And Catholics who had been accustomed to see the Church as coterminous with Roman Catholicism began to rejoice that the Lord had given his Holy Spirit to Protestant brethren also.[31]

Enlarge my heart, Heavenly Father, so that I look beyond denominational labels and differences in order to see people; precious souls for whom my Saviour died. Once my eyesight is improved in that way, I will all the more enjoy 'praying and praising God together with them'; friends and fellow pilgrims from all kinds of different churches. Continue to renew us all, Lord; slow and ponderous though that operation can be at times. Build your church, Lord.

**Your mercy will not fail us,
Nor leave your work undone;
With your right hand to help us
The vict'ry shall be won.
And then by earth and heaven
Your name shall be adored;
And this shall be our anthem:
One church, one faith, one Lord![32]**

27 December

**For this is what the high and exalted One says –
he who lives for ever, whose name is holy:
'I live in a high and holy place,
but also with the one who is contrite and lowly in spirit,
to revive the spirit of the lowly
and to revive the heart of the contrite.'
(Isaiah 57:15)**

Jesus taught more severely about the judgment of God than any of the Old Testament prophets ever did. Remember, it was Jesus who taught about the two ways a man could go: one led to God and the other led to destruction. There were two groups a man could belong to: wheat, destined for the barn, or weeds, destined for the fire. There were two destinies that awaited men: inside the joyous feast, or outside where there was weeping and gnashing of teeth. The teaching of Jesus flies straight in the face of our easy-going optimism that God is a good fellow and won't be too fussy about our achievements. He is good, and therefore he will be extremely fussy. He is the ethically upright God that our conscience uncomfortably suggests he is. He is deeply concerned at the fundamental difference between right and wrong, and will not pretend that the distinction is unreal . . . The Almighty does not owe us forgiveness, any more than the world owes us a living. Forgiveness is never cheap.[33]

Not cheap at all, Lord; my forgiveness cost you everything. Maybe I don't always realize, or remember, the horrific depths to which you were prepared to go, in Christ, in order to save my soul. Maybe I am, sometimes, inclined to misunderstand or underestimate your holiness. At such times, Lord, lead me back to the cross. Confront me afresh with your perfection, for that will only ever do me good. Abba Father, never let me go, not even in my drifting patterns of thought. Thank you, Lord God, for the sheer beauty and worth of today's Bible text; this speaks so wonderfully of holiness and humility.

28 December

**Every animal of the forest is mine,
and the cattle on a thousand hills.
(Psalm 50:10)**

If heaven were the reward of merit, it would be ghastly. If I got there because I did my best, pushed my way in, and established my own claims no matter who got hurt in the process, it would be intolerable. If heaven were peopled by self-made men waving their own beastly goodness around under everyone else's nose, it would be hell. Ascot is bad enough, with everyone showing off their clothes for all they are worth. Is heaven to be one long Ascot? Perish the thought!

I found a gravestone once, in an ancient church. It enshrined superbly this idea that I do my best and God ought to be very pleased with it, and it shows how repulsive that idea really is. It comes from king Ethelred the Unready, and it runs like this:

I, Ethelred, king of Albion, in order that on the awful day of judgment I may, by the intercession of the saints, be deemed worthy to be admitted to the heavenly kingdom, do give Almighty God the possession of three lands [i.e. farms] to be held for ever for the monastery of the aforesaid martyr.

That shows up the proud attitude of 'I do my best. What more can I do more?' in its true colours. It is disgusting. God will not have his heaven cluttered up with the smug and the self-satisfied. The very idea is obscene.[34]

Apart from anything else, Lord, the irony of this is that all I possess is yours in the first place. I can only ever give you that which by right belongs to you anyway. Even the love by which I am drawn to you is on loan from you – I did not even have that in my heart until you put it there! Oh, Lord, forgive such follies. Forgive us.

29 December

My brothers and sisters, if one of you should wander from the truth and someone should bring that person back, remember this: whoever turns a sinner from the error of their way will save them from death and cover over a multitude of sins.
(James 5:19–20)

It is . . . a constant element in the New Testament doctrine of salvation, that a man is only safe as he is in union with Christ. There are many verses that make it certain that Christ will never repudiate the man who trusts in him, but there are others which make it plain that becoming a Christian does not rob a man of his self-determination, and if he chooses to sin against the light in departing from the safety of relationship with God, God will respect the integrity of his free will even in the hell of his own choosing . . .

James is saying . . . that such a man is not gone beyond the hope of recall. He can, by loving friendship and patient counsel, be won back. The Christian brother who undertakes this work can rest assured that it is perfectly possible, as well as vitally important.[35]

God of grace, I pray for 'backsliders'; those who have drifted away, turned away, or been away for a long time. Bring them home. Turn them around. Those who have fallen, Lord, let them fall back, into mercy.

There is a time for everything,
and a season for every activity under the heavens:
a time to be born and a time to die,
a time to plant and a time to uproot,
a time to kill and a time to heal,
a time to tear down and a time to build.
(Ecclesiastes 3:1–3)

No movement in Christendom should exist for itself. If it does so, it deserves to die, and it will not long be of service to the wider Church. A spiritual movement is a signpost to what the whole Church should be like. This Catholicism should not be a denomination or a party, but a powerful exhibition of and pointer to that wholeness which Christ wills for all his people. Evangelicalism should not be a party within Christendom, or a subculture spanning the denominations. It is, at best, a pointer to that loving outreach with the New Testament gospel of Christ which should characterise all God's people. Equally, the charismatic movement has little to offer if it is just a body of enthusiasts at a particular stage in history, but everything to offer if it demonstrates to the Church universal that dependence on the grace of God, that expectancy of his active intervention, which marked the earliest Christians but is all too rare nowadays.[36]

Teach us, Lord, of life and death, the value and benefit, church-wise, of letting go of that which has served its purpose and had its day, and is being kept on life support for no particularly good reason. Teach us, Lord of endings and renewals, how your church may be hindered by the dead weight of encumbrances that have long since reached their use-by date. And teach us, perhaps most of all, the enriching experience of clearing the decks so that new beginnings may have their moment.

31 December

And in conclusion . . .

> Ascribe to the LORD, all you families of nations,
>   ascribe to the LORD glory and strength.
> Ascribe to the LORD the glory due his name;
>   bring an offering and come before him.
> Worship the LORD in the splendour of his holiness.
> (1 Chronicles 16:28–9)

The sheer grace of salvation as it appears in the Bible, where God intervenes for the unworthy, the unlovely and the ungodly is something that strikes a note of amazement in the many loveless, lonely people of our modern world.[37]

Lord of our modern world, reach out in love. Or, as I should say, continue to reach out and intervene in love. Hear and answer every prayer in these pages, most merciful Father. Touch this modern world with the meaning of salvation, that individuals from all kinds of backgrounds may come to the Saviour. Thank you for redemption's wondrous plan. I give to Jesus glory!

Bibliography

Green, Michael, *The Empty Cross of Jesus: Seeing the Cross in the Light of the Resurrection* (Michigan: Eerdmans, 2023, ISBN: 9780802882578). Reprinted by permission of the publisher.

Green, Michael, *I Believe in the Holy Spirit: Biblical Teaching for the Church Today* (Michigan, Eerdmans, 2023, ISBN: 9780802882561). Reprinted by permission of the publisher.

Green, Michael, *The Meaning of Salvation: Redemption and Hope for Today* (Michigan: Eerdmans, 2023, ISBN: 9780802882585). Reprinted by permission of the publisher.

Green, Michael, *Why Bother with Jesus? You Must be Joking!* and *New Life, New Lifestyle* (London: Hodder & Stoughton, 1997) [three books published in one volume]. Reprinted by permission of the Wakebankes Trust.

Notes

January

1. Original footnote: *Encyclopaedia of Religion and Ethics* (1920), article 'Salvation'.
2. Thomas Buchanan Kilpatrick (1857–1939), Scottish Presbyterian minister, author, professor and social reformer.
3. Written in 1956.
4. Original footnote: 'Salvation is the central theme of the whole Bible, and as such is related to every other biblical theme.' A. Richardson, *Interpreter's Dictionary of the Bible* (1962).
5. Original footnote: See G.E. Wright, *God Who Acts* (1950), and Wright and Fuller, *The Book of the Acts of God* (1960).
6. Michael Green, *The Meaning of Salvation: Redemption and Hope for Today* (Michigan: Eerdmans, 2023).
7. The Early Church doctrine of a preparation for the gospel among cultures yet to hear the message.
8. *The Meaning of Salvation.*
9. Michael Green, *Why Bother with Jesus?* (London: Hodder & Stoughton, 1997) [three books published in one volume].
10. Michael Green, *I Believe in the Holy Spirit: Biblical Teaching for the Church Today* (Michigan, Eerdmans, 2023).
11. Michael Green, *The Empty Cross of Jesus: Seeing the Cross in the Light of the Resurrection* (Michigan: Eerdmans, 2023).
12. *The Empty Cross of Jesus.*
13. *Why Bother with Jesus?*
14. *The Meaning of Salvation.*
15. *I Believe in the Holy Spirit.*
16. *The Meaning of Salvation.*
17. *I Believe in the Holy Spirit.*
18. *The Empty Cross of Jesus.*
19. *The Empty Cross of Jesus.*
20. *Why Bother with Jesus?*
21. *I Believe in the Holy Spirit.*
22. *I Believe in the Holy Spirit.*
23. *The Empty Cross of Jesus.*
24. Or *chesed*, meaning merciful and compassionate behaviour between people (love and loyalty).

25 *The Meaning of Salvation.*

26 *Why Bother with Jesus?*

27 *The Meaning of Salvation.*

28 *I Believe in the Holy Spirit.*

29 *Why Bother with Jesus?*

30 *The Empty Cross of Jesus.*

31 *Why Bother with Jesus?*

32 *I Believe in the Holy Spirit.*

33 *Ruach* is a Hebrew word meaning wind, breath or life force.

34 *I Believe in the Holy Spirit.*

35 *The Meaning of Salvation.*

36 Written in 1984.

37 *The Empty Cross of Jesus.*

38 The Mishnah is the earliest written collection of Jewish oral law.

39 *Why Bother with Jesus?*

40 *The Meaning of Salvation.*

41 Original footnote: Persistence in sin separates a man or nation from God's saving activity (Isa. 59:1–2).

42 *The Meaning of Salvation.*

February

1 Michael Green, *Why Bother with Jesus?* (London: Hodder & Stoughton, 1997) [three books published in one volume].

2 Michael Green, *The Empty Cross of Jesus: Seeing the Cross in the Light of the Resurrection* (Michigan: Eerdmans, 2023).

3 Michael Green, *The Meaning of Salvation: Redemption and Hope for Today* (Michigan: Eerdmans, 2023).

4 Michael Green, *I Believe in the Holy Spirit: Biblical Teaching for the Church Today* (Michigan, Eerdmans, 2023).

5 *I Believe in the Holy Spirit.*

6 Prayer chorus written in 1926 by Daniel Iverson (1890–1977).

7 *Why Bother with Jesus?*

8 *The Empty Cross of Jesus.*

9 Stephen Poxon.

10 *I Believe in the Holy Spirit.*

11 *I Believe in the Holy Spirit.*

12 God who heals or God the Healer.

13 Original footnote: *Theological Word Book of the Bible*, ed. A. Richardson (1950), s.v. 'Save, Salvation'.

14 *The Meaning of Salvation.*

15 *The Empty Cross of Jesus.*

16 Stephen Poxon.

17 *The Meaning of Salvation.*

18 *I Believe in the Holy Spirit.*

19 *The Empty Cross of Jesus.*

20 *The Empty Cross of Jesus.*

21 *Why Bother with Jesus?*

22 *The Meaning of Salvation.*

23 Original footnote: Commentary on *Hebrews* (1892), p. 296.

24 Original footnote: 'When applied to God . . . the emphasis is upon the graciousness of the act rather than its cost, even though the latter is still present', G.A.F. Knight.

25 *The Meaning of Salvation.*

26 *Why Bother with Jesus?*

27 *I Believe in the Holy Spirit.*

28 *I Believe in the Holy Spirit.*

29 *The Empty Cross of Jesus.*

30 *Why Bother with Jesus?*

31 The text recited at the Seder on the first two nights of the Jewish Passover. (Seder: religious meal served in Jewish homes to commence the festival of Passover.)

32 *The Meaning of Salvation.*

33 Original footnote: F. Michaeli in *Vocabulary of the Bible* (1958), *s.v.* 'Salvation'.

34 Original footnote: See also Neh. 1:10; Ps. 78:42f.

35 LXX means the Septuagint, which is the Greek translation of the Hebrew scriptures.

36 Original footnote: See L. Morris, *Apostolic Preaching of the Cross* (1955), p. 17.

37 Original footnote: Though here the primary meaning in the religious sense appears to be that of protector rather than redeemer (A.R. Johnson, *Supplement to Vetus Testamentum*, i (1953), pp. 67ff.), this does not alter the costliness of the action.

38 *The Meaning of Salvation.*

39 From the hymn *Depth of Mercy* by Charles Wesley (1707–1788), written in 1740.

40 *Why Bother with Jesus?*

41   *I Believe in the Holy Spirit.*

42   *The Empty Cross of Jesus.*

March

1   Michael Green, *I Believe in the Holy Spirit: Biblical Teaching for the Church Today* (Michigan, Eerdmans, 2023).

2   Michael Green, *Why Bother with Jesus?* (London: Hodder & Stoughton, 1997) [three books published in one volume].

3   Michael Green, *The Empty Cross of Jesus: Seeing the Cross in the Light of the Resurrection* (Michigan: Eerdmans, 2023).

4   Original footnote: G.A.F. Knight, *A Christian Theology of the Old Testament* (1959), pp. 294ff.

5   Michael Green, *The Meaning of Salvation: Redemption and Hope for Today* (Michigan: Eerdmans, 2023).

6   *The Meaning of Salvation.*

7   *The Empty Cross of Jesus.*

8   *Why Bother with Jesus?*

9   *Why Bother with Jesus?*

10   Stephen Poxon.

11   *I Believe in the Holy Spirit.*

12   *Why Bother with Jesus?*

13   *The Empty Cross of Jesus.*

14   *The Meaning of Salvation.*

15   From Charles Wesley's hymn *Jesu, lover of my soul* (1740).

16   *Ruach* is a Hebrew word meaning wind, breath or life force.

17   *I Believe in the Holy Spirit.*

18   *The Meaning of Salvation.*

19   *Why Bother with Jesus?*

20   Michael Green, *You Must be Joking!* (London: Hodder & Stoughton, 1997) [three books published in one volume].

21   *The Empty Cross of Jesus.*

22   *You Must be Joking!*

23   *You Must be Joking!*

24   *I Believe in the Holy Spirit.*

25 *I Believe in the Holy Spirit.*
26 *The Meaning of Salvation.*
27 *You Must be Joking!*
28 *You Must Be Joking!*
29 *I Believe in the Holy Spirit.*
30 *The Empty Cross of Jesus.*
31 *The Meaning of Salvation.*
32 *The Empty Cross of Jesus.*
33 *You Must be Joking!*
34 *I Believe in the Holy Spirit.*
35 *The Empty Cross of Jesus.*
36 *Luther's Works*, 26:21–22.

April

1 Michael Green, *The Meaning of Salvation: Redemption and Hope for Today* (Michigan: Eerdmans, 2023).
2 From the hymn by Joachim Neander (1650–1680). The date of its composition is unknown, but it was translated from its original German into English by Robert Bridges (1844–1930) in 1899.
3 *The Meaning of Salvation.*
4 Michael Green, *The Empty Cross of Jesus: Seeing the Cross in the Light of the Resurrection* (Michigan: Eerdmans, 2023).
5 From the hymn *To God be the glory* by Fanny Crosby (1820–1915), written in 1875.
6 *The Meaning of Salvation.*
7 Michael Green, *You Must be Joking!* (London: Hodder & Stoughton, 1997) [three books published in one volume].
8 *You Must be Joking!*
9 Original footnote: Josephus, *Ant.* 13.10, 6.
10 Original footnote: Josephus, *B.J.*, 2.8, 14.
11 *The Meaning of Salvation.*
12 *The Meaning of Salvation.*
13 Michael Green, *I Believe in the Holy Spirit: Biblical Teaching for the Church Today* (Michigan, Eerdmans, 2023).
14 *The Empty Cross of Jesus.*

¹⁵ *I Believe in the Holy Spirit.*

¹⁶ Original footnote: They regarded the Oral tradition as a 'fence for the Law', and claimed for their traditions equal authority with the Torah. See Mk. 7.13 and *Aboth*, 1.1. where it is claimed that the oral law derived from Moses and was transmitted through the prophets to the men of the Great Synagogue i.e. the 'elders' from the days of Ezra to their own.

¹⁷ *The Meaning of Salvation.*

¹⁸ Original footnote: It is not surprising that an increasing concern with personal salvation marks this period of national frustration, quite apart from the growing influence on Judaism of the Greek emphasis on the individual.

¹⁹ Original footnote: Early second century BC.

²⁰ Original footnote: See the similar emphasis on 'works' in Baruch, 51.7, 'But those who have been saved by their works, and to whom the Law has been a hope . . . they will behold a world which is now invisible to them.'

²¹ *The Meaning of Salvation.*

²² *You Must be Joking!*

²³ *I Believe in the Holy Spirit.*

²⁴ From the hymn of the same title by William Freeman Lloyd (1791–1853), written in 1824.

²⁵ *The Empty Cross of Jesus.*

²⁶ *The Empty Cross of Jesus.*

²⁷ *You Must be Joking!*

²⁸ Original footnote: Another composite work, usually dated to the first century AD.

²⁹ *The Meaning of Salvation.*

³⁰ *I Believe in the Holy Spirit.*

³¹ *The Meaning of Salvation.*

³² *You Must be Joking!*

³³ From Charles Wesley's *Hark! the herald angels sing*, written in 1739. Lyrics altered by George Whitefield (1714–1770).

³⁴ *You Must be Joking!*

³⁵ *I Believe in the Holy Spirit.*

³⁶ *I Believe in the Holy Spirit.*

³⁷ *The Empty Cross of Jesus.*

³⁸ *I Believe in the Holy Spirit.*

³⁹ *You Must be Joking!*

⁴⁰ *The Meaning of Salvation.*

⁴¹ *I Believe in the Holy Spirit.*

May

[1] Michael Green, *You Must be Joking!* (London: Hodder & Stoughton, 1997) [three books published in one volume].

[2] Michael Green, *The Empty Cross of Jesus: Seeing the Cross in the Light of the Resurrection* (Michigan: Eerdmans, 2023).

[3] From the inscription on the tombstone of Immanuel Kant in Kaliningrad. The inscription is lifted from Kant's work *Critique of Practical Reason*.

[4] Michael Green, *I Believe in the Holy Spirit: Biblical Teaching for the Church Today* (Michigan, Eerdmans, 2023).

[5] Michael Green, *The Meaning of Salvation: Redemption and Hope for Today* (Michigan: Eerdmans, 2023).

[6] John Leonard Wilson, Anglican Bishop of Singapore from 1941 to 1949, during the time of Japanese occupation.

[7] *You Must be Joking!*

[8] Original footnote: F. Cumont, *Les Religions Orientales* (1906), p. xxii.

[9] *The Meaning of Salvation.*

[10] *The Empty Cross of Jesus.*

[11] *The Empty Cross of Jesus.*

[12] From Charles Wesley's hymn of the same title, written in 1749.

[13] *I Believe in the Holy Spirit.*

[14] *I Believe in the Holy Spirit.*

[15] *The Meaning of Salvation.*

[16] *You Must be Joking!*

[17] *I Believe in the Holy Spirit.*

[18] Original footnote: When Paul on the Areopagus (Acts 17:22ff.) addresses the philosophers in their own language, he says, 'God is not far from any one of us; for in him we live and move and have our being . . . for we are his offspring.' This phrase is a quotation from a Stoic poet Aratus (*Phaenomena*, 5), and although Paul meant by it something very different from the Stoic pantheism of Aratus, the language would be readily understood.

[19] *The Meaning of Salvation.*

[20] Original footnote: *The Environment of Early Christianity* (1914), p. 226.

[21] *The Meaning of Salvation.*

[22] *The Empty Cross of Jesus.*

[23] *You Must be Joking!*

24. Anselm of Canterbury (d. 1109), https://www.goodreads.com/quotes/5152-for-i-do-not-seek-to-understand-in-order-that (accessed 5 June 2023).
25. Original footnote: Gilbert Murray, *Five Stages of Greek Religion* (1925), ch. 4.
26. Original footnote: This word was used in a messianic sense, in view of Isa. 40:1; 49:13; 51:3; 61:2; 66:13. The 'horn' metaphor was derived from the wild ox (wrongly translated 'unicorn' in the AV), which was famous for its strength (e.g. Num. 24:8; Deut. 33:17). The phrase was probably widely used of the Messiah; as early as Ps. 132:16–17 the 'horn of David' is associated with salvation in this sense. But in Ps. 18:2 God himself is called 'the horn of my salvation'. We may possibly have another messianic metaphor in *anatolē*, verse 78, if, as Jacoby argued, it means shoot or sprout in the sense of Zech. 3:8 and Isa. 11:1 (*Zeitschrift fur neutestamentliches Wissenschaft* (1921), pp. 205ff.).
27. *The Meaning of Salvation.*
28. Original footnote: See most recently A.N. Sherwin-White, *Roman Society and Roman Law in the New Testament* (1963).
29. *The Meaning of Salvation.*
30. *I Believe in the Holy Spirit.*
31. *I Believe in the Holy Spirit.*
32. *The Book of Common Prayer* 1662.
33. *The Empty Cross of Jesus.*
34. *The Meaning of Salvation.*
35. *You Must be Joking!*
36. *The Empty Cross of Jesus.*
37. *I Believe in the Holy Spirit.*
38. *The Meaning of Salvation.*
39. Original footnote: I take this to be the meaning of this difficult verse; but it is *varie tentatus*.
40. *The Meaning of Salvation.*
41. *The Empty Cross of Jesus.*
42. *The Empty Cross of Jesus.*
43. *I Believe in the Holy Spirit.*

June

1. 'This world is not the product of intelligence. It meets our gaze as would a crumpled piece of paper . . . What is man but a little puddle of water whose

freedom is death?' This quote is attributed to Sartre by Michael Green in *You Must be Joking!*

2   Michael Green, *You Must be Joking!* (London: Hodder & Stoughton, 1997) [three books published in one volume].

3   Michael Green, *I Believe in the Holy Spirit: Biblical Teaching for the Church Today* (Michigan, Eerdmans, 2023).

4   Michael Green, *The Empty Cross of Jesus: Seeing the Cross in the Light of the Resurrection* (Michigan: Eerdmans, 2023).

5   Michael Green, *The Meaning of Salvation: Redemption and Hope for Today* (Michigan: Eerdmans, 2023).

6   Original footnote: The one exception is Stephen's use of this phrase at his death, Acts 7:56. It is distinct from the title in Revelation 'one like unto a son of man'.

7   Original footnote: Added by some MSS. To Lk. 9:56, Matt. 18:11.

8   Original footnote: The literature on the subject is enormous. The latest massive treatment of it is by A.J.B. Higgins, entitled *Jesus and the Son of Man* (1964). His conclusions appear to me to be most improbable.

9   *The Meaning of Salvation.*

10   From the hymn *Praise to the Holiest in the height* by John Henry Newman (1801–1890), written in 1865.

11   The Spirit of the Lord.

12   *I Believe in the Holy Spirit.*

13   *The Empty Cross of Jesus.*

14   *The Empty Cross of Jesus.*

15   *I Believe in the Holy Spirit.*

16   *I Believe in the Holy Spirit.*

17   Unlearned rural workers: people of the land.

18   Original footnote: See Holzman's *Neutest. Theol.*, 1.132ff.

19   Original footnote: See also 2 Es. 7.51,52,59ff. Needless to say, the dislike of the scholars for the common people was returned with interest. Pesaḥim 49b recalls a saying of R. Akiba, which refers to the time when he was an *'Am-ha'arets*. He used to say, 'I wish I had one of those scholars, and I would bite him like an ass.' His disciples said, 'You mean, like a dog?' He replied, 'An ass's bite breaks the bone; a dog's does not.'

20   *The Meaning of Salvation.*

21   *You Must be Joking!*

22   *I Believe in the Holy Spirit.*

23   *The Empty Cross of Jesus.*

24   *I Believe in the Holy Spirit.*

25 *The Empty Cross of Jesus.*
26 *The Empty Cross of Christ.*
27 *The Meaning of Salvation.*
28 Original footnote: See Lk. 7:39; Mk. 7:1–23.
29 Original footnote: See Matt. 23.
30 Original footnote: Thus they can plot the death of Jesus on the Sabbath without a twinge of conscience. But if he heals a man on the Sabbath, they fly to the defence of their broken tradition concerning what may and what may not be done on the Sabbath (Mk. 3:1–6).
31 *The Meaning of Salvation.*
32 *The Empty Cross of Jesus.*
33 *The Empty Cross of Jesus.*
34 From Charles Wesley's hymn *And can it be,* written in 1738.
35 Original footnote: The latter are content if some of the sheep are in the fold; Jesus is not willing for a single one to be lost.
36 Original footnote: Whether or not the Jews at this time had the right to inflict the death penalty, or whether it would have been administered for adultery, is much debated. Jews were certainly allowed to inflict the death penalty on any Gentile who entered the inner court of the Temple, and, whether allowed to or not, they killed Stephen and James, though in both instances these were mob killings rather than judicial executions. However, the point here is the contrast in *attitude* between Jesus and the Pharisees to the adulterous woman.
37 *The Meaning of Salvation.*
38 *I Believe in the Holy Spirit.*
39 *You Must be Joking!*
40 From a prayer/chalice hymn of St Richard of Chichester (1197–1253), https://www.stmatthewsworthing.org/the-prayer-of-st-richard (accessed 5 June 2023).
41 *I Believe in the Holy Spirit.*
42 *I Believe in the Holy Spirit.*
43 *The Empty Cross of Jesus.*
44 'Made perfectly whole'.
45 *The Meaning of Salvation.*
46 From Charles Wesley's hymn *Love divine, all loves excelling,* written in 1747.
47 *I Believe in the Holy Spirit.*
48 *I Believe in the Holy Spirit.*

July

1 Michael Green, *You Must be Joking!* (London: Hodder & Stoughton, 1997) [three books published in one volume].

2 From the hymn *Tell me the old, old story* by Katherine Hankey (1834–1911), written as a poem in 1866.

3 Original footnote: On some occasions, indeed, Jesus deliberately withdraws from situations where the healing ministry was occupying too much of his time (Mk. 1:34,37,38); on others he refuses to perform a 'sign' (Mk. 8:12), and on yet others he bewails the hardness and blindness of heart which remains satisfied with the miracle without penetrating to its meaning (Mk. 8:14–21; Jn. 6:26–7).

4 Original footnote: Not all healings are messianic; these ones are. See A. Farrer, *A Study in Mark* (1951), p. 223. See also the connection Matthew makes between the healing of a man both blind and dumb and the fulfilment of the prophecy of the Servant (Isa. 42:1–4) recorded in the words immediately preceding (12:17–22), not to mention his view that the healings are the fulfilment of Isa. 53:4 (Matt. 8:17).

5 Michael Green, *The Meaning of Salvation: Redemption and Hope for Today* (Michigan: Eerdmans, 2023).

6 Michael Green, *The Empty Cross of Jesus: Seeing the Cross in the Light of the Resurrection* (Michigan: Eerdmans, 2023).

7 Michael Green, *I Believe in the Holy Spirit: Biblical Teaching for the Church Today* (Michigan, Eerdmans, 2023).

8 *I Believe in the Holy Spirit.*

9 Original footnote: Both these words are loaded. Following Jesus is used of the Christian life (Mk. 1:18; Jn. 1:37), and the Way is an early name for Christianity (Acts 9:2; 19:23; 24:24).

10 Original footnote: The way in which disease is made an illustration of sin in the Gospels must not, of course, mislead us into supposing that Jesus shared the common belief that all suffering was the result of specific sin. This is expressly repudiated in Lk. 13:1–5; Jn. 9:2–3 – without denying that some illness may be due to previous and particular sin.

11 *The Meaning of Salvation.*

12 *The Empty Cross of Jesus.*

13 Original footnote: See also Mk. 9:23; 11:24; Lk. 8:50.

14 Original footnote: This is not by any means the same as modern 'faith-healing', or the influence of mind over matter. It is the one in whom faith is placed, Jesus, who heals. Faith is particularly linked with salvation in Lk. 8:12, a point not made by the other evangelists at that juncture.

15 Original footnote: One of the remarkable things about the Gospels is how little they record of the characteristic doctrine of salvation of the early Christians. This suggests that they are either an example of conscious archaism unparalleled in antiquity, or else a remarkably faithful record of the actions and sayings of Jesus on this and other subjects.

16 *The Meaning of Salvation.*

17 *The Empty Cross of Jesus.*

18 *I Believe in the Holy Spirit.*

19 Original footnote: The evidence from the New Testament is hard to contravene; e.g. Acts 2:22 (party of the *kerygma*); Mk. 3:22; Jn. 11:47. And there is plenty of rabbinic evidence to support it, e.g. 'Jesus practised magic and misled Israel (*Sanh.* 43a, 107b). See E. Stauffer, *Jesus and His Story* (1960), pp. 19f. for further evidence. He concludes, 'the polemics of the rabbis completely assume and admit the brute fact that Jesus worked miracles'. Indeed, it would seem that exorcisms were relatively common in the Hellenistic world (Acts 19:13; Just. *Dial.* 85; Iren. *A.H.* 2.6.2; and, of course, the Life of *Apollonius of Tyana, passim*). The crucial differentia in the case of Jesus was that they took place in the context and in substantiation of his messianic claims.

20 Original footnote: See G. Aulen, *Christus Victor* (1931), p. 77; H. Schlier, *Principalities and Powers* (1961), pp. 40ff.

21 *The Meaning of Salvation.*

22 From the hymn of the same title by Civilla D. Martin (1866–1948), published in 1913.

23 *The Empty Cross of Jesus.*

24 *The Empty Cross of Jesus.*

25 *The Meaning of Salvation.*

26 *The Meaning of Salvation.*

27 *The Empty Cross of Jesus.*

28 *I Believe in the Holy Spirit.*

29 *I Believe in the Holy Spirit.*

30 *The Empty Cross of Jesus.*

31 *You Must be Joking!*

32 *You Must be Joking!*

33 Original footnote: Similarly, Paul's delightful description of the state of Christians who have died is simply this: they are 'with the Lord' (Phil. 1:23; 1 Thess. 4:14). His own expectation of death is 'to depart and be with Christ, which is far better' (Phil. 1:23) while his most awful description of hell is 'everlasting destruction from the presence of the Lord' (2 Thess. 1:9). Heaven and hell are basically a matter of relationship with God.

34 Original footnote: *Honest to God* (1963), p. 80.

35 *The Meaning of Salvation.*

36 *I Believe in the Holy Spirit.*

37 *The Meaning of Salvation.*

38 *The Meaning of Salvation.*

39 *The Empty Cross of Jesus.*

40 *The Empty Cross of Jesus.*

41 Original footnote: See Acts 4:12, etc., where salvation is attributed to the *name* of Jesus.

42 Original footnote: It is noteworthy that to Matthew, Jesus is also the new Moses (see W.D. Davies, *The Setting of the Sermon on the Mount* (1964), ch.2). Like Moses, Jesus was snatched from death under a cruel tyrant. Like him, he was tempted in the wilderness. Like him he was a prophet, miracle worker, lawgiver and supremely Saviour.

43 LXX means the Septuagint, which is the Greek translation of the Hebrew scriptures.

44 *The Meaning of Salvation.*

45 *I Believe in the Holy Spirit.*

46 From the hymn of the same title by Justin W. Van De Venter (1855–1939), published in 1896.

47 *I Believe in the Holy Spirit.*

48 *The Empty Cross of Jesus.*

August

1 Original footnote: This verse makes it perfectly plain that the woman was saved because of her faith in Christ, not as a reward for her act of love, as a cursory reading of 7:47 might imply. This would, of course, make nonsense of the preceding parable of the debtors. The woman, like the debtor, loves much because she had been forgiven already.

2 Michael Green, *The Meaning of Salvation: Redemption and Hope for Today* (Michigan: Eerdmans, 2023).

3 *The Meaning of Salvation.*

4 Michael Green, *You Must be Joking!* (London: Hodder & Stoughton, 1997) [three books published in one volume].

5 Michael Green, *I Believe in the Holy Spirit: Biblical Teaching for the Church Today* (Michigan, Eerdmans, 2023).

6 Original footnote: Not 'to you' as in A.V. Nestle gives Acts 13:26 as a quotation from Ps. 107:20. If so, it is remarkable that Luke has inserted the words 'of this salvation' into the text of the Psalm, just as he lengthened his quotation of Isa. 40:3 in Lk. 3:6 to include the salvation reference.

7 *The Meaning of Salvation.*

8 *I Believe in the Holy Spirit.*

9 Michael Green, *The Empty Cross of Jesus: Seeing the Cross in the Light of the Resurrection* (Michigan: Eerdmans, 2023).

10 Original footnote: Van Unnik, *op. cit.,* p. 51.

11 Original footnote: In some ways, it may be parallel to the extended treatment of the Passion at the end of the Gospel where not all the anti-God forces arrayed against Jesus were able to prevent his bringing salvation to the world.

12 Original footnote: Both at the turning point (13:47 and at the conclusion of his book (28:28), Luke cites the Gentile prophecy of Isa. 49:6: in both cases it is set in a context of Jewish rejection of salvation.

13 *The Meaning of Salvation.*

14 *You Must be Joking!*

15 *The Meaning of Salvation.*

16 Original footnote: *The Interpretation of the Fourth Gospel* (1953), pp. 144–50.

17 *The Meaning of Salvation.*

18 Ernest Renan, French scholar and author of *Life of Jesus.*

19 David Friedrich *Strauss, German theologian and writer.*

20 *The Empty Cross of Jesus.*

21 *The Empty Cross of Jesus.*

22 *I Believe in the Holy Spirit.*

23 From Charles Wesley's hymn *Love divine, all loves excelling.*

24 From the Latin *opere citato*, meaning 'in the work cited', referring, in this case, to *The Interpretation of the Fourth Gospel* (1953), which Michael Green quoted elsewhere in *The Meaning of Salvation.*

25 *The Meaning of Salvation.*

26 From the hymn *The day thou gavest, Lord, is ended* by John Ellerton (1826–1893), written in 1870.

27 *The Empty Cross of Jesus.*

28 *I Believe in the Holy Spirit.*

29 Original footnote: H.D.B. article 'Salvation'. (H.D.B. might possibly refer to *Hastings Bible Dictionary* – Ed.)

30 Original footnote: E.g. P. Bonnard, s.v. 'Salvation in the New Testament' in *Vocabulary of the Bible* (1958).

31 *The Meaning of Salvation.*

32 Karl Theodor Keim, German Protestant theologian.

33 *The Empty Cross of Jesus.*

34 From the hymn *When I survey the wondrous cross* by Isaac Watts (1674–1748), written in 1707.

35 In full, at length.

36 *The Meaning of Salvation.*

37 Original footnote: The necessity for the sufferings of the Messiah was a cardinal point on Christian apologetic. In 3:18 it is stated; in 26:23 (Greek) it is argued. In 1 Peter 1:11 it reappears, as it does in Lk. 24:26,27,46. The Old Testament does not specifically teach a suffering Messiah – but then it never speaks of a Messiah as such at all! It assuredly does look for a Suffering Servant, and the early Christians followed Jesus himself in interpreting his Messiahship in terms of the Servant prophecies.

38 Original footnote: Ps. 16 is used not only here but in 13:35 and may have had wide currency in the early Church. But Ps. 110:1 was fundamental to the preaching of the Gospel, and is cited independently in Mark, Acts, Paul, Hebrews and 1 Peter. See Dodd, *According to the Scriptures*, p. 35.

39 *The Meaning of Salvation.*

40 *I Believe in the Holy Spirit.*

41 *The Empty Cross of Jesus.*

42 *The Empty Cross of Jesus.*

43 *I Believe in the Holy Spirit.*

44 *The Meaning of Salvation.*

45 I wrote this poem about, and for, a friend who was in meltdown, for reasons that weren't mine to judge.

46 Original footnote: 'O our Lord, come!' It is probably to be divided thus, and seen as a prayer, rather than *Maran-atha* ('Our Lord has come') and seen as a primitive creed. However much or little content they put into the word 'Lord', which can, of course, mean anything from 'sir' to 'almighty God', it

is remarkable because it is used as an *invocation*. One does not invoke a mere rabbi!

47 *The Meaning of Salvation.*

48 *I Believe in the Holy Spirit.*

49 *The Empty Cross of Jesus.*

50 One definition is 'refuge from enemies'.

51 *The Meaning of Salvation.*

52 *You Must be Joking!*

September

1 Michael Green, *The Meaning of Salvation: Redemption and Hope for Today* (Michigan: Eerdmans, 2023).

2 *The Meaning of Salvation.*

3 From the carol of the same title by Cecil Frances Alexander (1818–1895), written in 1848.

4 Original footnote: It is frequently a matter for complaint among those who doubt the historicity of these speeches that the Pauline speeches are too Petrine, and Peter's speeches too Pauline. Why should not the essence of the primitive *kerygma* have been common ground for both? Indeed, it is impossible to explain the growth of the early Church if they spoke with a divided voice. The attitude displayed by such criticism is, as J. Munck has shown, an unrecognized but real vestige of the discredited Tübingen hypothesis (*Paul and the Salvation of Mankind* [1959], especially ch. 3).

5 Original footnote: See Strack-Billerbeck, *Kommentar zum neuen Testament aus Talmud und Midrasch* (1922), vol. 3, pp. 15–22.

6 *The Meaning of Salvation.*

7 Michael Green, *The Empty Cross of Jesus: Seeing the Cross in the Light of the Resurrection* (Michigan: Eerdmans, 2023).

8 *The Empty Cross of Jesus.*

9 Original footnote: See W.M. Ramsay, *Bearing of Recent Discovery on the Trustworthiness of the New Testament* (1915), pp. 136ff. and 173–98, and his *Teaching of Paul in Terms of the Present Day* (1913), pp. 95ff.

10 Original footnote: Professor C.F.D. Moule has kindly drawn my attention to an article on 'The Guild of Zeus Hypsistos' in *Harvard Theological Review* (1926), pp. 39ff.

11 Original footnote: See Westcott's note on Heb. 7.1 and Pearson on *The Creed* (1859), p. 136, for a conspectus of the evidence, also *T.W.N.T.*, vii, p. 1006 (Götter als σωτήρες). As we have seen, 'Saviour' was a common Old Testament name for God. It was meaningful both for Jew and pagan. (*Theologisches Wörterbuch zum Neuen Testament* – Ed.)

12 Original footnote: He was addressed as Apollo Paean, Apollo Medice, by the Romans (Macrobius, *Sat.* 1.17.15).

13 Original footnote: The Delphic Oracle was his shrine; that is why he was called the Pythian god, after the snake (python) of Delphi. Hence, too, the name pythoness for his female prophetesses.

14 Original footnote: Augustus venerated him highly, and built him a temple on the Palatine, because his famous victory of Actium occurred near the temple of Apollo.

15 *The Meaning of Salvation.*

16 *The Meaning of Salvation.*

17 Michael Green, *I Believe in the Holy Spirit: Biblical Teaching for the Church Today* (Michigan, Eerdmans, 2023).

18 From 'The Gallican Rite', taken from *Prayers of the Early Church* https://ccel.org/ccel/potts/prayerearly/prayerearly.pr43.html (accessed 5 June 2023).

19 *The Meaning of Salvation.*

20 *I Believe in the Holy Spirit.*

21 *I Believe in the Holy Spirit.*

22 Michael Green, *You Must be Joking!* (London: Hodder & Stoughton, 1997) [three books published in one volume].

23 *The Empty Cross of Jesus.*

24 *I Believe in the Holy Spirit.*

25 The prayer of St Patrick, taken from https://www.journeywithjesus.net/PoemsAndPrayers/Saint_Patrick_Prayer.shtml (accessed 5 June 2023).

26 *The Empty Cross of Jesus.*

27 'The transgression of law'. Or, in Greek drama, a digression from the script.

28 *The Meaning of Salvation.*

29 *The Empty Cross of Jesus.*

30 *The Meaning of Salvation.*

31 *The Empty Cross of Jesus.*

32 'The Good Friday prayer for the Jews', revised by Pope Benedict XVI.

33 *I Believe in the Holy Spirit.*

34 *I Believe in the Holy Spirit.*

35 *The Meaning of Salvation.*

36 *I Believe in the Holy Spirit.*
37 *I Believe in the Holy Spirit.*
38 *The Empty Cross of Jesus.*
39 *I Believe in the Holy Spirit.*
40 *The Meaning of Salvation.*
41 *The Meaning of Salvation.*
42 Christian fellowship (with God and with fellow Christians).
43 *I Believe in the Holy Spirit.*
44 *I Believe in the Holy Spirit.*

October

1   Michael Green, *The Empty Cross of Jesus: Seeing the Cross in the Light of the Resurrection* (Michigan: Eerdmans, 2023).
2   *The Empty Cross of Jesus.*
3   Michael Green, *You Must be Joking!* (London: Hodder & Stoughton, 1997) [three books published in one volume].
4   From a much longer poem of the same title by C.T. Studd (1860–1931).
5   *You Must be Joking!*
6   Michael Green, *The Meaning of Salvation: Redemption and Hope for Today* (Michigan: Eerdmans, 2023).
7   *The Empty Cross of Jesus.*
8   Michael Green, *I Believe in the Holy Spirit: Biblical Teaching for the Church Today* (Michigan, Eerdmans, 2023).
9   Original footnote: On Christ's victory over evil powers, see, e.g. H. Schlier, *Principalities and Powers* (1962) and C.D. Morrison, *The Powers that Be* (1960).
10 *The Meaning of Salvation.*
11 *The Meaning of Salvation.*
12 From the hymn *Saviour, teach me, day by day* by Jane Eliza Leeson (1808–1881), written in 1842.
13 *The Empty Cross of Jesus.*
14 *The Empty Cross of Jesus.*
15 *You Must be Joking!*
16 Not an exact translation but 'not to say, but not to be silent'.
17 *The Empty Cross of Jesus.*
18 *The Empty Cross of Jesus.*

19   *I Believe in the Holy Spirit.*
20   *The Meaning of Salvation.*
21   *I Believe in the Holy Spirit.*
22   *The Meaning of Salvation.*
23   *I Believe in the Holy Spirit.*
24   *The Empty Cross of Jesus.*
25   Original footnote: For an acute interpretation of Paul's hopes for the salvation of Israel, see F.J. Leenhardt's *Commentary on Romans* (1961) . . . See also J. Munck, *Paul and the Salvation of Mankind* (E.T. 1959), though he spoils his case by exaggeration.
26   *The Meaning of Salvation.*
27   Attributed to Jim Elliot (1927–1956), an American missionary and one of five people killed during Operation Auca, an attempt to evangelize the Huaorani people of Ecuador. This quote emerged from Elliot's distaste for Western consumerism in the light of eternal priorities.
28   Original footnote: And it allowed a lot. See H. Chadwick, 'All things to all men' in *New Testament Studies* (1955), pp. 261ff.
29   Original footnote: This seems to be the meaning of the verse. Alternatively it may mean that God is the preserver of all men, and especially (i.e. in the distinctively Christian sense) of believers.
30   *The Meaning of Salvation.*
31   *I Believe in the Holy Spirit.*
32   *I Believe in the Holy Spirit.*
33   *The Empty Cross of Jesus.*
34   A prayer of St Clement of Rome, taken from *Daily Prayer,* https://dailyprayer.us/daily_devotion.php?day=4331 (accessed 5 June 2023).
35   *The Meaning of Salvation.*
36   *You Must be Joking!*
37   From Jane Eliza Leeson's hymn of the same title, written in 1842.
38   *I Believe in the Holy Spirit.*
39   The Spirit of the Lord.
40   *I Believe in the Holy Spirit.*
41   *You Must be Joking!*
42   Paul Althaus, German Lutheran theologian.
43   *The Meaning of Salvation.*
44   From the hymn *I Come to the Garden Alone* by C. Austin Miles (1868–1946), written in 1913.

November

1. Michael Green, *The Empty Cross of Jesus: Seeing the Cross in the Light of the Resurrection* (Michigan: Eerdmans, 2023).
2. Michael Green, *The Meaning of Salvation: Redemption and Hope for Today* (Michigan: Eerdmans, 2023).
3. *The Empty Cross of Jesus.*
4. Michael Green, *You Must be Joking!* (London: Hodder & Stoughton, 1997) [three books published in one volume].
5. Original footnote: *The Faith of a Moralist* (1930), vol. 1, p. 400.
6. Original footnote: *Op. cit.*, vol. 1, p. 421.
7. *The Meaning of Salvation.*
8. *The Meaning of Salvation.*
9. Michael Green, *I Believe in the Holy Spirit: Biblical Teaching for the Church Today* (Michigan, Eerdmans, 2023).
10. Original footnote: On the recovery through Christ of man's original status as creature made in God's image, see A.M. Ramsey, *The Glory of God and the Transfiguration of Christ* (1949).
11. Original footnote: He was increasingly . . . called *Sōtēr* in the first century, particularly in the Eastern Mediterranean.
12. *The Meaning of Salvation.*
13. *The Empty Cross of Jesus.*
14. *I Believe in the Holy Spirit.*
15. *I Believe in the Holy Spirit.*
16. *The Empty Cross of Jesus.*
17. From the hymn *O love that wilt not let me go* by George Matheson (1842–1906), written in 1882.
18. *The Empty Cross of Jesus.*
19. *I Believe in the Holy Spirit.*
20. Attributed to Howard Kingsbury (1842–1878), though this is disputed. Composition date unknown.
21. 'Alone with the Solitary One' or 'Alone with the Alone'.
22. *The Meaning of Salvation.*
23. *You Must be Joking!*
24. *You Must be Joking!*
25. From the hymn *There is a green hill far away* by Cecil Frances Alexander, written in 1848.

26 *I Believe in the Holy Spirit.*
27 Original footnote: *Sanhedrin,* 90 b.
28 *The Meaning of Salvation.*
29 *The Empty Cross of Jesus.*
30 *The Empty Cross of Jesus.*
31 A Covenant Prayer in the Wesleyan tradition, taken from *The Connection,* https://sites.duke.edu/theconnection/2012/08/01/wesley-covenant-prayer/ (accessed 5 June 2023).
32 *I Believe in the Holy Spirit.*
33 From the hymn *Lord Jesus, thou dost keep thy child* by Jean Sophia Pigott (1845–1882), written (possibly) in 1876.
34 *The Empty Cross of Jesus.*
35 Original footnote: See F.J. Hort's commentary (1898).
36 *The Meaning of Salvation.*
37 *You Must be Joking!*
38 *You Must be Joking!*
39 *The Empty Cross of Christ.*
40 *I Believe in the Holy Spirit.*
41 *The Meaning of Salvation.*
42 *I Believe in the Holy Spirit.*

December

1 Michael Green, *The Empty Cross of Jesus: Seeing the Cross in the Light of the Resurrection* (Michigan: Eerdmans, 2023, ISBN: 9780802882578).
2 *The Empty Cross of Jesus.*
3 Michael Green, *You Must be Joking!* (London: Hodder & Stoughton, 1997) [three books published in one volume].
4 *The Empty Cross of Jesus.*
5 Michael Green, *I Believe in the Holy Spirit: Biblical Teaching for the Church Today* (Michigan, Eerdmans, 2023).
6 *I Believe in the Holy Spirit.*
7 *The Empty Cross of Jesus.*
8 *The Empty Cross of Jesus.*
9 *You Must be Joking!*
10 *You Must be Joking!*

11 People who believe that Christians are released by grace from the obligation of observing the moral law.

12 Original footnote: See the magisterial indictment of this attitude in a modern setting in D. Bonhoeffer's *The Cost of Discipleship*.

13 Michael Green, *The Meaning of Salvation: Redemption and Hope for Today* (Michigan: Eerdmans, 2023).

14 *The Meaning of Salvation.*

15 *I Believe in the Holy Spirit.*

16 *The Empty Cross of Jesus.*

17 *You Must be Joking!*

18 *You Must be Joking!*

19 *I Believe in the Holy Spirit.*

20 *The Empty Cross of Jesus.*

21 *You Must be Joking!*

22 *The Empty Cross of Jesus.*

23 Not a literal translation, but something akin to 'the one who would save the inhabited world from danger'. This title was ascribed to several characters believed to be deities.

24 *The Meaning of Salvation.*

25 *I Believe in the Holy Spirit.*

26 *I Believe in the Holy Spirit.*

27 *The Empty Cross of Jesus.*

28 'The faith which you are said to have'.

29 Original footnote: It is interesting to note the different content given to 'works' in Paul and James. James is advocating the loving deeds which prove faith (see 2:8; 1:25) while Paul is attacking acts performed to win merit from God (cf. Rom. 4:2–4).

30 *The Meaning of Salvation.*

31 *I Believe in the Holy Spirit.*

32 From the hymn *Thy hand, O God, has guided* by E.H. Plumptre (1821–1891), written in 1864.

33 *You Must be Joking!*

34 *You Must be Joking!*

35 *The Meaning of Salvation.*

36 *I Believe in the Holy Spirit.*

37 *The Meaning of Salvation.*

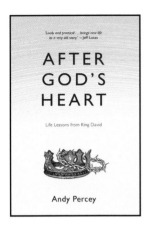

After God's Heart

Life lessons from King David

Andy Percey

The Bible devotes more verses to David than anyone else except Jesus. God called David a man after his own heart, yet he made monumental mistakes. So why was this flawed king so esteemed and what can we learn?

Touching on universal themes such as being overlooked, family tensions, conflict and temptation, Percey draws out biblical truths that gently challenge us to look at our lives and draw closer to Jesus.

David's life gives hope to all of us who make mistakes and whose hearts are easily moved that we too can learn to be after God's own heart.

978-1-78893-284-4

Authentic

We trust you enjoyed reading this book
from Authentic. If you want to be
informed of any new titles from this author
and other releases you can sign up to the
Authentic newsletter by scanning below:

Online:
authenticmedia.co.uk

Follow us: